Critical Muslim 55

Fascism

Critical Muslim is published quarterly by C. Hurst & Co. (Publishers) Ltd. on behalf of and in conjunction with Critical Muslim Ltd. and the Muslim Institute, London.

All editorial correspondence to: editorial@criticalmuslim.com

C. Hurst & Co (Publishers) Ltd., New Wing, Somerset House, Strand, London, WC2R 1LA

ISBN:9781805264354 ISSN: 2048-8475

To subscribe or place an order by credit/debit card or cheque (pounds sterling only) please contact Kathleen May at the Hurst address above or e-mail kathleen@hurstpub.co.uk

A one-year subscription, inclusive of postage (four issues), costs £60 (UK), £90 (Europe) and £100 (rest of the world), this includes full access to the *Critical Muslim* series and archive online. Digital only subscription is £3.30 per month.

A Cataloguing-in-Publication data record for this book is available from the British Library.

EU GPSR Authorised Representative
Easy Access System Europe Oü, 16879218
Address: Mustamäe tee 50, 10621, Tallinn, Estonia
Contact Details: gpsr.requests@easproject.com, +358 40 500 3575

Critical Muslim

Subscribe to Critical Muslim

Now in its fourteenth year in print, *Critical Muslim* is also available online. Users can access the site for just £3.30 per month – or for those with a print subscription it is included as part of the package. In return, you'll get access to everything in the series (including our entire archive), and a clean, accessible reading experience for desktop computers and handheld devices — entirely free of advertising.

Full subscription

The print edition of *Critical Muslim* is published quarterly in January, April, July and October. As a subscriber to the print edition, you'll receive new issues directly to your door, as well as full access to our digital archive.

United Kingdom £60/year
Europe £90/year
Rest of the World £100/year

Digital Only

Immediate online access to *Critical Muslim*

Browse the full *Critical Muslim* archive

Cancel any time

£3.30 per month

www.criticalmuslim.io

CM55

SUMMER 2025

CONTENTS

FASCISM

Speak! Your lips are free
Speak! Your tongue, is still yours
Your graceful body, is still yours
Speak! Your life, is still yours

Look, in the blacksmith's shop
Fierce flames rise, red is the iron
Locks begin to open their jaws
Garments of shackles fall

Speak! This brief time is abundant
Before body and tongue fall silent
Speak! Truth is still alive
Speak! Declare what must be said.

Bol by Faiz Ahmed Faiz
translated by Ebrahim Moosa

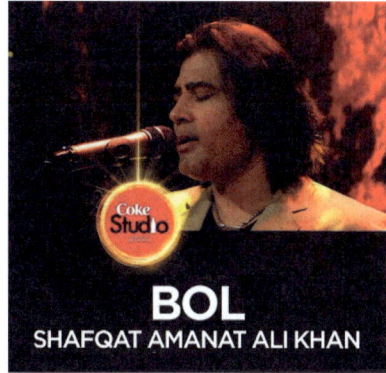

Coke Studio (Pakistan), Season 10
https://youtu.be/9FwoR8mh8T0

ART AND LETTERS

REVIEWS

ET CETERA

FASCISM

INTRODUCTION: SPRINGTIME FOR FASCISM

Hassan Mahamdallie

Reactionary national political formations are multiplying at a frightening rate. So much so that the lexicon by which we describe them is also expanding: authoritarianism, dictatorship, totalitarianism, the far-right, autocracy, kleptocracy, tyranny, autocracy, the police state, fascism, neo-fascist, post-fascist, techno-fascist, accelerationist, capitalist nihilist, and so on. The fever dreams of crackpots have moved from the ridiculed fringe to seemingly grip millions in the mainstream of societies across the world. Doomsday cultists, violent preachers of the End Times, are these days more likely to be found around the dinner tables of industrialists, billionaires, Silicon Valley elites, and their hangers-on than in the South American jungle, Californian hippie communes, or Texas fortified encampments.

For the first time in many decades, fascist organisation, ideology, and symbols are rapidly re-entering the mainstream with varying degrees of popular support, and able to draw on backing from sections of big business. In the US the richest man in the world (at the time) Elon Musk made the Nazi stiff-armed salute not once but twice during Donald Trump's inauguration ceremonies. Open fascists and white supremacists, and every other kind of ugly, are appointed to positions in the Trump cabinet and governmental posts. No one would be shocked to find out that members of the Proud Boys, Oath Keepers, and the other armed far-right militia, who organised the storming of the Capitol building on 6 January 2021, have now been absorbed into the ranks of the feared ICE deportation snatch squads openly harassing and scooping up people on the basis of their presumed ethnic origin or political outlooks. In recent times Hungary, Brazil, Italy, and Israel have seen fascist politicians and parties enter governmental office and begin the job of making fascism respectable again. Other European countries, most notably France, have been teetering on the verge of giving power to political parties who have ancestral roots in pre-World War Two fascism.

The political commentator Richard Seymour argues in *Disaster Nationalism: The Downfall of Liberal Civilisation*, 'there hasn't been a better time to be a fascist since 1945'.

But how do we recognise fascism when we see it? We all know what fascism looked like in the twentieth century, largely through the prism of the 1930s and World War Two: the demagogic party-building, the role of the old political class and big business in facilitating their seizure of power, the mass rallies, the Brownshirts, the elimination of their enemies, the terror, the pogroms, the torture and butchery, brutal wars of territorial expansion, the millions slain, and the grim march to the death camps and the gas chambers. We know of the depths of depravity and barbarism these regimes sank to because of the post-war generation that survived and lived to testify, and historians of the period have since meticulously gathered the evidence. The slogan 'Never Again!' was a powerful, popular invocation post war (and continues to be so even as the political firewall is breached in multiple places).

But did the spectre of fascism ever really fade away? The West in particular, where fascism had first arisen and seized power, never really managed to rid itself of the stamp of the jackboot. The whole of Eastern Europe, including a partitioned Germany, emerged from World War Two under the totalitarian grip of Stalin and a new Russian Empire. Stalin and his proxies refined terror in vassal states such as East Germany in such a vast and penetrating way that it corrupted the nature of even the most intimate of human relations – between husband and wife, mother and daughter, lover, friend, neighbour, or workmate.

In Spain, the brutal Franco dictatorship stretched from the 1930s, through the war, and only ended with his death in 1975. In neighbouring Portugal, the dictator Salazar's rule lasted from 1932 to 1968, with democracy only being finally restored by the popular revolution of 1974. In Italy, post Mussolini, the secret state employed a 'strategy of tension', utilising neo-Fascist terror bombings and murders to destabilise democracy in preparation for a *coup d' etat*. In Greece, the generals seized power in 1967 and ruled as a military junta until 1974. Everywhere, in Europe, in South America, the Middle East, Asia, and Africa the CIA sought to sabotage and destroy democratic and radical movements and governments they considered against American interests. If there ever was a Golden Age of Democracy it certainly wasn't to be found in the post-war era.

The German (and later American) historian and philosopher Hannah Arendt was born into a Jewish socialist family in Linden in 1906. She was active against German fascism in the 1930s, before being forced to flee to France and then to the US in 1941. By the time she came to write her influential book *The Origins of Totalitarianism* in 1950 the Axis forces had been defeated. Although it is an early attempt to explain the rise of Hitler, his use of anti-Semitism, the nature and mechanics of fascism and totalitarianism, and their psychological and societal impact, the book does not read in the slightest as a backward exercise in historical accounting. It is written with the insight that humanity had crossed a line from which there would be no return. Fascism would remain an ever-present danger. As the Black American writer James Baldwin wrote in his 1963 book *The Fire Next Time* the coupling of 'Europe' and 'Civilisation', as a historical claim to superiority over the other races on the face of the earth had definitively ended with the inferno of World War Two and the Holocaust. Arendt wrote with the understanding that the roots of fascism ran deep in European societies in particular, and their remained the possibility of a repeat. Arendt's writings have a strong contemporary resonance. In the introduction to *The Origins of Totalitarianism*, she writes:

> Never has our future become more unpredictable, never have we depended so much on political forces that cannot be trusted to follow the rules of common sense and self-interest – forces that look like sheer insanity, if judged by the standards of other centuries. It is as though mankind has divided itself between those who believe in human omnipotence (who think that everything is possible if one knows how to organise the masses for it) and those for whom powerlessness has become the major experience of their lives.

One of Arendt's novel contributions at the time was her understanding of the connective tissue between European colonialism and the totalitarian project of European territorial expansion and internal control by force. She argues that Hitler's drive to create a pan-German Empire and Stalin, a pan-Slav Empire, by forced territorial assimilation (invasion, occupation, subjugation, and sometimes expulsion) were drawn directly from the colonial model practised over the centuries by the European powers, that had expanded their rule on the basis of the superiority of one race over another. Arendt notes that 'not even concentration camps are an invention of totalitarian movements. They emerge for the first time during the Boer War, at the beginning of the century, and continued to be used in South Africa as well as India for 'undesirable elements'; here, too, we first find the term 'protective custody' which was later adopted by the Third Reich'. Furthermore, If the colonial powers could rule over their 'subjects' by decree in the colonies and still pretend to be custodians of the inalienable 'rights of man' , why shouldn't Hitler transfer that model to the territories he occupied and even to Germany itself? Colonisation at some point always comes home, as those who have studied the history of European colonial rule and its influence on domestic polity know very well. The first twentieth century genocide, with the attendant exterminations, the forced labour, the concentration camps, the policy of starvation, the enslavement and medical experimentation, had been carried out against the Herero and Nama people in what is now Namibia between 1904-1908. Arendt notes:

> When the European mob discovered what a 'lovely virtue' a white skin could be in Africa, when the English conqueror in India became an administrator who no longer believed in the universal validity of law, but was convinced of his own innate capacity to rule and dominate, when the dragonslayers turned into either 'white men' of 'higher breeds'... the stage seemed to be set for all possible horrors. Lying under anybody's nose were many of the elements which gathered together could create a totalitarian government on the basis of racism. 'Administrative massacres' were proposed by Indian bureaucrats while African officials declared that 'no ethical considerations such as the rights of man will be allowed to stand in the way' of white rule.

Although *The Origins of Totalitarianism* was published in the aftermath of the defeat of Europe's fascist regimes, Arendt, and others writing in similar vein such as George Orwell, could discern that there was plenty of hatreds embedded in European societies, and the potential for a resurgence of extreme nationalisms allowing the remnants of fascism to regather were always there.

I have in my possession a leaflet from 1948 circulated in Manchester by the Union Movement – the successor to Oswald Mosley's pre-war British

Union of Fascists. Mosley had been interned in 1940 with his family in the grounds of Holloway Prison, London, before being released from gaol and put under comfortable house arrest in a country cottage in Hampshire for the rest of the war. When his liberty was restored to him in 1945 he went, unhampered by the authorities, back into the business of fascism. The Manchester Union Movement leaflet drips with antisemitism in its attempt to rewrite the entire history of World War Two, just three years after the defeat of Mosley's Fuhrer, Adolf Hitler:

> Who Are the Traitors? You have been told that MOSLEY and his followers were traitors. The principal accusers are Jews and Communists, their friends in the Labour Party and 'The National Council of Civil Liberties'. Do not let the Jewish-Communist-Socialist alliance puzzle you; remember that both Communism and Socialism owe their origin to the Jew, Karl Marx.

In a wholly opportunistic anti-Semitic twist, the leaflet goes on to list the terrorist assassinations carried out by the Zionist Stern Gang against British soldiers and politicians in the British Mandate of Palestine. An historical reminder to choose your political bedfellows carefully. Ten years later Mosley would be whipping up murderous violence against West Indian immigrants in Notting Hill, West London. And at the same time as the Union Movement were attempting to build in Manchester they were terrorising Jewish communities in east London, provoking ex-Jewish servicemen to form the 43 Group, an anti-fascist defence organisation that physically confronted Mosley and his thugs on the streets.

Mosley and his fascist successors in the UK were fought and pushed back in the late 1940s, the 1950s, the 1960s, the 1970s, the 1980s, the 1990s and the 2000s. For two decades, from 1985 to around 2005 I was involved in anti-Nazi activities in the UK. It taught me many things about both the nature of British fascism and fascism in general. A few points stand out.

First, I learned that anti-Semitism was never far below the surface – even though I understood perfectly well that Black and Asian people had become the murderous target of fascist thugs and the victims of their public propaganda, it was hatred of the Jews and anti-Semitic conspiracy theories that remained the infernal engine of their ideological worldview and motivating hatred. I don't think that has essentially changed. Maybe

Soros has replaced the Rothschilds as the prime representative of the devil on earth but that's about the extent of it.

Second, I learned that fear was their greatest currency – if they could make you feel isolated and afraid, if they could terrorise local minority populations into looking over their shoulders, or even into submission, they had won. That is why fascist and far-right organisations at a point in their development take to the streets in an effort to dominate them and normalise their public presence. I don't think that has changed. Where we see militant fascist or far-right organisations emerge today we see the ensigns, the badges, dress codes, salutes, torchlight parades, the menace and the violence, in a direct echo of the Blackshirt gangs and the Nazi night rallies. I can admit to succumbing to that fear at points – for example when in the late 1980s I was attempting to organise against the fascist British National Party in Rochdale, Lancashire, in the northwest of England. At that time the BNP was run by John Tyndall, a hardened Hitlerite who had first come to prominence in the White Defence League in the 1950s. Somehow the local BNP found out where I was living with my young disabled son and organised a 'demonstration' outside my house. I slept with a machete under my bed from that point onwards. I also remember the collective fear and dread across London when, in 1999, a young fascist follower of Tyndall named David Copeland planted and set off a series of nail-bombs across the capital killing three people and injuring nearly 180 others, many suffering terrible injuries including having their limbs blown off. Copeland targeted three areas of London – Brixton with its Black population, Brick Lane, home of the Bangladeshi population, and Soho, historic meeting place for the capital's LGBTQ+ community. I was a reporter at the time and remember being sent to Brixton in the direct aftermath of the first bombing. Glass from blown out shop fronts was everywhere and pools of blood could still be seen on the pavement outside the local Iceland food store, the injured having been taken to hospital, including a twenty-three-month-old baby boy with a nail lodged in his skull. Even at that point people suspected that a neo-Nazi terror campaign was now underway, and were mortally afraid of who would be next. A week later, Copeland hit Brick Lane.

I also learned that half of the battle against fascism was overcoming all the political obstacles one faced when attempting to mobilise coalitions against them. In Britain, we celebrate the 1936 Battle of Cable Street, when London's East Enders came out to successfully oppose a provocative march by the British Union of Fascists through their neighbourhoods. Less talked about is that the British Home Secretary refused to ban the march, indeed providing the Mosleyites with a mounted police escort, and that the Labour Party leadership and most of the Jewish establishment including the Board of Deputies and the *Jewish Chronicle* argued that Jews should stay indoors and away from the counter-demonstration. Although the Battle of Cable Street did not destroy Mosley's organisation and support, it was a decisive victory against his street movement.

The major problem we face today is that there are 'respected' forces propagandising for extreme forms of nihilism and destruction. The irrationality of it is certainly difficult to grasp. Although the societal causes and political programmes may be different, 'American Taliban' is no longer confined to the John Walker Lindh's of the past. There are now legions of (mostly) white American (mostly) men who believe in the codification of misogyny and control over women's bodies, glorifying terrorism and violence, stoking civil war, killing their opponents, stoning homosexuals, rationalising slavery, and fetishising a distorted masculinity and repressed sexuality. All wrapped up in a jagged religious identity, cherry-picked from Biblical texts interpreted by psychotic preachers to justify and lend a moral purpose to their all-consuming hatreds and bigotry. Who knew that the endpoint of the 'war on terror', unleashed by the American political and military establishment and its international allies in 2001, would be the emergence of a home grown western terroristic religious fundamentalist movement, the mirror image of their perceived Islamic enemies, now relentlessly dismantling the freedoms and liberties they told us they were going to war in Afghanistan and Iraq to defend.

The failures and fractures of liberalism and liberal western-style democracies were the focus of the previous issue of this journal, but it is worth reiterating the point that writer-activist Walden Bello makes when he argues we should view modern-day fascism as liberal democracy's doppelgänger, or evil double. When one sets about analysing what is happening in America under the second term of Donald Trump, whether or not we see him as a fascist or a catalyst moving American society towards fascism, it is the case that for some this is not a newly threatening experience encroaching upon their world. Minority communities in liberal democracies, for example African-Americans in the US, have for generations lived under wildly fascistic, violent and repressive states of oppression and persecution. In July 1937, Langston Hughes, the luminary of the Harlem Renaissance, addressed an international gathering of writers in Paris with these words:

> We are the people who have long known in actual practice the meaning of the word fascism—for the American attitude toward us has always been one of... discrimination: In many states...Negroes are not permitted to vote or to hold political office. In some sections freedom of movement is greatly hindered... All over America we know what it is to be refused admittance to schools and colleges, to theatres and concert halls, to hotels and restaurants...Negroes do not have to be told what fascism is in action. We know. Its theories of Nordic supremacy and economic suppression have long been realities to us.

Or take Hughes's compatriot in New York, the Jamaican radical Claude McKay who wrote the defiant poem 'If We Must Die' in 1919 when America (and Britain) was in the grip of murderous anti-Black pogroms in the aftermath of World War One:

If we must die, let it not be like hogs
Hunted and penned in an inglorious spot,
While round us bark the mad and hungry dogs,
Making their mock at our accursèd lot.
If we must die, O let us nobly die,
So that our precious blood may not be shed
In vain; then even the monsters we defy
Shall be constrained to honour us though dead!
O kinsmen! we must meet the common foe!
Though far outnumbered let us show us brave,
And for their thousand blows deal one death-blow!
What though before us lies the open grave?
Like men we'll face the murderous, cowardly pack,
Pressed to the wall, dying, but fighting back!

According to the National Association for the Advancement of Colored People (NAACP) From 1882 to 1968, 4,743 lynchings were carried out in the US. In Nazi Germany the regime and complicit citizenry sometimes attempted to hide their worst atrocities; in America there was a trade in postcards depicting gruesome lynchings that white people would collect and even send through the post to their friends and relatives, much as one might send greetings from a summer holiday resort.

The drive to deliberately speed the destruction of humankind and the planet is another example of Arendt's category of sheer insanity. Far right forces are at work hastening the collapse of the biosphere. As Richard Seymour writes in *Disaster Nationalism*, 'if the interwar fascism thrived on a crisis of democracy exploding from the volcanic mouth of raging class civil wars and decadent imperialism, disaster nationalism is already beginning to insinuate itself into a more intractable climate crisis', or as Donald Trump stupidly sums it up: 'Drill, Baby, Drill'.

When it comes to further insanities, the miasma of conspiracy theories to attempt to create an alternate universe is one thing, as is rounding up and expelling low paid migrant workers that significant sections of industry and agriculture rely on to keep their businesses operating and in profit. Turning Orwell's dystopic warning *1984* into a White House media relation handbook is yet another, but the feverish adoption of apocalyptic Christian zealotry is something else. The conviction that humanity will soon face the 'End Times' or 'The Rapture' as the Christian evangelical right describe it; the Second Coming when the righteous will ascend to meet Christ, leaving the ungodly behind to their fate is seemingly adhered to by millions in America.

And this vision is being articulated by some of the most powerful men on Earth. Peter Theil, the backer of US vice-president JD Vance, and founder of PayPal and Palantir Technologies, sometimes described as the 'intellectual architect of Silicon Valley's contemporary ethos' now delivers four-part lectures on the topic of 'the Biblical Antichrist'. According to Thiel, the climate and human rights activist Greta Thunberg is a shoo-in for the role of the satanic beast.

The conscious despoliation and wrecking of the planet goes hand-in-hand with another disaster theory propagated by the far right – accelerationism. This has been described as the 'deliberate propulsion of technological development' without guardrails. The aim is to supercharge unfettered capitalism until the system (and the planet) burns itself out. At that point the uber-rich will abandon the masses to their fate, as they retreat to corporate island states and underground bunkers, or in the case of Elon Musk, to terraform Mars. New Zealand is the destination of choice for many of the super-wealthy seeking to protect themselves from the very catastrophe they are hastening. New Zealand is favoured because it's 7,000 miles from what they believe will be the epicentre of the coming apocalypse, the US itself. As Canadian writers Naomi Klein and Astra Taylor put it in their *Guardian* essay, 'The Rise of End Times Fascism', 'if the world teeters on the edge of catastrophe, these folk, well aware that their own business and personal behaviour contributes mightily to that existential predicament, build fortified bunkers. The rest of the world can simply fuck off'.

Is America driving towards fascism? It could be. The elements are all certainly there or in embryo. But it is not there yet. Is Trump a fascist? I think not, although when he dies or moves aside, a much more determined political actor, with a coherent fascist programme may replace him. Will a future fascism manifest itself in a direct repeat of twentieth century fascism? Probably not, but for us to better understand what fascism is and might be, we do need to go back to examine it at its previous moment of triumph.

The historian Robert O. Paxton argues fascism takes to the stage when there 'is a sense of overwhelming crisis beyond the reach of any traditional solutions'. Donny Gluckstein in his essay for this issue of *Critical Muslim* 'What is Fascism?' argues that today we do have multiple crises developing at a social, political, and economic level in many countries, but it is not as severe as the descent into chaos and panic that fuelled the rapid rise of fascism in the aftermath of the 1929 Wall Street Crash: 'The capitalist world economy collapsed in spectacular fashion in 1929. The Wall Street Crash reduced world trade fall two thirds. The elite was now determined that the rest of society must bear the economic brunt...Of the twenty-four European countries which enjoyed some form of democracy in the interwar period only eleven remained by the later 1930s. The rest were under authoritarian regimes'. However Gluckstein counsels that today 'this does not make the danger of fascism any less, but it explains why far right politics has not crystallised in such a sharp, concentrated way [compared to the 1930s]. Political scientists like to talk of a broad spectrum of far-right parties ranging from 'populist right', to 'radical right', and 'neo-fascist'.

Given this I would argue that Donald Trump, at least for now, can best be understood as the leader of a populist radical right movement that combines nativism (White America First) and growing authoritarianism with populism – the pretence that there are simple solutions to complex problems. Underpinning this are widespread resentments and distrust of unaccountable corrupt elites, anger at deprivation and rage at a perceived loss of a national identity fuelling hatred and scapegoating against refugees and migrants, Muslims, transgender people, and others. Trump sits on top of a coalition of sometimes contradictory forces; aggrieved poor and small business voters on the one hand and his billionaire cronies on the other, between the Steve Bannons who pretend to represent the hardworking man and the distant Tech-bros such as Elon Musk and Peter Thiel and the barons of industry. Trump himself oscillates between personal greed, monstrous egotism, reptilian cunning, authoritarian cravings, racist hatreds, and flailing attempts to 'Make America Great Again' on the world stage. That is not to say he is an extreme danger even now – if you are of Hispanic descent in America today, do you fear that you are living under a fascistic regime, where you can be snatched off the streets and disappeared? Very much so.

The lessons of the holocaust have evaporated. In his essay, 'Excavating the Warsaw Ghetto', Martin Smith pieces together the fragments that reminds us of the barbarism of Hitler and his Final Solution. Smith describes how he started out intending to be an academic focusing on the far right in contemporary times, but after he was offered a part time job working as a researcher at the site of the Treblinka extermination camp, turned his efforts to uncovering and documenting the crimes of the Nazis and the voices of those who survived to tell of them. Smith offers 'some insights into the unimaginable horror that was Treblinka and the desperation and degradation of the Jewish Ghetto in Warsaw'. Amongst those whose testimony he includes in the essay is that of Treblinka camp survivor Samuel Willenberg, who described to Smith firsthand the moment he discovered his sisters had been murdered:

> My first day in the sorting hut I was instructed to bundle together some coats. On the floor I recognised a brown coat, it had belonged to my little sister

Tamra, next to it was a skirt worn by my older sister Itta. At that terrible moment I knew that my sisters had been killed, a silent rage and anguish engulfed my body... I vividly remember looking outside the sorting shed, the factory of murder continued working as normal.

As Arendt notes in *The Age of Totalitarianism*, 'the real horror of the concentration and extermination camps lies in the fact that the inmates, even if they happen to keep alive, are more effectively cut off from the world of the living than if they had died, because terror enforces oblivion'. Smith also gives voice to the resistance to the Nazis by Jewish fighters in the Warsaw Ghetto in 1943. As one of the participants Marek Edelman put it, 'our inspiration to fight was not to allow the Germans alone to pick the time and place of our deaths.'

The same dark period but from another perspective is the focus of historian Marko Attila Hoare, who describes the Chetnik genocide of Muslim Bosniaks (Bosnian Muslims) and Croats in East Bosnia that took place between 1941 and 1945. Hoare shows how 'the extreme Serb-nationalist Chetnik movement, under the umbrella of Fascist Italy's occupation forces and later of the Germans, massacred tens of thousands of people, above all Muslims but also Croats, with the goal of creating an ethnically pure "Great Serbia"'. In the period before fascist occupation, Bosnians had been wrestling over historic divisions and inequalities rooted in the former Ottoman rule and subsequent partition. In time these polarised political conflicts may or may not have been resolved, but the Axis invasion put a deadly end to it all. Instead, as Hoare writes 'the occupation of Yugoslavia and Bosnia in April 1941 by the German Nazis and Italian Fascists – moral nihilists who systematically promoted and exploited ethno-national and other divisions in the lands they occupied – was a recipe for bloodshed and disaster'. So it proved to be. The genocide only came to an end when large numbers of the Muslim and Croat population joined the Partisans 'giving them a decisive edge' against the Chetniks, the Croat fascist *Ustashas*, and the Italians and German occupiers, leading to liberation and the establishment of the post-war Yugoslavian state under General Tito. However as Hoare concludes, tragically, 'the Bosnian question was not...resolved, and half a century later, the heirs of the Chetniks repeated their genocidal experiment'.

A distorted version of masculinity notwithstanding, how can we explain the attraction of female supporters to far-right parties? Judith Orr, in her essay 'Women and Fascism', argues that today women are actively involved at every level of the far right, from three women – Marine Le Pen in France, Alice Weidel in Germany, and Georgia Meloni in Italy – who lead the three most significant and powerful fascist organisations in Europe today, to 'the trad wives and far-right influencers on TikTok'. How is it, Orr asks, that women would attach themselves to a political movement that seeks to put them back into the home and curtail their hard-won freedoms? Orr argues that we should not deny women who get involved in fascism their agency – they are not being duped, or suffering from naivete – it is their conscious choice. Their gender is important to the fascist project. As Orr explains 'the striking difference with the past is not just the female fascists in the leadership, but also their effective use of their gender to promote their ideas to a wider audience. The most important way they do this is a common feature across today's far-right and fascist parties in western Europe – a fervent Islamophobia that paints Muslims as a threat to women's rights'. For example, Marine Le Pen, leader of Rassemblement National (National Rally) in France, denounces Islam 'as an inherently sexist religion'; Muslim men are characterised as sexual predators and Muslim women as inherently submissive and oppressed. Le Pen has stated, 'I am scared that the migrant crisis signals the beginning of the end of women's rights'. Orr's essay leaves you not only with a greater understanding of the centrality of women's role in fascism, but the sophistication of the fascist project in its modern, post-feminist incarnation.

That incarnation has a great deal to do with digital media. In 'From Fear to Fascism', Tahir Abbas, explores the digital dominance that the far-right has managed to achieve. He argues that modern European fascism 'demonstrates a potent adaptation for the twentieth-century by effectively monopolising digital media and leveraging burgeoning legislative power. This contemporary iteration excels at retrofitting the propaganda tactics of the 1930s for the digital age, bypassing traditional media gatekeepers and directly engaging with target audiences'. Abbas gives the example of Germany's Alternative for Germany (AfD) who have become particularly adept at using digital platforms to spread anti-migrant and Islamophobic tropes: 'This often takes the form of viral disinformation campaigns that falsely attribute rising crime rates and the spread of disease directly to refugees and immigrants. These campaigns are frequently bolstered by inflammatory imagery and sensationalised headlines designed to provoke fear and resentment'. Abbas also demonstrates how the internet is facilitating transnational dialogue and organisation between these national movements. He also describes a new fascist cultural project – the never-ending culture wars that 'seek to erase pluralism, replacing it with a mythic past where racial purity and hierarchy are naturalised': 'Orbán erects statues of medieval kings to frame Muslims as "invaders", and Italy's Meloni revives fascist-era symbols like the fasces to legitimise nationalism. Education systems are co-opted: Poland's curriculum whitewashes colonial atrocities, while Texas bans critical race theory to suppress discussions of systemic racism…Social media accelerates this erasure, with algorithms amplifying content that frames diversity as 'cultural suicide'. It's not history repeating; but a new and even more dangerous remix.

The extreme violent rhetoric in the digital arena can move rapidly into the physical world, ushered on by internet conspiracy theories that provide the framework for actual murderous plots. Lous Ordish describes how in France in 2021 'a coup plot nicknamed "Operation Azur", led by Rémy Daillet, a former local politician for the liberal Democratic Movement (Mouvement Démocrate), was thwarted by police. Daillet showed a …belief in QAnon theories, opposing 5G towers and chemtrails. Further radicalised during the pandemic, Daillet attempted to build a network of soldiers ready to attack vaccination centres, masonic lodges, and journalists'. A year earlier a similar plot had been uncovered in Germany involving members of the far-right Patriotic Union (Patriotische Union) group plotting a civil war and monarchist coup, led by Heinrich XIII Prinz Reuss, the grandson of a German colonial official. The decentralised nature of the internet and social media is also generating radicalised far-right 'lone wolves' who it is virtually impossible to identify let alone stop before they attack.

Ordish decries 'the intimate embrace' between centrist political parties and far-right policies. The *cordon sanitaire* is breaking across Europe. For Ordish, the centrality of racism and xenophobia in the programme of the far right has to be matched with the centring of anti-racism and a defence of embattled minorities in the movement against it: 'Organising without a serious commitment to anti-racism risks reproducing the very exclusions it seeks to challenge'. This has been the case in France where the left and far-left parties have collapsed into Islamophobia, thus curtailing any prospect of a unified push back against Marine Le Pen. Ordish seeks to unite both race and class to build a movement of true resistance.

In a personal and political account, Sean Goodman traverses the landscape of Christian Zionism and its ideological and religious fixation on and support for the genocidal Israeli settler-state. He explains that most Christian Zionists believe that 'the Second Coming will occur only after multiple nations attack Israel. For this prophecy to be fulfilled, Jews will need to have Israel, the Palestinian territories, Jordan, Syria, Lebanon, and Egypt'. Do these beliefs matter? Goodman argues they do. He points out that: 'There are over 70 million evangelical Christians in the United States, and over 80 percent of them support Israel. Christians United for Israel, or CUFI, is the largest Zionist organisation in the world, and claims to have over 10 million members… American evangelicals make up 40 percent of tourism to Israel each year'. Goodman warns there is also a strand of far-right anti-Zionism rooted in antisemitism that we need to be aware of and not align ourselves with. Far right, influential social media figures such as Tucker Carlson and Candice Owens may advocate for Palestine, but their motives are the polar opposite of Goodman's and the vast majority of those engaged in pro-Palestinian support and advocacy today.

Stepping outside of Europe, and in a reminder that fascism has mutated into a worldwide disorder, Sufyan Hatia pulls aside 'the Saffron Curtain' of Hindutva to reveal it toxic nature and that twists Hinduism into a 'voter base primed for violence'. Like other modern forms of fascism, 'Hindutva offers a fusion of mythic nostalgia tied to a unique form of nationalism epitomised by victimhood and hatred of the Muslim other…Only an awakened Hindu majority can restore its lost glory and remove the cancer of the alien once and for all'. In one significant respect Hindutva resembles classical twentieth century fascism – the creation of a mass volunteer paramilitary movement – the Rashtriya Swayamsevak Sangh (RSS) and its affiliates gathered in its umbrella organisation the Sangh Parivar (Family of the RSS) whose tentacles reach inside every aspect of civil society and its parliamentary representation, the Bharatiya Janata Party (BJP), the ruling party under Narendra Modi. It was the Sangh Parivar that led the mobs to demolish the sixteenth century Babri Masjid in 1992 and who are responsible for organising terror attacks and pogroms against Muslims and other targets.

Hatia identifies three myths at the heart of Hindutva ideology: 'Pakistan betrayal, demographic siege, Kashmiri treason — interact to create a climate where Muslim visibility triggers rage. Friday prayers overflow into a park? "Land jihad". An Eid goat market? "Hurt sentiments". Islamic missionary gatherings? "Corona jihad"... This mindset supersedes any single policy and cements Muslims as a permanent enemy to saffron fiction, thus justifying violence as "historical correction"'. Not all adherents to Hindutva, either in India or internationally, are to be regarded as fascists, that would be a terrible mistake to make. However, it is the case that Hindutva activists are attempting to align themselves with far right counterparts abroad, and the relationship between Modi, Hindutva, Zionist organisations and the Israeli government is well documented.

What of the role of culture in combatting the far right and pulling people, especially young people, towards solidarity and defence of those under attack? In her thoroughly researched and enlightening essay, art historian Marjorie Allthorpe-Guyton examines perhaps the most ubiquitous anti-fascist artwork ever produced: Pablo Picasso's *Guernica*. The painting was created in response to the brutal Nazi bombing of the Basque town of Guernica on 26 April 1937. Allthorpe-Guyton chronicles the mixed reception the painting received when it was first shown in public. Critics were divided. If it was meant to be an intervention to help change the course of history then it was a failure in that the Republicans lost the Spanish Civil War and Francisco Franco and the fascist forces were victorious. But that is much too high a bar to set a singular artistic expression against. Allthorpe-Guyton posits that its success (putting aside its status as an antiwar visual icon) is the influence it has had on subsequent generations: 'Its greatest and enduring impact was on artists: from Max Ernst, Henry Moore, John Craxton, Merlyn Evan to Francis Bacon and Jackson Pollock. Most recently, the late British artist Donald Rodney's exhibition at the Whitechapel 2025 included a photograph of his lost work Soweto/Guernica 1988, a collage of Picasso's work and a photograph of the schoolboy, Hector Pieterson, murdered by the South African authorities'. Allthorpe-Guyton notes, 'Guernica's latent power is generative'.

Art can also be in the service of reaction in obtuse and complicated ways that goes beyond simple propaganda. Boyd Tonkin describes an encounter in 1942 when 'a German writer called on Pablo Picasso at the artist's studio in Paris. There, on the rue des Grands-Augustins, the visitor 'had the impression that I was looking at a magician'. Picasso's magic cast a strong spell over the German…The pair chatted amiably about art, and current affairs, before the entranced author departed'. The visitor was Ernst Jünger, 'distinguished creator of novels, memoirs, treatises, and essays in Germany'. Jünger's 'sensational front-line memoir of trench warfare on the Western Front, *Storm of Steel*, had established the multiply-decorated veteran as a literary firebrand in the early 1920s'. In his essay Tonkin wrestles with the conundrum of Jünger, the master of 'concealment and misdirection' who drank with Bertolt Brecht and had a friendship with the Nazi-supporting legal theorist Carl Schmitt. Tonkin cites the writer Jean Cocteau who quipped, 'some people had dirty hands, some people had clean hands, but Jünger had no hands'. Tonkin describes how 'Jünger himself knew how to swim in many seas of thought, without ever getting soaked'. Hitler venerated the author of *Storm of Steel* and Josef Goebbels wanted to find a use for Jünger's 'sharp pen'. But Jünger rebuffed approaches by the Nazi leadership to exploit his reputation. Tonkin writes that Jünger's vast body of work 'offers a singular example of a Fascist ethos and aesthetic unbendingly pursued alongside a consistent revulsion from Fascist politics in practice'.

How can a society recover from the wastelands of fascist and totalitarian rule? Robin Yassin-Kassab explores this immense challenge in his vivid and layered account of the journey back to his homeland Syria following the fall of the Assad dictatorship in December 2024. He arrives, with his wife, in Damascus via a taxi from Beirut. Robin has not been in Syria since brief visits in 2013 and his wife since 2006 when she was compelled to leave for being part of an outlawed human rights organisation. As they head towards the Syrian border their taxi driver informs them that Damascus has just been bombed by the Israelis. Peace remains still out of reach. As he reaches the capital Yassin-Kassab is surprised to discover that: 'The city centre was a time capsule. Almost everything was exactly the same – the same restaurants, shops, residential blocks – only with a thicker layer of grime on the surfaces. I walked towards the flat I'd lived in that had felt most like home. My way was lined by the same shops selling more or less the same items. The same restaurant opened its doors on the alleyway corner. And there was our balcony. It looked exactly the same, except someone new was sitting on it'. But as he looks closer Yassin-Kassab notices that 'many people were wearing clothes and shoes that were threadbare…There were queues for bread, and long queues outside the banks as a result of the liquidity crisis'. Outside of the city centre travelling through the suburbs he finds the situation to be even worse. Rebel held areas have been bombed to bits by the Assad regime: 'The rubble stretched for mile after mile. We drove on over pulverised dust to what had once been the suburb of Harasta'. In another town he finds the people to be 'war blasted…Men missing legs were propped on broken wheelchairs at roadside'. He visits Sednaya Prison, where tens of thousands were tortured and murdered: 'The sadism is difficult to understand. Like the destruction of the cities, the relentless torture of prisoners took organisation, energy, commitment, hard work'. Yassin-Kassab asks himself (and us) 'How to come to terms with all this?' It is far too early to advance a definitive answer. There are many possibilities, including bloodletting and indiscriminate revenge. He cites the sectarian atrocities carried out by militias that took place against Alawite communities on the coast in March 2025.

What of a future post-fascism? Yassin-Kassab informs us that the majority of the population presently support Ahmad al-Sharaa, the leader of Hayat Tahrir al-Sham (HTS) that brought down the regime. But as our author wryly comments 'Syria desperately needs him to succeed, but not too much'. If Syria is allowed to have a future, Yassin-Kassab is convinced that one must put hopes for recovery in the hands of the Syrian people themselves. His hope is with them.

We can only hope that, to use Arendt's words, 'the rules of common sense' will triumph over 'sheer insanity'. But we would have to stand up and make sure this is the case.

WHAT IS FASCISM?

Donny Gluckstein

The global growth of the far right should alarm anyone who believes in freedom, equality, and social justice. Its political leaders detest all three. If there is any doubt, the shocking record of President Trump's treatment of his country's ethnic minorities, the genocide in Gaza, the world economy, legal rights, and academic freedom, should convince them. These movements take a variety of forms from purely electoral (so-called 'populism') to more openly fascist street violence. To see such hateful politics prospering in Germany and Italy, the lands of Hitler's and Mussolini's murderous dictatorships, is especially disturbing.

Fascism is a version of far-right politics, and knowing your enemy is essential to defence. But defining it is not straightforward. Firstly, these extremists try to dissociate themselves from their tainted past. Ironically, in doing so they follow Hitler by hiding behind 'the grossly impudent lie' which 'always leaves traces behind it even after it has been nailed down'. Consider Austria's FPÖ. Its founder, Anton Reinthaller, SS Brigadeführer, and jailed Nazi Reichstag member, called it the *Freedom* Party. Britain's Tommy Robinson has fronted numerous misnamed organisations like 'the Football Lads Alliance' or 'Democratic Football Lads Alliance'. What did the arson attacks on refugees in August 2024 in Rotherham have in common with soccer?

An additional complication is that well-intentioned opponents may label any authoritarian or bullying behaviour as fascist. When campaigning against Reform UK in a recent by-election someone came up and said, 'Farage is a fascist' but immediately added, 'And the Tories are fascists too!' Whatever one thinks of Tories we were not living in a fascist Britain from 2010 to 2024 when the Conservatives were in power. The current Labour government of Keir Starmer uses heavy police tactics against Palestine and climate protesters, but appalling as that is, he is not a fascist either. Applying the term too widely blunts it as a tool for combating the genuine article.

Conventional analyses of the contemporary far right are hardly more useful. One takes claims of respectability at face value and concludes that what we see today has no meaningful connection to the pre-war dictatorships. Approaching the question in this narrow way ignores the dynamic and dangerous nature of current political trends and the deepening parallels with the past.

Another view centres on the idea we are witnessing a defensive cultural backlash against immigration or 'woke' policies. The flaw here is that there is no correlation in Britain or anywhere else, between support for the far right and levels of immigration or ethnic minority presence. Indeed, there is often an inverse relationship. Take the 2024 general election in Britain. London has around three times the national average of ethnic community people living there, yet Reform UK got half the vote share it received in England overall. Scapegoats are not to blame for their own oppression.

Social Roots

The answer lies elsewhere. Fascism is best understood as the product of class relations generated during periods of social crisis. In 1932, the year before Hitler became German chancellor, the Russian socialist Leon Trotsky noted the central role played by the petty bourgeoisie: 'When the social crisis takes on an intolerable acuteness, a particular party appears on the scene with the direct aim of agitating the petty bourgeoisie to a white heat and of directing its hatred and its despair against the working class'.

What was true in the 1930s remains true of the far right's social composition today. A recent report by a large scale and widely respected European Social Survey says:

> in terms of occupational class, populist voting was strongest among the petty bourgeoisie (typically small proprietors like self-employed plumbers, or family-owned small businesses)... Voting support for these parties is more likely to come from older generations living in rural villages, rather than inner-city urban areas.

This section is not to be confused with other so-called 'middle class' people who, in fact, are white-collar wage earners. The petty bourgeois person aspires to become a big bourgeois, but sits between them and the working class.

Autocratic rule and the persecution of ethnic minorities is not new, but fascism is a distinctly recent development. It first arose in the early twentieth century in places where there was a parliamentary-style democracy and capitalist economy. Here the petty bourgeoisie split away from mainstream politics and mobilised as a semi-independent and deadly force.

But how could this group, usually the bastion of conventional social respectability, turn towards extreme reaction? To understand that we need to look at the ideas which social classes hold in their heads. We are socialised into a capitalist society that consistently displays several key features. Firstly, it is a system of competition between firms and states. Secondly, it depends on exploitation by a narrow group. Hierarchical authority is exerted top-down from bosses to workers. Living in such a society makes the rivalry and inequality of nations or people (or 'races' as they used to be called) seem natural and common sense. This pervasive ideology is the breeding ground for discrimination and oppression. Everyone is affected and while no class is ever homogenous, class location generally influences how this ideology is interpreted in practice.

Big business takes a pragmatic approach. While happily exploiting labour wherever it can, at home its representatives stress 'national interest' as a convenient cover for its selfish goals. This is supplemented by weaponising competition and hierarchy to divide and rule the population. Scapegoats are routinely identified to divert discontent.

Like the big bourgeois, the petty bourgeois strives to succeed *within* the capitalist framework, but it lacks the means. Feeling it has a stake in the system ruling idea is generally accepted without qualification. Capitalism is taken to be a system of unbreachable 'economic laws', which means every group must struggle over a limited pot of resources, and so on. Nationalism has a particular attraction for a group which operates chiefly within the local economy. Because it is also a disparate grouping in which individuals often compete one against the other, they find in 'the nation' a sense of collective identity seeing themselves as its very embodiment.

Working-class attitudes are tempered by the reality of the daily grind which contradicts such thinking. Pressure from the boss at work, poverty, and gross inequality, cut across the idea of an undifferentiated national community where 'we are all in it together'. For this reason, the working class has a history of fending off capitalism's worst excesses by forging a culture of solidarity based on concepts of equality, free speech, and the right to vote and form unions. Consciousness of the capitalist/worker antagonism pushes back against discrimination and prejudice. Nonetheless, there are some workers who come to share the petty bourgeois mentality; they suffer like others but think they are more entitled than others who are seen as rivals for limited resources.

Classical Fascism

In the triangular class interplay of capitalists, the petty bourgeoisie, and workers parliamentary democracy – and accompanying liberal freedoms – reflects a certain configuration of relations. These reforms were established by the struggle of ordinary people from below. Though an advance on past practices, they were always a compromise between the wealthy elite and the mass of the population. By conceding things such as the franchise, profit-making could continue undisturbed. Democratic 'rule' always stopped short of granting significant economic rights to workers, or undermining the state's function of safeguarding capitalist interests home or abroad. Nonetheless, the concession was real.

In the early twentieth century this system of elections and 'middle ground' politics had taken root as the 'normality' in parts of Western Europe and beyond. Here the petty bourgeoisie, hoping to become big bourgeoisie someday, supported the latter's political representatives and backed centre or right-wing parties like the Conservatives and Liberals. However, the capitalist crisis up-ended everything. This was when fascism first appeared.

In 1914, economic competition turned into military conflict between rival imperial blocs. The trauma of the First World War was ended by left-wing revolutions beginning in Russia in 1917 and spreading to Germany and Austro-Hungary a year later. This alarmed big business and its representatives on political grounds. Then the capitalist world economy collapsed in spectacular fashion in 1929. The Wall Street Crash reduced world trade by two thirds. The elite was now determined that the rest of society must bear the economic brunt. Living standards plummeted everywhere. In many countries the ruling classes concluded that earlier compromises such as parliaments were no longer tolerable. In some places they took matters directly into their own hands. Of the twenty-four European countries which enjoyed some form of democracy in the interwar period only eleven remained by the later 1930s. The rest were under authoritarian regimes.

It is significant that fascist dictatorships were only set up in Italy and Germany. Studying these countries tells us what conditions led to this happening and helps predict where the risks lie today. Unlike the other European countries which fell to non-fascist authoritarianism, Germany and Italy were industrialised and had a significant working-class presence. Class compromise was long-standing and the concessions made not easily withdrawn. In the midst of crisis, the Italian and German ruling classes would eventually find an unexpected saviour in petty bourgeois fascism, but that lay ahead along a twisted path.

Early on it was not the fascists but radical workers who made the running. In 1918, mass uprisings ended the First World War and forced the German Kaiser to abdicate. Italy experienced the *biennio rosso* (two red years) which culminated in the Occupation of the Factories. However, these moves towards the revolutionary overthrow of capitalism stopped half-way. Capitalism was allowed to survive and the Italian and German ruling classes resolved to avoid a repetition. Yet their own numbers were miniscule, and they lacked reliable means of defence. Germany's military forces had mutinied and what remained were reduced in number by the Versailles peace treaty. Italy's army was demoralised, and its officers were unsure whether the rank and file would shoot their own people to protect elite property.

Enter the fascists. Mussolini founded Italy's *fasci di combattimiento* (fighting bands) in 1919, giving fascism its title. The National Fascist Party (PNF) followed. Hitler set up the German Nazi party (NSDAP) a year later. These movements were neither puppets nor initiated by the ruling class itself. Led by political adventurers like Hitler and Mussolini they had their own agenda. Indeed, these ruling classes were so thoroughly discredited due to disastrous war and then the Wall Street Crash, that *only* movements standing outside their ranks stood a chance of marshalling significant support.

Fascism marked an organisational severance of the petty bourgeoisie from conventional politics. Both Hitler and Mussolini posed as anti-establishment. This sounded radical, but they did not reject its ideology. Far from it. What they called for was full and unrestrained implementation of its dogma. Their criticism was not directed against capitalist society but at its political set-up which was judged not reactionary enough. As a sign of petty bourgeois desperation fascism demanded counter-revolution against parliament and democratic freedoms.

Symbolic of this were the forces Mussolini and Hitler initially mobilised: an extreme right-wing ex-army rabble thrown on to the streets by the ending of war. Dressed in paramilitary uniforms – black shirts (Italy) and brown shirts (Germany) – they used physical violence against any group they disapproved of. They would get help and finance from some hard-line members of the elite, but as yet these rag-tag formations were far too weak to carry through a programme of totalitarian rule. A mass political movement was necessary.

That was delivered by systemic crisis. The traditional allegiance of the petty bourgeoisie was to its 'superiors', but its world was turned upside down by the very people and system it admired. Furious but feeling privileged over those 'below', it channelled its anger downwards. Classical fascism was a movement that combined the initial street gangs born of wartime bloodshed with an 'anti-party' mass party backed by many petty bourgeois voters.

The rulers of Italy and Germany did not immediately warm to outsiders like Mussolini or Hitler. Their squads might be useful for cracking the skulls of class enemies, and their votes offset those of left parties, but neither regime wanted to cede its own state positions. They were also suspicious of the way the demagogues publicly denounced the establishment to attract followers. However, a moment came when intractable crisis meant feelings of distaste were outweighed by a realisation that things would be even worse if fascists were not given political authority.

In Italy, fascists began with attacks against organised labour in the countryside at the behest of landowners. This gave the blackshirt leader enough confidence to demand state power for himself, using the threat of still more violence to gain it. To maintain his radical credentials

Mussolini would claim he conquered the government, but the truth was more prosaic:

> In reality, the March on Rome, in the strict sense, was a colossal bluff. The city was defended by 12,000 men of the regular army... who would have been able to disperse the Fascist bands without difficulty. Many of the Fascists failed to arrive at their point of concentration; they were travelling by train and were stopped by the simple expedient of taking up a few yards of track. Those who did arrive were poorly armed and they were short of food. They could do nothing except hang around miserably in the torrential autumn rain.

Despite Mussolini's hollow threat the King made him Prime Minister. To have trounced fascism at that point would have emboldened the working-class movement which was the greater enemy.

Hitler attempted to emulate the March on Rome, but his Beer Hall *Putsch* of 1923 ended in failure and arrest. Germany's weakened army High Command dared not take the risk of enabling open counter-revolution so soon after the Kaiser's downfall. Hitler realised that:

> Instead of working to achieve power by armed conspiracy we shall have to hold our noses and enter the Reichstag... If outvoting them takes longer than out-shooting them, at least the results will be guaranteed by their own constitution.

Under the post-war Weimar Republic this strategy also failed dismally. It was only when the 1929 Crash shattered stability that Hitler's made headway. When mainstream political parties lost all trust the Nazi party gained millions of votes, particularly from the petty bourgeoisie. But the industrialists and military leaders still hoped to hold on. They sidelined the Reichstag parliament to rule directly with Field Marshal Hindenburg, the President, as figurehead. It was they, not Hitler, who effectively ended democratic rule. Hitler was refused the chancellorship in July 1932 when he got his highest vote (37 percent) in a free election.

A new election, in November 1932, saw the NSDAP haemorrhaging support. Paradoxically that was the very moment the establishment decided to put Hitler in power. The elite had relied on balancing the far-right masses against the working class. But when it looked like his movement might disintegrate, fear of the left outweighed any reservations they had. This conversation between the sitting Chancellor and head of the army says it all:

> We were both convinced that the only possible future Reich chancellor was Hitler. Any other decision would generate a general strike, if not a civil war, and thus lead to a totally undesirable use of the army against the National Socialists, as well as against the left.

Hitler was appointed Chancellor in January 1933 with only one third of the electorate behind him.

The first priority of fascism was to smash working-class organisations, both unions and parties, and it had a weapon unlike anything possessed by conventional state forces. At the time of his accession to power Mussolini had some 200,000–300,000 *squadristi* while Hitler's stormtroopers numbered some 400,000. Their totalitarian counter-revolution penetrated every corner. It then became clear that fascism in government differed from when it was a rising movement. Now the leaders of the petty bourgeoisie had fulfilled that grouping's dream of personally becoming members the ruling class, they wielded an unlimited domination over *all* of society, the petty bourgeoisie included.

Those duped into being foot-soldiers of counter-revolution had served their purpose and were now cast aside. This exposed an intrinsic contradiction contained in the fascist project. It is organisationally independent of the ruling class but ideologically enslaved to it. Unlike the embattled workers whose role in production makes them indispensable, the independent social weight of the petty bourgeoisie is negligible. In 1923, Mussolini dissolved the fascist squads. In the infamous 'night of the long knives' of 1934, Hitler massacred the leadership of the brownshirts to discipline the Nazi base. All power was concentrated at the top through Italy's corporatist state and Germany's massive conglomerates. Beneath these small businesses were swallowed up or collapsed.

There was also a sinister policy dynamic that came into play. Mussolini and Hitler saw their duty as curing the capitalist crisis. This was to be at the expense of the petty bourgeoisie along with all others, but they still wanted to retain popularity over a mass base for use as a bargaining chip in power struggles at the top. Smashing workers' organisations and persecuting target groups might temporarily satisfy the craving of the supporters, but it did nothing to actually improve their lives. To resolve the dilemma fascist leaders turned to ever more aggressive policies at home and abroad. This led to a spiral of what historians call 'cumulative radicalisation' at the end of which lay Auschwitz.

There were national differences. It took Mussolini four years of manoeuvring before he could proclaim himself dictator or dissolve all rival parties to the PNF. Hitler did that in five months. Mussolini allowed employers' organisations like Confindustria to take the economic reins more-or-less directly. Hitler wanted his gang to be the dominant element in the ruling class partnership. In both cases collaboration between the fascist state and big business was extensive. With that came an imperialist agenda that ultimately led to the Second World War, the Holocaust, and the destruction of both regimes.

One important contrast between classical fascism and the situation today concerns racism. Unsurprisingly, mainstream histories of classical fascism play down how its primary role was to establish pro-capitalist dictatorship through crushing the working class. Instead, what is noted, and unavoidably so, is that Nazi racism targeted Jews. Other victims – Roma, leftists, gays, and so on – are commonly overlooked.

Yet racism was a side consideration in comparison with counter-revolution. Despite Jews being Europe's most significant target of ethnic persecution, in fascist Italy they were welcomed into the PNF as members of 'the nation'. Their presence in that party was three times higher than their share in the population. It was only in the late 1930s, at the insistence of Hitler, now an ally in the Rome-Berlin Axis, that anti-Jewish measures were enacted. In Germany, 95 percent of Nazi public propaganda was devoted to petty bourgeois fears of socialism and communism, and rejection of the parliamentary *status quo.*

The class character of the fascist phenomenon is therefore key to understanding it. Nonetheless, a fabricated conspiracy with Jews at the helm played an internal role for the NSDAP and continues to this day as a perverted way the far right understands the world. Antisemitic politics began in the 1880s when the Kaiser's private chaplain founded the first anti-Jewish party to divide and rule the socialists. Like the rest of establishment ideology, the Nazis took this over, inventing a Jewish-Bolshevik plot to control everything. That served to bind and motivate the inner core of 'true believers'. When Germany declared war on Russia this delusion led to genocide.

Fascism Today

Fascists did not disappear after 1945, but the landscape had changed. Mass wartime resistance movements led by the left had torn out their roots and they were associated with concentration camps, Axis invasions, and the Holocaust. During the sustained economic boom which lasted until the mid-1970s, they were consigned to the dustbin of history and 'normality' reigned.

However, the fundamental conditions that gave birth to classical fascism have returned. Despite differences there is important continuity with the past. Firstly, capitalism has been experiencing declining profit rates and intermittent crises ever since the 1970s. This has been accompanied by business concentration at the top, neoliberalism, globalisation, and austerity, all of which render the position of the petty bourgeoisie increasingly precarious. Like its forbears it is turning away from the discredited centre parties. While its accepts the basic tenets of capitalism and vents its fury downwards, for the moment the main target is ethnic minorities.

That is not how mainstream commentators see it. They suggest the entire population is in the grip of reactionary ideas (hence their use of the loaded term 'populism'), and that all politicians must therefore respond to the demands of far-right leaders 'legitimate concerns'. This is a distorted approach that puts cause and effect the wrong way round.

It was reactionary politics from the mainstream that *preceded* far right electoral success. Tariq Ali has called this development the emergence of an 'extreme centre'. With nothing to offer their populations in the midst of capitalist crisis, centre politicians and the media have been competing with each other to distract attention by attacking immigrants, Muslims, and others, while they support the super-rich. The far right saw an opportunity to escape the ghetto and jumped on this bandwagon, making it their main selling point. They outbid the mainstream by insisting it does not go far enough. And then the mainstream politicians are surprised that they are losing votes. This justifies a further move by the 'centre' towards the right to appease the reactionary forces they themselves have conjured up. What we are witnessing is a creeping form of cumulative radicalisation without fascist governments necessarily being in charge.

Another difference concerns fascist strategy. In the interwar period, the sequence began with organised violence preceding the building of a mass petty bourgeois base. Counter-revolution was to the fore. Nowadays the order is reversed. The far right, whether direct descendants of fascism or not, typically avoids the stigma of the past and its street armies. It shuns uniforms, dresses smartly, and tries to sound respectable (albeit not too much) to woo electors but deliver the dog whistle messages of reaction. It remains to be seen whether, if the far right attains government, the authoritarian tendency inherent of the enraged petty bourgeoisie will indeed be satisfied by the use of conventional state coercion. But a potential recourse to extra-judicial violence to bully their political competitors or smash their opponents, is not excluded. Examples are the Tommy Robinson pogrom in UK (2024), fire-bombing of Roma in Italy (2011), and PEGIDA actions in Germany (2014–17). We saw how Trump was prepared to countenance violence by the Proud Boys and suchlike in the assault on the Capitol on 6 January 2021 but now uses state agencies like ICE (Immigration and Customs Enforcement) to terrorise opponents.

There is also a difference in pace. The period we live in has been described as the 1930s in slow motion. Today traditional left parties are weaker than at that time and therefore not seen as needing to be immediately eliminated. This does not make the danger of fascism any less, but it explains why far-right politics has not crystallised in such a sharp, concentrated way. Political scientists like to talk of a broad spectrum of far-right parties ranging from 'populist right', to 'radical right', and 'neo-fascist'. By contrast, the Bolshevik revolution of 1917 and Wall Street Crash gave an urgency to the counter-revolutionary programme of the angry petty bourgeoisie that is lacking today. Classical fascism was therefore overt, extreme, and explicit in both word and deed.

It took Mussolini three years from founding his movement to being appointed 'Il Duce' or dictator. Hitler's NSDAP was the sole party in Germany just thirteen years after its foundation. Post-war France and Italy are examples of the modern fascist trajectory. Jean-Marie Le Pen set up the Front National in 1972 and its first electoral breakthrough was in 1988. Today, though making headway it is still seeking power. The Italian fascist movement was re-founded in 1946, but it was not until 2022 that Georgia Meloni became prime minister. Austria's FPÖ was established in 1956 and has had three bouts in office as part of coalition governments. The country's parliamentary institutions, diverse political parties, and trade unions have survived till now.

The situation is dynamic and unstable. Ultimately, despite differences of pace, the unfolding logic of petty bourgeois reaction is highly dangerous. Refugees trying to save their lives by crossing the Channel in small boats may be the primary target of petty bourgeois outrage today. But if far-right ideas take hold the danger of a full-blown fascist-style dictatorship or something akin to it is very real and extends far beyond the scapegoats of today. Above all, the working class could be dramatically weakened once again. Its powers of resistance curtailed, society as a whole would be forced to pay the full price of an accelerating capitalist crisis.

The Working Class

A sense of urgency on our side is essential despite the longer timescale and more diffuse far right movement. Luckily, we are forewarned by history, anti-fascist resistance is not yet facing the repression of the inter-war period, and there is much that we can do.

A class analysis of fascism reveals both its strengths but also its weaknesses. The reactionary petty bourgeoisie is important but is a diminishing section of society. As producers the working-class majority has greater social weight, and diametrically opposed interests. So, an understanding of where workers stand is the starting point for defence. The situation is not simple. The electoral scores achieved by the far right could not be achieved without some working-class voters. Analysis of election patterns shows these supporters tend to be white, male, and manual with a low level of educational achievement.

Since the beginnings of the crisis in the mid-1970s this segment, like the rest of the working class, has seen its living standards and quality of life slashed. The problem has been aggravated by a shift of manufacturing to countries in the Global South. The political conclusion drawn from this situation could have gone either way. There might have been a decision to fight back by joining with the rest of the working class, adopting a genuinely critical posture toward capitalism, and voting left. This did not happen because mainstream left party leaders have betrayed this group along with the entire class. These leaders see their role, especially during crises, as nurturing big business in the hope that one day some crumbs will be shared from the table. That is why Rachel Reeves, Britain's Chancellor of the Exchequer talks endlessly of growth – by which is meant profits. Such people are barely distinguishable from traditional representatives of the right and have paid a heavy electoral price.

Consequently, a minority of workers falls into the far-right camp. They are seduced by an ideology that whispers that being white and male makes them superior. Others believe they are protesting against the system, rather than bolstering it and worsening their fate. Voting this way does nothing to end the vicious cycle of poverty leading to low educational achievement. It merely perpetuates the disadvantage they feel compared to those in better paid, skilled, more knowledge-based jobs.

But we should not be mesmerised by this lapse in judgement. Many white, male, manual workers do not vote far right, and in any case this category is a declining element of the working class overall. Taken in the round working class consciousness is expanding to encompass areas such as education, health, services, 'white collar', and 'professional' spheres that once were regarded as middle class in status and mentality. The contemporary working class is broad, multigender, and multi-ethnic.

Furthermore, while far-right electoral advances cannot be overlooked, voting itself is only one part of a much larger picture. Disillusionment with the failure of the current political system extends well beyond election times. For decades parliament has not reflected or acted on major public priorities such as social services and living standards. OECD surveys show almost half the population have little or no trust in politicians, and many don't vote at all. Abstainers tend to come from the very group of low paid, educationally poorly qualified people that the far-right hopes to win. But it is only gathering part of this group to its reactionary message. Since abstention took off in the 1970s, those who stay home outnumber far-right voters by a ratio of two to one in Britain and are equal to them in France and Germany. In Italy the largest party among workers is neither on the left nor on the right, but non-voters.

This means there is a huge reserve of working-class people for anti-fascists and anti-racists to appeal to. And this is not just a theoretical claim. Despite the noise about all-conquering 'populism' which requires its constant presence on our screens, we never hear about a far *more* popular counter-trend in public opinion. In 2002, the Europe-wide Social Survey put three countries in the category of being most favourable to immigration. That number was eight a decade later. As Marine Le Pen's party challenges for the presidency, French polls suggest 'there is no sign of a long-term move to the right. Rather it is the inverse that is seen.' A 2024 British Social Attitudes report on immigration finds that in 2014, 30 percent thought that immigration had a positive impact on the economy; by 2021, this figure had increased to 59 percent. As one writer summarises it, 'despite a rise in populism on the continent, Europeans seem to be getting more liberal'.

The key issue, therefore, is how to mobilise this force. One powerful factor is the distaste felt by most ordinary people for fascism and its record. That even includes some who cast their ballot for the far right in the mistaken belief that is a way to protest. The effectiveness of calling out fascism and racism has been seen in recent mobilisations, both electoral and on the streets in France and Germany. Classic examples from earlier history are the Anti-Nazi League and Unite Against Fascism in the UK at the end of the 1970s (which destroyed the National Front and British National Party), and KEERFA which broke Golden Dawn in Greece.

As class analysis also shows, it is a mistake to restrict our strategy to opposing the far right alone. Lying behind its growth is economic crisis, mainstream political decay, the precarious situation of the petty bourgeoisie and workers, and divide and rule tactics driven from the top. Therefore, as well as combating fascism it is necessary to challenge the source of the contagion – capitalism. There are many fronts to this: anti-imperialism, Palestine solidarity, strikes, social justice campaigns, fighting oppression of women, LGBTQ, and more. All these should be seen as part of the common fight. Offering a left alternative to social despair is a necessary antidote to fascism.

There is no room for passivity or complacency. Arch-reaction is on the move, but so are its opponents. There are many people who can and should be mobilised on our side, and let's face it – this must be done if humanity is to have a viable future.

THE FAR RIGHT IN EUROPE

Louis Ordish

In December 2022, German police carried out a series of arrests against members of the far right Patriotic Union (Patriotische Union) group in order to stop a plot to provoke a civil war and carry out a monarchist coup. In total, twenty-five people were arrested and three hundred and eighty firearms seized. Allegedly, the group was led by Heinrich XIII Prinz Reuss, the grandson of a German colonial official. Heinrich XIII, who was to be installed as the new monarch following the coup's success, was driven by an anger originating in the expropriation of his familial assets under East Germany's Communist regime. The extreme monarchist beliefs of the group frequently saw it open to ridicule, notably by other neo-Nazi groups. This dismissal often served to obscure the serious threat they posed.

During the pandemic, the Patriotic Union saw a boost in popularity and played a key role in protests against the German government's Covid-19 measures. Its members not only included a former member of the Bundestag for the Alternative for Germany (AfD) party, a celebrity chef and former paratrooper, but also adherents to a reformed QAnon with European characteristics. In this version, American narratives about elite paedophile rings were easily adapted to local contexts, merging post-9/11 'War on Terror' constructions of Muslim otherness with older Islamophobic tropes that cast Muslims as culturally incompatible and sexually predatory. The result has been the creation of a conspiracy theory ecosystem in which Muslim communities across Europe are increasingly portrayed as central to imagined, transnational paedophile networks. Heinrich XIII himself highlights the connection to historical narratives of the far right, lamenting the loss of the Second World War and espousing antisemitic conspiracy theories about the Rothschild family, views that aligned with the groups opposition to government surveillance, migration, and the 'deep state'.

While the Patriotic Union took on its own German characteristics, the movement was not unique to the country. In France, a coup plot nicknamed 'Operation Azur', led by Rémy Daillet, a former local politician for the liberal Democratic Movement (Mouvement Démocrate), was thwarted by police. Daillet showed a similar belief in QAnon theories, opposing 5G towers and chemtrails. Further radicalised during the pandemic, Daillet attempted to build a network of soldiers ready to attack vaccination centres, masonic lodges, and journalists. Around the same time, just days before the German arrests, a retired train driver carried out a mass shooting that targeted Paris's Kurdish community. The man, who had a history of racist violence, was described as having a 'pathological' hatred of foreigners but could not be linked to a wider far-right group. In another incident, a man attacked a migrant centre in Dover with firebombs, injuring two people before he took his own life. His Facebook page was filled with Covid-19 conspiracies and Islamophobic posts, including one where he wrote, 'I have put in freedom of information request how many people cannot speak English right ... all of these people should be excluded from benefit,' echoing broader anti-immigrant narratives that portrayed welfare access as a drain on resources, where support for migrants came at the expense of the 'native' working class.

These acts of violence reflect the decentralised yet connected nature of far-right extremism, increasingly fuelled by Islamophobia. Most recently, on 27 April 2025, Aboubakar Cissé, a young Muslim worshipper from Mali, was stabbed to death in a mosque in La Grand-Combe, southern France. The attacker shouted insults against Allah and filmed the dying man, in an act the French prime minister condemned as an 'Islamophobic atrocity'.

These patterns of far right radicalisation and violence across Europe cannot be separated from the broader socioeconomic context, where the fragmentation and isolation driven by neoliberal capitalism have eroded the community bonds and collective structures that once helped reduce the spread of the far right. Organisations, like trade unions, not only politically dominated these communities, but also played a direct role in forming cultural organisations and community groups. Similarly, anti-racist movements, often excluded from the wider trade union movement, played a fundamental role in uniting communities, building coalitions and driving anti-fascist politics. Movements spanned the national and local, from the Asian Youth Movements to the Broadwater Farm Defence Campaign. However, the dominance of neoliberalism has seen increasing division and disruption of communities that once existed. The differences between metropolitan cities and their tertiary towns have been increasingly exacerbated through governmental cuts squeezing cultural organisations in towns and small cities. The young and educated are increasingly driven towards cities, while, in turn, the extreme rise in rent is forcing the working class out of them. Amidst declining towns, individuals experience greater precarity in work, declining wages, and rising living costs. Individuals remain as isolated as their towns, whilst this experience of capitalism is becoming increasingly totalising across Europe.

The far right have clearly gained from this isolation by offering a faux-community. Identifying people's concentration on social media, driven by their social alienation, the far right have exploited the rise of these platforms more than any other political movement. Here disinformation and fringe opinions have been spread and normalised quicker than in any other political sphere. This issue was clearly exacerbated by Covid-19 lockdowns, not only benefitting from a state in which the majority of people were left to communicate online, but also left in a vulnerable state in which conspiracies could flourish as governments attempted to control narratives about the virus. It is not surprising that far right discourse did not only spread in this environment, but unify around an opposition to lockdowns, vaccinations, and mask mandates. The idea of connectivity and community is also driven in subtler ways, like the creation of words and phrases specific to members of far-right communities. This shared discourse plays a key role in the contradictory sense of community within lone wolf far-right attacks. Not only did the Christchurch shooter's manifesto reference political ideas such as the 'Great Replacement' it also contained many references to memes specific to online communities. Similarly, many of Europe's lone wolf attackers have frequently made use of symbols and gestures shared by QAnon supporters.

The far right has also managed to create organisations that are increasing in number, though are not yet mass organisations. This not only represents the growth of paramilitary organisations like that of the Patriotic Union, it also encapsulates groups that have sought to fill in gaps in communities, while slowly spreading a far-right agenda. Since 2021, there has been an increasing number of 'Active Clubs'. Originally started in the US, the group seeks to establish networks between 'clubs' across Europe, North America, and Australia. These 'clubs' not only share a belief in the 'Great Replacement' and 'White Genocide', conspiracy theories claiming that white Europeans are being systematically replaced by non-white, often Muslim, migrants through immigration and higher birth rate, but also use these ideas to frame Muslim communities as an existential threat to Western civilisation, thereby justifying Islamophobic violence and exclusionary policies. At the same time, they share methods of organising: masquerading as sports clubs that promote male bonding and physical fitness, while in reality functioning as militia-style formations that foster radicalisation and prepare members for political violence. In other cases, members of the far right have set up groups to offer support for victims of sexual exploitation in order to access and pressure victims to spread narratives of 'Pakistani grooming gangs'. With the legitimacy of legality created by these organisations, far right groups have been able to transform discourse online into civil society. Unlike the moral panics of the twentieth century, the media and politicians today are left to react to the growth of these narratives. But, as has been the case in recent public debates on the topic, they have shown no wariness in replicating it.

Not only have clandestine far-right groups and lone wolf attacks dramatically increased, but the far right has seen increasing electoral success across Europe since the onset of austerity in the 2010s. The liberal victory exemplified by Emmanuel Macron's defeat of Marine Le Pen in France's 2017 presidential election has been short-lived, with 2024 and 2025 representing the years in which the far right became the clear emergent force in European politics. The AfD – recently declared a rightwing extremist force by Germany's spy agency – has increased its popularity from seventh place to Germany's second largest party in 2025, gaining eight million new voters. Notably, it now leads in all five former East German states. Similar dynamics are clear in Belgium, France, Austria, and the Netherlands, where far-right parties sit on the fringes, polling to take power in the countries' next elections. The far right is not only ascendant, it is also in power across Europe. Italy represents the largest European country with a far-right party, Brothers of Italy (Fratelli d'Italia), which invokes Mussolini's call for 'God, family and fatherland', led by Giorgia Meloni. Meloni's government has also been in frequent conflict with journalists, with staff at the state broadcaster RAI going on strike over 'suffocating control' from the government. Furthermore, amid an increased societal pressure on journalists, in which right wing papers published a list of 'anti-Meloni' journalists, physical and psychological attacks on journalists have increased. In Europe's other leading far right government, Hungary's Viktor Orban has repeatedly eroded the rights of LGBTQ communities, repeated ideas of a great replacement by migrants, alongside invoking 'globalist' conspiracy theories about George Soros.

Increasing in the middle of the decade, academic and public discourse rapidly struggled to keep pace, both in understanding and defining the new far right. Wary of diluting the term 'fascist', many other phrases have been suggested, like 'populist right' and 'national populist'. However, Enzo Traverso argues that to define these groups under the category of populist is to define them by something 'ungraspable', style rather than ideology. More convincingly, many have refused to differentiate the far right and fascist based on method. While many share a similar ideological basis, they clearly differ in strategy. While the examples of fringe organisations and lone wolves clearly represent a continuity with historical forms of fascism, the difference in approach between today's far right political parties and those of the past may lead many to see them as clearly different movements. When drawing comparisons to the past, we must question whether fascism was a unique historical phenomenon, specific to one conjuncture, or whether the movement is trans-historical. If the latter is the case, the question is, when do the fringe parties take centre stage? We must understand that what is not yet, is not necessarily different from fascism.

The danger that exists today is that this difference between the two strands is rapidly shrinking. First seen in 2016 with the assassination of British MP Jo Cox a week before the Brexit referendum, one would struggle to identify whether the attacker's beliefs originated in popular discourse or the online fringe. The attacker was not only obsessed with the South African Apartheid state and Nazi Germany, but also concentrated his belief on the European Union, identifying Jo Cox as a traitor to white people because of her campaigning for Remain. Notably, Nigel Farage would claim a week later that the Leave campaign had emerged victorious 'without a shot being fired'. By understanding these increasingly blurred lines we can begin to understand the far right today. The far right today are able to embolden other groups' violence, all while remaining in liberal structures. Of course, as touched upon earlier, Meloni's Italy is slowly unraveling democratic norms, similarly, Orban's Hungary is undergoing a democratic backslide. However, these changes have not seen a complete rupture in the political system, they are occurring generally in line with preexisting liberal norms. In this context, time would be better spent re-interrogating our understanding of liberalism and that today's rapid rise of the far right is a logical trend within it.

Historically, liberal democracy has been positioned as an antidote to far right tendencies. Europe often prided itself on its *cordon sanitaire* – a firewall to keep far-right parties who maintained continuity with wartime fascist parties from mainstream political debates. However, the last forty years have overseen an ever-decreasing pluralisation within the liberal politics of Europe, which has laid the foundations for the far right. As others have argued, the increased globalisation of capital has brought with it a series of systems imposed upon every nation. This process is possibly best encapsulated by Tariq Ali's phrase, the 'extreme centre'. This extreme centre has come to represent a politics wedded to the extreme transfer of wealth to the top of society, mass privatisation, disembodying of unions, and policing of community organisations. In most European nations, this has seen the convergence of previously social democratic and conservative parties, exemplified by Germany's Christian Democratic Union (CDU) and Social Democratic Party (SPD), or Blairite and Thatcherite politics. While the previous decade brought with it a reinvigoration of social democratic parties, whether it be Jeremy Corbyn's Labour or Syriza in Greece, it now seems as if social democratic failure is inevitable within a system that demands the opposition to decouple itself entirely from the system. In this sense, the lack of plurality in the system has created a replicating set of conditions. The system itself drives the majority of people into economic decline, leading them to demand an alternate society. However, the conditions are so that genuine change cannot be allowed. In this context, where a left opposition is the only movement capable of offering a different future, but faces limits on its existence, the far right will thrive.

Furthermore, we must not only argue that centrist political parties have created the conditions in which the far right has grown, they themselves have laid the foundations for far-right policies and discourse. Aijaz Ahmad chose to describe this as the 'intimate embrace' between centrist parties and the far right. While this idea has grown in popularity amid signs that the *cordon sanitaire* is breaking across Europe, the intimate embrace was ongoing at the beginning of the century. In Britain, it was Blair's Labour that took steps to increase the surveillance and policing of Muslim communities. In 2005, then Home Secretary Hazel Blears stated that Muslims can expect to be targeted by anti-terrorist legislation. Similarly, Labour has a history of invoking nativist approaches to class politics, from Margaret Hodge's call to deliver council houses to Brits first, or Gordon Brown's pledge of 'British jobs for British workers'. Recently of note is Keir Starmer's commitment to right wing discussions of 'stopping the boats', not only bashing the Conservatives for failing to reduce boat crossings, but also praising Italy's far-right PM Meloni for her schemes to clamp down on immigration.

In Europe today, liberal parties have shown the greatest push to demonise and halt mass protests. In Germany, in reaction to the organisation of protests against Israel's genocide in Gaza, officials initiated a preemptive ban, with then vice-chancellor Robert Habeck warning of deportation for those without permanent residence permits found guilty of burning the Israeli flag. Notably, the left has invoked Germany's special responsibility to combat and educate on antisemitism, all while left-wing figures like Yanis Varoufakis were deplatformed and shut out of debates due to their support of Palestine. Highlighting the ever flexibility of far-right politics the AfD – which has on multiple occasions invoked the Nazi slogan 'Everything for Germany' and lamented Germany's 'monument of shame' for the Holocaust – brought forward initiatives to ban the Boycott, Divestment, Sanctions movement. While many will attempt to diminish the threat of the far right due to their acceptance of these liberal structures and debates, it is because of their confidence in their ability to constantly exploit and use them for their own purposes. In this sense, the far right achieves its goals of rewriting the lessons of the Holocaust. It can be anti-immigrant and antisemitic, but it will support the state of Israel.

If the far right is increasingly accepted within liberal structures, we must question how it can be defeated. The approach of many political figures has been to argue that the far right must be learnt from. In the most notable case, Germany's Sahra Wagenknecht Alliance (BSW) sought to tie anti-immigrant and culturally conservative messaging to left-wing interventionist economics. Winning 4.98 percent of the vote in Germany's 2025 election, BSW failed to make any real impact, winning over only one in eighty AfD voters and instead making stronger strides in Die Linke's and the SPD's vote. If anything, BSW's embrace of a nativist approach served to further normalise AfD-driven culture wars. In a similar vein, Labour's poor performance in the UK's recent local elections has seen the first wide wave of criticism from MPs toward the party's approach. While many left-wing voices have called for the scrapping of austerity policies targeting Personal Independence Payments and the Winter Fuel allowance, the Labour party seems more open to falling into its tradition of listening to 'legitimate grievances'. Just recently, Blue Labour's Maurice Glasman described Reform's success as a working class insurrection, calling for Labour to lead the insurrection and ensure 'the protection of our borders'.

This belief is predicated on the growing notion that Reform and other far-right parties are representatives of the working class, something clearly driven by a lack of representation of the working class in politics. While of course, we cannot deny the popularity of the right among workers – as Richard Seymour argues, their victories could not be growing so comprehensively if they did not win over many workers - we must acknowledge that the far right's support is more often among a strategically significant group of working class voters. It is neither a plurality or a majority. The results of the 2024 General Election show that almost 80 percent of Reform voters had previously voted Conservative. While, of course, the fracturing of Labour's vote in 2019 must be taken into account, the tight contests in seats in former industrial towns was more representative of a low turnout and growing apathy than a former left that now flies the flag of the right. In fact, like most historical far-right movements, Reform is growing among homeowners, who are now feeling the extreme squeeze on the middle-class that has been increasing since the onset of austerity. The media and mainstream political parties often do as much work as the far right to further their spectacle of class struggle.

However, as far right discourse is further normalised and local issues of housing and work precarity increase, it should come as no surprise that white working class support grows.

Learning from the far right has not just come to mean the liberal embrace of nativist policies, but also the idea that the progressives can learn from how the right mobilises swathes of the population and increases popular support for their politics. The call for a left Joe Rogan or stronger progressive 'media ecosystem' have grown and are symptomatic of many peoples' division from community politics. Social media strategies work for the far right as these platforms offer the greatest affordances to them. Any growing local or international movement can be instantly jumped upon, with a clear right-wing agenda being pushed regardless of facts. The right's main strength lies in making anger and a politics of division feel organic to any specific issue. In contrast, the left can be strongest where the far right is weakest. As we have shown, the far right's rise has been inseparable from decades of neoliberal economic policy and the dismantling of collective institutions. This means that the only meaningful struggle against it must be interventionist and strive for economic inequality, rooted in demands for material change alongside broader progressive causes. By making clear earlier that the right thrives upon a lack of community, we must see that the struggle against the far right must be grounded in community organising. The movement can only feel organic and authentic when it is connected to communities everywhere across Europe. In this way, the left must embrace what it has always been, a broad collective of movements, driven to demand economic change and oppose the far right out of necessity. The politics of this cannot be artificially formed, but is made through the process of contention and solidarity between these movements. The threat of the far right requires strong and long-term mobilisation that can only come through supporting groups wherever they sprout.

In Britain, the ability of progressive groups to quickly organise was clearly evident during the 2024 riots, with tens of thousands taking to the streets in response to far-right rioters. However, while this rapid mobilisation was encouraging, we must also be clear about the narratives that followed. Both migrant centres and mosques were attacked, yet the riots were repeatedly framed as 'anti-immigrant.' Many have criticised this framing, as it possibly serves to legitimise a form of racism that casts Muslims as perpetual foreigners, even when they are British citizens. This underscores the need to resist narratives that diminish the racialised and religious nature of such violence, and to centre anti-racism explicitly alongside class struggle. Furthermore, links between organisations must be deepened, particularly across deindustrialised areas that have experienced a decline in collective organising. In making this argument, we must resist the simplistic narrative of the 'left-behind' white working class, a trope that too easily perpetuates nativist politics. What we face is not an abandoned working class, but rather an abandonment of the working class in all its diversity. Any future movement must be grounded in that understanding.

Importantly, we cannot combat the far right if we only build a movement of reaction. We must organise on the fight against increased economic exploitation and racism, continuing to build deeper than demonstration to play active roles in communities across Europe. At the same time, reversing the neoliberal conditions that have fuelled the far right cannot happen without some engagement with party politics. This not only requires some level of support for the social-democratic parties that remain, but also holding them accountable on both class and anti-racist issues. In Europe today, the recent electoral boost of Germany's left-leaning Die Linke should not be treated as a moment of success amidst the growth of the far right, but as a reminder to adapt and deepen engagement with communities. Belgium's Workers Party (PTB) has recently received much attention for the extent of its success in pushing struggles against economic inequality, believing that class represents the unifying force between diverse communities. However, the PTB should not be celebrated merely for what some identify as a discursive 'return to class', but for actually organising through class—the former prioritising populism, the latter centring solidarity. This has only been achieved by directly intervening in communities, through schemes like Medics for the People, which encourages qualified party members to provide free medical care in disadvantaged areas.

At the same time, criticisms of the PTB's record, particularly regarding its engagement with migrant communities and Islamophobia, should be noted. These failings show that class-based organising without a serious commitment to anti-racism risks reproducing the very exclusions it seeks to challenge. Underscoring the importance of centring anti-racism alongside class organising. Without this, efforts to build broad-based solidarity risk undermining the anti-racist and anti-fascist struggle. In a similar light, any hope of building a truly lasting movement can only be done with the assistance of unions. With increasing reports of far-right attempts to build support among trade union members, anti-racist groups must support them in educating members and keeping the far right out. The struggle against the far right continues to be a struggle shaped by both race and class. And, while our focus has remained on Europe, the reach of far-right networks are unmistakably global, from the anti-Communist Ibero-American Madrid Forum to the presence of far-right Hindutva groups in Britain. The struggle against the far right cannot be siloed. It must be as locally focused as it is international, anti-fascism must emerge from within the community, rooted in the everyday struggles of the working class.

WOMEN AND FASCISM

Judith Orr

There has been a common misconception about the rise of far-right and fascist movements today, that these are fundamentally male organisations, or even an extreme expression of masculinity. A cursory look around Europe undermines this view and in recent years academics and commentators have taken the role of women in the rise of these movements more seriously. Today women are actively involved at every level of the far right, from Marine Le Pen in France, Alice Weidel in Germany, and Georgia Meloni in Italy – who lead the three most significant and powerful fascist organisations in Europe today – to the 'trad wives' and far-right influencers on TikTok.

Of course, women have joined fascist and far-right movements in the past. However, this has never been in the numbers we see today and their current role in the leadership is unprecedented and contrasts with the period of twentieth century classical fascism. Today women are more – though still not evenly – represented in every part of society and political activity, should it be a surprise that they are also joining and leading fascist organisations?

Yet it seems to be an unfathomable contradiction. What is attractive to women about a political ideology that appears to want to turn back the clock on the gains women have made since the 1960s and idealises women's traditional roles as mothers and homemakers? Why would women join organisations that often preach misogynistic ideas and seem intent on restricting for example, women's hard-won reproductive rights?

There is no doubt that women are joining, supporting, and voting for the far right in greater numbers than ever before. For example, for the first time a higher percentage of women voted for Marine Le Pen in France in last presidential election than men.

One of the key driving forces of contemporary fascism is racism, this can come in many forms, whether it is Islamophobia, antisemitism, or generalised racism against immigrants. So it is important to point out from the start that racism is not, and never has been, the sole preserve of men. It may seem paradoxical that this simple fact needs to be stated, but such are the gendered expectations in society that women are still, even in the twenty-first century, assumed to be naturally gentle, caring, and empathetic. This has meant that women are too often assumed to hold political ideas that are seen as flowing from these 'natural' attributes. Such assumptions mean that women of the far right are too often seen to be aberrations of their gender, going against what assumed to be natural female characteristics.

Another long-held assumption about politics in general, and studies of fascist movements in particular, is that women simply follow male figures in their lives – boyfriends, husband, and fathers – into far-right movements. This patronising view denies women any agency, as if the only explanation for women's action is that they are 'standing by their man'. It also, exposes the inability to accept that women could, of their own volition, choose to get involved in fascist politics.

The role of women in the right contradicts such stereotype of what is 'natural' for women. Yet at the same time such assumptions do help soften the image and perception of far-right movements in which women are leading or visible. As the American writer, Seyward Darby, puts it, 'women are the hate movement's dulcet tones and its standard bearers'.

This is why it is worth looking at what is driving women to get involved in far-right and fascist movements, because the support of women, 50 percent of the population after all, is becoming a significant aspect of the growth of these organisations, particularly those looking to an electoral path to power. Remember, despite his well-publicised misogynistic behaviour, Donald Trump won 55 percent white women voters in the 2024 US presidential election, which helped him into the White House.

Women also helped earlier fascist movements get into power. In Italy, the fascist party led by Benito Mussolini's had a women's section, Fasci Femminili (Female Groups). Set up in 1919, it had over a million women members by 1942. Women were told they would get the vote, but that their most important role was in the family as mothers. In Germany, at the height of the power of the Nazi regime an estimated 13 million women were active in the Nazi party. This represented one third of the female population, but women's political roles in German society and the party were strictly constrained

Britain also provides examples of female fascists. Women made up over 20 percent of the active membership of the British Union of Fascists, led by Oswald Mosley from the 1930s. Historian of the movement, Martin Durham, pointed to the fact that thousands of fascist women took part in in rallies, marches, and elections at the movement's height. Many middle- and upper-class women who had previously supported the Tories shifted allegiance to Mosley. Although it was a male-dominated organisation, imbued with conservative ideas about women's role in society, it also looked to recruit women who had recently acquired the right to vote with its policies that supported women's suffrage and equal pay. Durham described a whole infrastructure to encourage the involvement of women: 'There was a women's section, women's branches, women's organisers, women's pamphlets, a women's page in the BUF paper and even an attempt to launch a magazine, the Woman Fascist'.

We rightly celebrate the tremendous resistance of the 100,000 anti-fascist men and women in East London who fought the Mosley's Blackshirts (BUF) and stopped them from marching at the famous battle of Cable Street in 1936. What is less well known is the fact that 300-strong contingent of fascist women in their 'black blouses' also marched with Mosley on the other side of the Cable Street barricades. Over the years of the BUF's growth, Mosley often referred to the contribution of women to the party's impact, once stating that 'without the women I could not have got a quarter of the way'.

Today the striking difference with the past is not just the female fascists in the leadership, but also their effective use of their gender to promote their ideas to a wider audience. The most important way they do this is a common feature across today's far-right and fascist parties in western Europe – a fervent Islamophobia that paints Muslims as a threat to women's rights. So let's take a look at Europe's three leading fascist females in turn and how they use racism and ideas about women's role in society to promote their political views.

First is the most longstanding of Europe's fascist women leaders, Marine Le Pen of Rassemblement National, (National Rally) in France. It is worth examining her role in some detail as it has become a model for those wanting to modernise the far right in western Europe. Le Pen has deployed her openly racist narrative over many years. She came second in the last presidential elections in 2022 with 41.45 percent of the vote – the party's highest share ever. At the time of writing, despite a recent court decision that bars her from standing in future elections, Le Pen is top of the polls. Her project has been to detoxify the party in an attempt to distance itself from its fascist roots. This has involved a name change, from Front National, and expelling her father Jean-Marie Le Pen. He was a direct link to the fascist collaborators of the Second World War and referred to the Holocaust in which six million Jews were murdered as 'a mere detail of history'.

Marine Le Pen has played a vital role in making the party's politics part of the mainstream. A *cordon sanitaire* no longer surrounds the party and she routinely appears on talk shows and political debates like any mainstream politician. She talks about her experiences as a single mother and won a growing number of women voters. Polling on the day of the European Parliament elections in 2024 showed that for the first time the percentage of female voters supporting National Rally at 33 percent outstripped men, at 30 percent. This is a 12 percent increase in women voters compared to the previous European election in 2019.

Le Pen may have been successful at detoxifying the party's image, but her political strategy involves rehashing longstanding racist tropes and lies. These include the superiority of western European culture; the civilising nature of western imperialism; and the need to protect western women from predatory black and brown men. These views, which go back to the days of justifying slavery and colonial domination across global empires, have been updated for today's audience.

So, the 'civilised' and 'enlightened' cultures of western Europe are said to include the achievement of women's equality, even liberation and therefore immigrants are portrayed as importing 'backward' views on women. Islam is denounced as an inherently sexist religion; Muslim men are characterised as sexual predators and Muslim women as inherently submissive and oppressed. Le Pen has stated, 'I am scared that the migrant crisis signals the beginning of the end of women's rights'.

This Islamophobic narrative reflects ideas rooted in the history of France's imperialist past, when Algerians and other colonised peoples were deemed inferior in contrast to the 'civilising' nature of the enlightened invaders. Remember, these ideas are not consigned to the history books in Britain either. It was not so long ago that our own government dusted them down to justify supporting the US invasion of Afghanistan in 2001, in the name of 'liberating' Afghani women. During this invasion Cherie Blair, wife of Britain's prime minister Tony, and Laura Bush, wife of US President George W, famously wore a scrap of blue fabric on their lapels during the invasion and occupation. They claimed these were to represent the burkas of Afghan women whose freedom they claimed their husbands' armies were pursuing. The anti-war movement at the time pointed out that bombing women and their families was a perverse method of liberation.

Today, this Orwellian distortion of the meaning of liberation continues. So, in France immigrants and Muslims are portrayed not simply as a threat to the sanctity of women – as might have been the narrative of the past – but to the liberated lives of sexual and gender equality they claim French women all lead. The implicit assumption is that French women have achieved equality and liberation, and sexism no longer exists in the country.

Put simply, the progressive cause of women's rights has been weaponised by the right to pursue a racist agenda. But it is significant that this is an agenda that is not solely being pursued by the fascists and the far right, it is utterly mainstream. It was the government under conservative President Jacques Chirac that, in 2004, banned the hijab in state-run schools and government institutions. This ban was then expanded, by another conservative government under President Nicolas Sarkozy, to Muslim women delivering public services in 2007. Three years later the same government banned the wearing of full-faced veils in public in 2010. Restrictions continue to be tightened, most recently in 2023, school students were banned from wearing abayas.

What makes such legislation more shocking is not only that it was mainstream politicians who imposed it, rather than the far right, but the fact that such restrictions have been supported by much of the left and feminist campaigners in France. This support is justified by invoking the French concept of *laïcité*, secularism and the separation of church and state. But in a country where saints' days are public holidays and the prime minister talks of Catholicism being part of the life blood of the nation, using laïcité to justify the targeting of Muslim community is simply an attempt to give progressive cover to a complete collapse into Islamophobia. Most importantly it also denies Muslim women any agency in how they choose to live their lives.

Dictating what women should and shouldn't wear, should be anathema to anyone claiming to advocate for women's liberation. Not only that but by supporting these policies feminists and much of the left have opened the door for the far right to push for even more restrictions. Marine Le Pen now declares she wants to ban the hijab being worn anywhere in public in France. These policies led to the shocking sight of police harassing Muslim women wearing modest burkinis on beaches in 2016 in areas of the south of France controlled by National Rally mayors. The police insisted women remove their chosen clothing or leave the beach, as if simply being unclothed was part of French 'superior' liberated culture around women's bodies.

Similar racist narratives about women being at risk from immigrants and Muslims are at play in Britain and throughout Europe. In Britain, the scandal of police ignoring allegations of young women in vulnerable situations when they reported that they had been abused, has been distorted by fascists pursuing a racist agenda. For example, fascist Tommy Robinson has claimed that the police have protected Muslim men because of 'political correctness' and that such men were more likely to be abusers in 'grooming gangs'. This has been taken up by Tory politicians, and Elon Musk. Yet the police's own figures show that vast majority of such offences are carried out by white men.

In Germany this narrative was played out most dramatically after a number of thefts and sexual assaults took place at New Year's Eve celebrations in the cities of Cologne and Munich in 2015. These crimes were quickly, without evidence, blamed on immigrants and their 'inability' to integrate into a culture that supported women's rights was the cited cause. The events and their aftermath gave a boost to the far right and fascists, whose leading party today, Alternative für Deutschland (AfD), has just experienced its best ever election result.

Alice Weidel is co-leader of the AfD and, unlike Le Pen, she sees no need to distance herself or her party from Nazi roots. Her grandfather was a Nazi judge and her supporters chant 'Alice für Deutschland!' evoking 'Alles für Deutschland', or 'Everything for Germany'. This chant is banned in Germany as it was used by Hitler's Nazi stormtroopers. She has been described as an unlikely candidate for a far-right leader, because she is a lesbian and she has two children with her partner who is Sri Lankan – the party opposes the right of LGBT people to marry. But she says she is in the AfD because of her sexuality, not despite it, because the party addresses what she claims is the homophobia of immigrants and Muslims.

Again, there should be no illusions that Weidel might represent a softer aspect of the AfD's xenophobic politics. For example, in a speech to the German parliament in 2018 she said of immigrants: 'Burqas, girls in headscarves, knife-wielding men on government benefits and other good-for-nothing people are not going to ensure our prosperity'. Under her leadership the party's vote doubled to over 20 percent in February's national election, making them the second largest party in Germany. Three months later Germany's intelligence agency designated the party as 'extremist' because of its policies on ethnicity and excluding certain groups from equal participation in society. The AfD is suing the agency saying the move will 'delegitimise millions of votes'.

Then there is Georgia Meloni, Prime Minister of Italy since 2022. She began her political activism in the Movimento Sociale Italiano (Italian Social Movement, MSI), set up to keep fascist politics and organisation alive after the Second World War. As a leading light in its youth movement in 1996, she told French TV that, 'I think Mussolini was a good politician. Everything he did, he did for Italy. And we haven't had any politicians like that in the past fifty years'.

Today she leads the party she created, the Fratelli d'Italia (Brothers of Italy), and is feted in Europe as a politician with whom everyone can work, and someone who the US President listens to – a 'Trump whisperer'. Yet whatever her protestations that fascism is consigned to history, her party doesn't hide its political roots. Her supporters make no secret of echoing Benito Mussolini's politics. In 2024, an undercover reporter recorded the party's National Youth wing doing fascist salutes, using racist and antisemitic language, and chanting 'For a cleaner world, come back, Uncle Benito' and 'Sieg Heil!'. Meloni's first response was to condemn the tactic of a reporter infiltrating the youth group, only later did she criticise the actions of the party members.

These three women are not outliers, there are other women leaders in leading positions of far-right and fascist parties in Europe: Riikka Purra is Deputy Prime Minister of Finland and leader of the far-right Finns Party. She was exposed as having commented online about a confrontation with a group of immigrants in 2008 saying that 'if they gave me a gun, there'd be bodies on a commuter train, you'll see'. Pia Kjærsgaard, founded and led the far-right Dansk Folkeparti (Danish People's Party), and has spent forty years in the Danish parliament. Siv Jensen of Norway's extreme right wing Progress Party has been in the Parliament for over two decades and is the country's longest serving finance minister. Beata Szydło is a leading member of the Polish Prawo i Sprawiedliwość (Law and Justice Party), a member of the European parliament and former Prime Minister of Poland. She once used a speech at a memorial ceremony at the Auschwitz-Birkenau Nazi death camp to promote the party's nationalist anti-migrant policies.

These are some of the women that are the new face of fascism in Europe today, and they are integral to its rise.

Women are attracted to these movements by many aspects of their ideology, including the perception that the far right values the role of women as mothers and the importance of families. Glorifying the role of motherhood has long been a staple feature of fascist movements. Hitler's Nazi party talked of the importance of '*Kinder, Küche, und Kirche*' ('children, kitchen, and church'). Mussolini coined his campaign to get women to have more babies, the 'Battle for Births'. Today there is once again a modern spin on the propaganda. It is that feminists, and others who challenge what the right see as biologically dictated gender roles, have conned women into thinking that being exploited as a minor cog in the system is an achievement. Such exploitation is counterposed to the fulfilling lives they could have raising children fulltime. This narrative plays into the very real anxieties many women have about coping with the double burden of work, often with long hours and low pay, and being a good mother. It also expresses the alienation many women and men feel as workers in modern capitalism.

However, these ideas have another important and sinister purpose: promoting 'natalism' – that is, encouraging women to have more children – although not all women. Just as in Nazi Germany, when German women were told it was their moral and national duty to be breeders of the master race, it is white women who are told they must reproduce more children. In a replay of eugenicist ideas, a racist ideology that originated in Britain at the start of the twentieth century, the far right say white women must have multiple babies to avoid white populations being 'replaced' by immigrants. The 'Great Replacement Theory' is invoked by the far right across the US and Europe, and this racist conspiracy is deployed to tell women that their ability to reproduce is the first defence against the 'threat' of immigration. Far right politicians like to cite differences in 'culture' to justify their opposition to immigrations, however, at its core pronatalism is an expression of pure biological racism based on ideas of keeping a nation's bloodline 'pure'.

These ideas are central to government policies in Hungary and Italy for example. In Hungary the government under far-right leader Victor Orban gives substantial financial and tax incentives to Hungarian women to have large families, posing this as a direct alternative to immigration. He hosts biannual demographic summits on addressing falling birth rates of 'native' European populations. In Italy similar propaganda programmes encourage women to have many babies. At one such summit in 2024 Italian Prime Minister Meloni declared she wanted to 'reverse the narrative' on women having children: 'For decades, it has been said that bringing a child into the world would compromise freedom, dreams, career, in some cases beauty, and that it was therefore a choice that, in the end, was not "convenient"'. She also invokes the threat that Italy might be 'replaced' by immigrants unless women reproduce more.

These programmes do not just have echoes of fascist regimes in the past, they are in some cases direct lifts of policy from Mussolini and Hitler. Such racist conspiracist views are now common across the spectrum of the right. Even Britain's Tory Leader, Kemi Badenoch, has said the problem of looking after an ageing population was 'people not having enough children' and that immigration was not going to solve the problem.

What about younger women, is the far right attracting the next generation? This is where the 'femosphere', a term coined by academic Jilly Kay, comes in. Much has been written about the toxic nature of the 'manosphere', the online world of misogynist often far-right men, less known is the online world of far-right women.

On the surface, the femosphere looks like a lot of content posted by any mainstream 'influencer'. Authors such as Eviane Leidig, in her book *The Women of the Far Right*, have interviewed far-right women with large online followings. Leidig writes that such women, often coined 'trad wives', pride themselves on creating 'relatable' content to draw women in, such as advice on makeup, yoga, and gym routines. Yet beneath the surface the racist messaging is what matters, among the social media entries about recipes and home schooling are posts with headlines such as 'Need to breed'. Creators go to lengths to ensure their content doesn't get flagged by TikTok rules. For example, one video of a women applying makeup has a voice over in which she says: 'Take that foundation and cover up all of your face's imperfections. Just like your history teachers have covered up all of Islam's crimes throughout history'.

Some women are attracted to far-right influencers because they feel they are victims of 'woke' culture and part of a counterculture against the elites and establishment who want to undermine women's true purpose in life. So, influencers talk of women being freed from 'soul sucking nine to five' in order to fulfil their 'true' role as mothers and homemakers. Such ideas are often mixed in with a form of New Age mysticism and wellness culture, ideas that were also popular within the fascist movements of the early twentieth century. This advocate going back to nature, which today means avoiding toxins and 'Big Pharma'.

Of course, some of these online accounts are on the fringes, but many have garnered mass audiences. US right wing commentator Brett Cooper started her own programme on YouTube in January and had the 'second-fastest growing political YouTube channel in the first quarter of 2025 with over 900,000 new subscribers'.

It must be pointed out that there is a contradiction among the women who are most prolific online, on TikTok, and elsewhere extolling the virtues of fulltime homemaking and breeding. By working full time on social media output, they are not practising what they preach. Some describe how they have been criticised by men in their own movement for not being married or not having children and acknowledge this reflects sexist ideas. Some describe how far-right men use the term being 'feminised' as shorthand for something or someone becoming weak and experience the widespread use of deeply misogynist language to denigrate all women.

So, it would be mistaken to think that the presence of leading women means sexism has been eradicated in these movements, far from it.

At a time when the wider far right is on the rise the question of attracting women is central to the project of winning elections and continuing to move their political ideology into the mainstream. Looking to an electoral road to power means widening your political base, so winning women becomes a key part of the strategy. The experience of the last decade or so shows that the growing involvement of women in fascist and far-right organisations does not indicate any actual tempering of the reactionary ideas and racism of such groups. But the presence of women leaders and activists can help create the illusion that these ideas are not a threat, and even, preposterously, that they are in tune with women's rights.

The more women who are visibly leading, supporting, and voting for fascist and far-right parties, the more these parties are normalised and appear non-threatening, in turn only increasing their reach and potential for growth. It's a dangerous combination.

FROM FEAR TO FASCISM

Tahir Abbas

'We live in interesting times', a phrase overused in today's world, feels particularly apt as President Trump reassumes leadership of the 'free world'. His policies, marked by 'making deals', self-aggrandisement, and erratic governance, from firing and rehiring key officials to fuelling stock market uncertainty and cryptocurrency volatility, flip-flopping over tariffs, herald a troubling era of hard-right, protectionist, and isolationist rule. This shift carries implications globally, especially for Europe, as a trading bloc but also as a political entity on the global stage, which has fallen below the consistently high standards that former German Chancellor Angela Merkel fervently contended to uphold for all of the European Union. Meanwhile, the resurgence of far-right movements worldwide has drawn comparisons to the fascism of the recent past, underlining the urgent need to re-examine what it means for us today in a political climate echoing the totalitarian ideologies of the 1930s. Throughout Europe, nationalist parties exploit economic insecurity and cultural fears to promote xenophobic narratives and historical revisionism. Mimicking their fascist predecessors, these leaders invoke nostalgia for a mythic past of glory and stability, positioning themselves as saviours of national rejuvenation. In framing immigrants and foreign influences as existential threats to national identity, they sow division and fear. This resurgence not only mirrors the rhetoric and symbolism of early fascist regimes but also paves the way for centralised power, undermining democratic institutions and eroding civil liberties.

Modern European fascism, a troubling evolution of historical far-right ideologies, has adopted to the twenty-first century by effectively monopolising digital media and leveraging burgeoning legislative power. This contemporary iteration excels at retrofitting the propaganda tactics of the 1930s for the digital age, bypassing traditional media gatekeepers, and directly engaging with target audiences. Germany's Alternative for

Germany (AfD) stands as a salient example of this shift. The party has become particularly adept at deploying platforms such as Facebook and YouTube to disseminate pervasive anti-Muslim and anti-migrant rhetoric. This often takes the form of viral disinformation campaigns that falsely attribute rising crime rates and the spread of disease directly to refugees and immigrants. These campaigns are frequently bolstered by inflammatory imagery and sensationalised headlines designed to provoke fear and resentment. The AfD's digital strategy allows them to cultivate an 'alternative news' ecosystem, mirroring tactics seen in other European far-right parties such as the Austrian FPÖ, which developed its own online broadcasting to circumvent mainstream media. This approach helps solidify a narrative that demonises minority groups and portrays established political parties and media as untrustworthy

Beyond national borders, transnational white nationalist groups such as the American Renaissance exploit various digital platforms, including their own websites and, where permissible, larger sites like YouTube and X, to propagate their ideology. A key element of their messaging involves the promotion of discredited and long-refuted IQ studies to argue for innate racial differences and assert the supposed intellectual inferiority of non-white populations. This pseudoscientific veneer is used to frame non-white immigrants as an inherent threat to the social cohesion and perceived progress of Western societies. Such rhetoric provides a disturbingly familiar 'rational' justification for policies that echo the darkest periods of history, including Nazi-era eugenics, by advocating for measures such as restrictive immigration bans and systems of racial segregation.

Meanwhile, parties like Italy's Brothers of Italy have successfully identified and exploited newer digital frontiers to reach diverse demographics. They have effectively harnessed platforms, such as TikTok, to deliver their nationalist and anti-immigrant messaging, specifically tailoring content to resonate with younger audiences who are heavy users of such platforms. This includes short, impactful videos that promote patriotic themes, often link immigration to societal problems, and reinforce a strong sense of national identity defined by exclusion. This multi-platform digital dominance allows modern far-right movements to not only disseminate their core ideological tenets widely but also to normalise extremist viewpoints and build dedicated online communities that can be mobilised for political action. The legislative power gained by some of these parties subsequently provides a worrying pathway to translate these digitally amplified, divisive narratives into concrete policies that impact civil liberties and the rights of minority groups.

Beyond these party-specific strategies, far-right groups have orchestrated broader digital campaigns, such as the 'It's Okay to Be White' initiative. Beginning in 2017, this effort flooded social media, Twitter, Reddit, and 4chan, with flyers and posts crafted to provoke outrage and mainstream the notion that white identity is under siege, a tactic that mirrors the AfD's disinformation campaigns but targets a transnational audience. Social media algorithms and online forums accelerate the spread of hate speech and conspiracy theories, creating echo chambers that radicalise users. State-aligned media outlets amplify these narratives while smearing dissenters and independent journalists, while repressive laws erode academic freedom and stifle civil society. This fusion of retrograde nationalism and digital-age manipulation suggests that fascism's dangerous appeal persists, not as a relic, but as a dynamic threat corroding European democracy today.

The resurgence of Europe's far-right demands a clear-eyed analysis of fascism's distinct traits and its overlaps with broader reactionary movements. Fascism, a totalitarian ideology, centres on ultranationalism, authoritarianism, and the violent rejection of liberal democracy. It consolidates power under a single leader or party, crushes dissent through repression and propaganda and enforces a myth of national purity. Mussolini's Italy (1922–1943) epitomised these doctrines: he dismantled democratic institutions, deployed paramilitary Blackshirts to terrorise critics, and fused militarism with nostalgia for imperial Rome. His corporatist economy subordinated individual rights to state-directed collaboration between labour and capital, framing it as national duty. These tactics, centralised control, cultural mythmaking, and systemic repression, reveal fascism's blueprint for power. While the far right spans diverse ideologies, from xenophobic populism to neo-Nazism, fascism represents its most virulent form: a relentless drive to replace pluralism with hierarchy, democracy with dictatorship, and empathy with exclusion.

Fascism and the far right, though distinct, share core tactics that fuel their resurgence in Europe: both instrumentalise public disillusionment with mainstream politics, exploiting anxieties over globalisation, cultural erosion, and economic precarity. They thrive by positioning themselves as rebels against a 'corrupt elite', a nebulous category spanning political establishments, wealthy elites, intellectuals, and institutions such as the EU, while claiming to defend the 'forgotten' masses. Islamophobic rhetoric, in particular, frames Muslim communities as agents of cultural contamination, stoking fears of a 'clash of civilisations'. This strategy taps into widespread grievances, from stagnant wages to crumbling social mobility, especially among younger generations, offering a seductive narrative of cultural purity and national revival. In fusing anti-establishment anger with xenophobic nationalism, these movements reframe democratic pluralism as weakness, positioning authoritarianism as the only shield against societal decay. While fascism embodies the far right's most violent extremes, its resurgence across Europe has normalised once-fringe ideologies, eroding democratic guardrails and mainstreaming xenophobia, Islamophobia, and anti-minority hostility.

Crucially, Islamophobia has become one of the far right's most effective tools for mobilising support, reinforcing a broader discourse of exclusion deeply embedded in European politic. Islamophobic tropes have long been embedded in European discourse, serving as a cornerstone for far-right ideologies. This is best illustrated by the Great Replacement Theory (GRT), which frames Muslims as existential invaders. The GRT is a prime example, originating in France and gaining global popularity in recent years. This theory suggests that there is a deliberate plan to replace white Europeans with non-white immigrants via mass migration and higher birth rates. Proponents argue that this replacement is facilitated by a globalist elite composed of politicians, corporations, and media, aiming to weaken Western societies. GRT is frequently associated with anti-Semitic and anti-Muslim rhetoric, promoting a dangerous belief that fosters racism and xenophobia. Historically, conspiracy theories such as GRT have been linked to the construction of race and religion as enemy subjects, with Jews often collectively targeted. Central to these theories is the dualism of good and evil, where conspirators are heavily stereotyped and deemed evil. In modern times, GRT has been amplified by waves of refugees from the Middle East and Africa, and it has been embraced by illiberal nationalist leaders such as Viktor Orbán of Hungary and Robert Fico of Slovakia. The theory's online presence has also contributed to its spread, exploiting insecurities and fears among the citizenry in the West.

This mainstreaming of Islamophobia has implications for social cohesion and national security, particularly in majority-white societies. A notable example is France's National Rally (formerly Front National), which successfully lobbied for bans on Islamic clothing namely the burqa and niqab. Marine Le Pen has mainstreamed GRT, declaring at a 2019 rally, 'we are facing a replacement of population, a replacement of civilisation'. These laws, framed as protecting secular values, disproportionately target Muslim women and reflect the party's broader strategy of exploiting cultural anxieties to justify exclusionary policies. In Austria, the Freedom Party (FPÖ) similarly pushed for restrictions on mosque construction and halal food practices, embedding anti-Muslim sentiment into official legislation. The Party for Freedom (PVV) in the Netherlands, led by Geert Wilders, epitomises the mainstreaming of Islamophobic rhetoric. Wilders has consistently advocated for strict immigration controls and the banning of Islamic symbols, framing Muslims as incompatible with Dutch culture. His party's success in parliamentary elections highlights the growing acceptance of far-right ideologies in mainstream politics. Meanwhile, Hungary's Prime Minister Viktor Orbán has adopted a political style reminiscent of Mussolini, using state-controlled media to disseminate nationalist propaganda while centralising power in his Fidesz party. Similarly, Italy's Matteo Salvini, leader of the League, echoes Mussolini's rhetoric by framing immigrants as threats to national identity and economic stability. These leaders use mass rallies, militaristic imagery, and authoritarian language to reveal their deliberate invocation of fascist symbols to legitimise their rule.

Far too many European nations today represent Muslim immigration as a deliberate assault on identity, justifying exclusionary practices, aligning with a wider far-right strategy of transforming conspiracy into electoral capital. The resurgence of far-right ideologies and xenophobic rhetoric in Western societies provides a critical lens through which to examine the intersections of race, class, and global capitalism. These movements reveal profound contradictions within the structures of modern capitalism, particularly regarding how racial identity often supersedes economic rationality in political mobilisation, whether it is opposition to immigration policies, resistance to multiculturalism, or the rise of populist nationalism. This phenomenon reveals how racial ideology continues to serve as a powerful tool for consolidating power, even when it works against the economic self-interest of its adherents. This normalisation of xenophobic discourse creates an environment conducive to hate crimes and social division.

At the core of this dynamic is the collision between economic necessity and racialised fear, a tension that fuels modern fascism's resurgence. Nowhere is this clearer than in debates over skilled immigration, a nexus where Silicon Valley's reliance on global talent clashes with populist narratives of cultural dispossession. In the US, opposition to programmes like the H-1B visa system exposes a paradox: while tech industries depend on foreign expertise to fill critical gaps, far-right movements frame this as a threat to white economic entitlement. Critics simplistically claim immigrant workers depress wages, yet this ignores the broader economic contributions of skilled migrants, from tax revenues to innovation-driven growth over time, even as these workers remain vulnerable to precarious employment and restrictive citizenship norms. Rational economic arguments falter against the visceral fear of displacement that conflate immigration with 'cultural suicide'.

This dynamic transcends borders: Brexit's triumph, fuelled by promises to 'reclaim sovereignty' from EU migrants, prioritised racialised nationalism over economic pragmatism, mirroring Hungary's Orbán or Italy's Salvini, who exploit migration as a scapegoat for systemic inequities. In 2016, Leave advocates promised that exiting the EU and curbing immigration would restore economic sovereignty, claiming it would yield more jobs and higher wages for British workers, despite immigrants' net positive contributions to the economy over time. This narrative mirrors fascist tactics by scapegoating migrants for systemic failures, offering exclusion as a populist salve for precarity. Such movements reveal how fascism's modern iteration leverages economic grievances to mask deeper anxieties about racial hierarchy, positioning exclusionary policies as both patriotic and economically necessary, even as they entrench inequality.

The current global economic order, dominated by Western interests and increasingly concentrated in tech monopolies, generates contradictions that manifest in numerous ways. Anxiety over immigration, whether skilled or unskilled, reflects a deeper crisis in white identity as global economic power gradually shifts away from its recent historical Western centre. For many white workers, whose connection to economic power structures is increasingly tenuous, racial identity becomes a crucial anchor, lest they lose even more preciously earned privileges that come automatically with dominant hegemonic whiteness. Challenges to white economic privilege are therefore perceived not just as economic threats but as existential catastrophes, exacerbating tensions between global integration and nationalist impulses. The intersection of race and class in this context reveals the persistent power of racial ideology in maintaining political alliances that often work against class interests. Tech companies' ability to attract global talent while maintaining support from nationalist politicians exemplifies the adaptability of capitalist structures in managing these contradictions. However, this arrangement appears increasingly unstable as economic realities clash with racialised expectations of privilege. The resulting tensions suggest that Western capitalism's reliance on racial hierarchy as a stabilising force may be approaching its limits, though the path toward a more equitable global order remains uncertain and contested. The implications of these developments extend far beyond immigration policy. They suggest that the future of Western capitalism will largely depend on its ability to navigate the contradiction between global economic integration and nationalist political movements grounded in racial identity.

This contradiction is precisely what fascism exploits, using economic systems to entrench racial hierarchies and frame racialised groups as existential threats to national prosperity. Historically, fascist regimes such as Nazi Germany leveraged economic crises, such as hyperinflation or unemployment, to scapegoat minorities, blaming Jews, Roma, and others for societal ills. This strategy diverted blame from structural failures, consolidating power by positioning the dominant racial group as the 'true' engine of economic vitality. Modern iterations mirror this logic: Hungary's Orbán frames Muslim migrants as 'economic parasites', justifying austerity measures that disproportionately harm marginalised communities while subsidising oligarchs. Similarly, Trump's 'America First' policies conflate immigration with job loss, masking how neoliberal capitalism's inequalities fuel precarity. Fascism's economic model, corporatism in Mussolini's Italy or today's crony capitalism, prioritises state-aligned monopolies (or oligarchies) that exclude racialised groups from wealth and labour rights. By tying economic survival to racial purity, fascism transforms inequality into a moral panic, ensuring that racial exclusion becomes both a cause and consequence of policy. The GRT exemplifies this: it frames non-white immigration as a plot to 'replace' white workers. In this way, fascism's economic agenda perpetuates racism, ensuring that racialised groups remain perpetual outsiders in systems designed to exclude them.

Fascism's political machinery hinges on constructing a mythic 'people' (the Volk, the nation) defined by racial and cultural homogeneity. This process requires the dehumanisation of others, who are cast as invaders, degenerates, or existential threats. Mussolini's fascism framed Ethiopia's invasion (1935) as a civilising mission, masking resource extraction as racial destiny. Hitler's Nuremberg Laws (1935) codified Jewish exclusion, legally redefining citizenship through bloodline. Today, parties such as Germany's AfD and France's National Rally deploy similar tactics, framing Muslims and migrants as 'enemies of the people'. Marine Le Pen's RN, for instance, claims Muslims 'refuse to assimilate', positioning secularism as a shield for Christian identity. Politically, fascism erodes pluralism by centralising power in a charismatic leader who embodies the 'will of the people', a dynamic that silences dissent as treason. Orbán's 'illiberal democracy' and Trump's 'deep state' conspiracies exemplify this: they delegitimise institutions (courts, media) as tools of 'elites', while framing racialised policies (border walls, Muslim bans) as patriotic acts. Orbán epitomises this fusion, weaving Islamophobia, economic scapegoating, and digital propaganda into a cohesive strategy. By branding Muslim migrants as 'economic parasites' and threats to Hungarian purity, he justifies restrictive citizenship laws while flooding state-aligned media and social platforms with anti-immigrant content, reinforcing a racialised 'Volk' that excludes outsiders. By collapsing political legitimacy into racial identity, fascism ensures that governance becomes a perpetual war against internal and external 'others', justifying authoritarianism as the only path to national survival.

Fascist policies operationalise racism by embedding exclusion into legal frameworks to legitimise violence and marginalisation. Nazi Germany's Nuremberg Laws (1935) stripped Jews of citizenship, banned interracial marriage, and laid the groundwork for genocide. Similarly, Italy's 1938 racial laws excluded Jews from public life, framing them as 'biologically inferior'. Modern far-right policies mirror these tactics: Hungary's 'Stop Soros' law (2018) criminalises aiding migrants, while Italy's citizenship laws deny rights to children of non-EU parents, despite birth on Italian soil. France's burqa ban (2010) and Austria's restrictions on Islamic education (2020) frame Muslim cultural practices as incompatible with 'European values', legalising Islamophobia. These policies are often draped in neutrality, 'public safety', 'integration', but their intent is racial control. GRT underpins such laws: by framing diversity as a threat, fascists justify surveillance, segregation, and exclusion. Even climate policies are targeted; Poland's coal-heavy energy agenda is framed as defending 'Polish jobs' against EU 'green imperialism', scapegoating migrants for ecological crises. Through law, fascism transforms racism from ideology into infrastructure, ensuring racialised groups remain perpetual outsiders in systems that criminalise their existence.

Fascism's cultural project seeks to erase pluralism, replacing it with a mythic past where racial purity and hierarchy are naturalised. Mussolini's regime glorified imperial Rome, while Hitler's Nazis exalted an Aryan 'golden age'. Today, this cultural warfare persists: Orbán erects statues of medieval kings to frame Muslims as 'invaders', and Italy's Meloni revives fascist-era symbols like the *fasces* to legitimise nationalism. Education systems are co-opted: Poland's curriculum whitewashes colonial atrocities, while Texas bans critical race theory to suppress discussions of systemic racism. Pop culture amplifies these myths: films like *300* (2006) reframe Persians as monstrous 'others', mirroring modern anti-Muslim tropes. Social media accelerates this erasure, with algorithms amplifying content that frames diversity as 'cultural suicide'. Elon Musk's X platform, for instance, hosts influencers who claim 'white genocide' via immigration, echoing GRT. By monopolising cultural narratives, art, history, media, fascism rewrites collective memory, positioning racial exclusion as a patriotic duty. This cultural hegemony ensures that racism is not merely policy but a shared worldview, where pluralism is weakness and hierarchy is destiny.

At the heart of this cultural war lies eugenics, the pseudoscientific belief in 'improving' human populations through controlled breeding, a cornerstone of fascist ideology that provides a veneer of 'rationality' to justify racial hierarchies. In Nazi Germany, eugenics underpinned the Holocaust, with policies targeting Jews, Roma, disabled individuals, and others deemed 'genetically inferior'. Today, eugenicist logic resurfaces in subtler forms, often masked by debates over immigration, public health, or genetic research. For example, Orbán frames Muslim migrants as 'biologically incompatible' with Europe, echoing eugenicist fears of 'racial dilution'. Similarly, far-right groups in Italy and France cite discredited studies on IQ disparities to legitimise anti-immigrant policies. Modern eugenics also intersects with neoliberalism: Silicon Valley's obsession with 'optimising' human potential, via gene editing or AI-driven 'talent', revives dangerous notions of genetic superiority. These ideologies dovetail with fascist goals, framing certain groups as 'undesirable' or 'burdensome', thereby justifying exclusion. In recasting eugenics as 'science', far-right movements exploit public trust in empirical research to mainstream racism, positioning it as a logical response to numerous societal challenges.

Scientific racism, the misuse of biology, anthropology, and genetics to hierarchise races, remains a critical tool for modern fascism. The far-right cherry pick data to claim non-white populations are 'inherently prone' to crime, disease, or cultural backwardness. France's National Rally, for instance, cites skewed crime statistics to argue that Muslim immigrants 'threaten' public safety, while Germany's AfD invokes debunked studies on 'genetic predispositions' to justify anti-refugee policies. This pseudoscience is amplified by think tanks like the New Century Foundation, which publishes 'research' linking race to intelligence or criminality, despite academic condemnation. Even the denial of climate change intersects with scientific racism: far-right figures such as the Danish Bjørn Lomborg argue that 'overpopulation' in the Global South, not systemic inequality, drives ecological crises, echoing colonial-era Malthusianism. By framing racism as 'evidence-based', these groups sanitise fascist ideals, making them palatable to educated elites.

Universities and journals, often unwittingly, provide platforms for such ideas, as seen in the *Journal of Bioeconomics'* flirtations with race-based genetic determinism. This intellectual veneer allows scientific racism to infiltrate mainstream discourse, normalising fascist exclusion under the guise of 'rational debate'.

The digital age has revitalised eugenicist and scientific racist ideologies, enabling their rapid dissemination through memes, algorithms, and 'alt-tech' platforms. Websites like *Unz Review* host essays advocating 'differential birth rates' as existential threats to white populations, while YouTube channels like Stefan Molyneux's promote 'race realism' to millions. Social media algorithms, optimised for engagement, prioritise inflammatory content. Elon Musk's X endorsed the 'IQ gap' myth, while TikTok's algorithm recommends videos linking immigration to 'genetic decline'. Gaming communities and 4chan forums further radicalise users with 'ironic' eugenicist memes, normalising hate through humour. This digital ecosystem mirrors historical fascist propaganda strategies, blending pseudoscience with mass mobilisation. Through framing eugenics as 'forbidden knowledge' suppressed by 'elites', far-right influencers position themselves as rebels against 'political correctness', recruiting tech-savvy youth to their cause. The result is a feedback loop where scientific racism evolves virally, adapting to evade content moderation while radicalising new adherents.

Eugenicist ideologies directly inform far-right policy agendas, eroding democratic norms under the banner of the 'public good'. Hungary's ban on gender studies and restrictions on LGBTQ+ rights are framed as 'protecting national DNA', echo Nazi policies criminalising 'degenerate' identities. Italy's Meloni government funds fertility programs for 'ethnically Italian' families while slashing healthcare for migrants, mirrors Mussolini's pro-natalist laws. In the US, far-right think tanks push policies tying welfare access to genetic testing, resurrecting eugenicist arguments about 'undeserving' populations. These policies are often justified through crisis narratives: Orbán claims low birth rates among Hungarians threaten 'racial survival', while France's Le Pen warns of Muslim birth rates 'swamping' Europe. In fuelling demographic anxiety, fascists reframe democracy as a threat to racial purity, positioning authoritarianism as necessary to 'protect the people'. This undermines pluralism, as seen in

Poland's criminalisation of abortion for foetal abnormalities, a policy rooted in eugenicist fears of 'defective' births. Such measures reveal fascism's core logic: substituting human rights with biopolitical control, where citizenship is contingent on genetic 'fitness'.

The resurgence of far-right movements in Europe indicates a chilling continuity with fascism's darkest legacies, recalibrated for the digital age. By marshalling Islamophobia, exploiting economic precarity, and manipulating cultural anxieties, these movements revive fascism's core tenets: ultranationalism, authoritarianism, and the violent rejection of pluralism. Digital platforms amplify propaganda once disseminated through rallies and radio, while legislative power consolidates control, echoing the erosion of democratic norms seen in Mussolini's Italy or Hitler's Germany. The GRT, a modern descendant of fascist conspiracy-mongering, mirrors the scapegoating of minorities that justified historical atrocities, now reframed as a 'clash of civilisations'. Yet this resurgence is not merely a replay of the past but a mutation, leveraging neoliberal capitalism's inequalities and algorithmic radicalisation to mainstream extremism. The far right's fusion of populism, xenophobia, and state-backed repression reveals fascism's adaptability, a warning that its toxic ideologies persist not as relics, but as evolving threats to democracy itself. To combat this, Europe must confront not only the symptoms of discontent but the fascist logic that seeks to exploit them, lest the shadows of the 1930s stretch further into the twenty-first century.

THE CHETNIK GENOCIDE

Marko Attila Hoare

The genocide carried out by Serb nationalists against Muslim Bosniaks (Bosnian Muslims) and Croats in the 1990s was the preeminent international crisis of its day. It dominated the pages and screens of the world media, preoccupied Western statesmen, and became a cause célèbre for a whole generation of activists. Yet, it is not widely known that the genocide was largely a repeat of a similar genocide that had taken place a half century earlier, during 1941–1945, in the chaos of World War II, when Bosnia-Hercegovina was occupied by Nazi Germany and Fascist Italy. The extreme Serb-nationalist Chetnik movement, under the umbrella of Fascist Italy's occupation forces and later of the Germans, massacred tens of thousands of people, above all Muslims but also Croats, anti-fascist Serbs and others, with the goal of creating an ethnically pure 'Great Serbia' – an expanded Serbia that would include Bosnia-Hercegovina and much of Croatia. This is a story of how foreign fascist occupation exacerbated national conflicts in an occupied country and catalysed the rise of local extremists seeking the most radical of solutions to them.

Bosnia-Hercegovina is a country that throughout its modern history has been demographically divided between three principal ethnonational groups: the Orthodox Serbs, Catholic Croats, and Muslim Bosniaks. While they speak the same language and share most cultural traits, their leaders have resisted integration to form a single multi-religious nationality. Instead, they have competed politically or collaborated tactically with each other. With none of the three enjoying an overall majority in Bosnia, none has succeeded in dominating it. Traditionally, Serb nationalists formally considered Bosnia a Serb land, and Muslims and Croats in Bosnia as Muslim and Catholic Serbs. They upheld this ideology while Bosnia was under the rule of the Habsburg Austro-Hungarian Empire in the period 1878-1918, when modern party politics in Bosnia was born. For some of this period,

Muslim Bosniaks and Orthodox Serbs collaborated against the foreign Catholic occupier. However, in 1918, the Austro-Hungarian empire collapsed with its defeat in World War I, and Bosnia and Serbia (as well as Croatia, Slovenia and other mostly South Slavic lands) became parts of the new state of Yugoslavia, formally named the Kingdom of Serbs, Croats and Slovenes. The new kingdom was in many ways an expanded Serbia, ruled from the Serbian capital of Belgrade through a Serbian-dominated army and bureaucracy, so initially seemed to fulfil the national aspirations of the Bosnian Serbs. But very quickly, Bosnian Serb nationalists became disappointed with the new order, largely due to the Muslim question.

Despite their history of common opposition to the Habsburgs, Serbs and Muslims in the predominantly agricultural country of Bosnia were divided from one another by the agrarian question. In Ottoman times, the landlord class in Bosnia was overwhelmingly Muslim, while most Serb peasants were subject to a system resembling serfdom; by the end of Ottoman rule in 1878, despite reforms, they still lacked ownership of their plots or farms and were required to pay their landlords a third of their produce and the state another tenth. After the Austro-Hungarians occupied Bosnia-Hercegovina in 1878, they largely preserved this system of agrarian class relations, ensuring that a class divide continued to exacerbate the national and religious differences between Muslims and Christians. This created a dilemma for the Serb political classes: they could not win the Muslim landlords and Orthodox Serb peasants at the same time. Either Serb politicians could seek to win the Muslim landlords and by extension Muslims generally to Serb national politics, at the price of alienating the Serb peasants, or they could win the popular support of the Serb peasants that made up most of the Bosnian Serb population, at the price of alienating the Muslims.

Belgrade's eventual compromise agrarian reform of 1921 satisfied neither Serbs nor Muslims. The Bosnian Serbs split politically between the mainstream nationalist People's Radical Party and the more anti-Muslim League of Farmers, which rejected the agrarian compromise and sought a more radical reckoning with the Muslim landlords. The Farmers would form the basis for the Bosnian wing of the genocidal Chetnik movement in World War II. The Muslims, by contrast, responded to the threat posed them by the new, Serb-dominated Yugoslav regime, by mostly uniting behind a single party of their own – the Yugoslav Muslim Organisation (JMO), emphasising that they rejected inclusion in Serb nationhood and effectively saw themselves as a separate national community that needed its own political party. Ironically, therefore, although the Serbs in this period demographically outnumbered the Muslims in Bosnia (comprising 43.87 percent of the Bosnian-Hercegovinian population according to the 1921 census, compared to 31.97 percent for the Muslims and 23.58 percent for the Croats and other Catholics) they were politically weaker. Thus, in municipal elections in 1928, the less numerous but united Muslims through the JMO won greater representation in local government than the more numerous but politically divided Serbs.

The JMO sought an agreement with the political classes in Serbia that would protect the Muslims from radical Bosnian Serb demands. In return for agreeing to vote, in the constituent assembly of 1921, in favour of a constitution that guaranteed Serbia's hegemony in the new Yugoslav state, it was able to extract important concessions: not just an agrarian reform that was less unfavourable to the Muslim landlords, but the preservation of Bosnia's traditional provinces and borders within the new state administration. In the years following, this would be blamed by the Bosnian Serb nationalists for their inability to break Muslim resistance in Bosnia. Priorities were different for the political classes of Serbia on the one hand, which prioritised some level of accommodation with the Muslims, to prevent them going over wholly to the side of the Croats, and on the other for the Bosnian Serb politicians, who prioritised their local political struggle with the JMO for control of Bosnia, and who gravitated toward collaborating with the Croats against it. This local struggle was a bread-and-butter issue: whether a municipality was under Serb (Radical, Farmer) or Muslim (JMO) control determined which nationality would enjoy the jobs and patronage in it.

Bosnian Serb frustration manifested itself during the 1920s in increasing use of paramilitary violence against the JMO and Muslims, but this failed to break their resistance. Milan Srškić, the leader of the Radicals in Bosnia and the leading Bosnian Serb politician, responded with an innovation in Serb-nationalist thinking: instead of upholding Bosnia as a unified 'Serb land', the country should be divided up territorially between Serb- and Croat-majority provinces, so that the Muslims would be fragmented and reduced to a minority everywhere. He was eventually able to put this plan into practice in 1929, when Yugoslavia's King Aleksandar established a royal dictatorship and appointed him minister of justice. Srškić reorganised Yugoslavia into nine large provinces or 'banovinas'. Bosnia was divided between four banovinas, three of which were joined to non-Bosnian territories of other Yugoslav lands (Serbia, Croatia, and Montenegro), while the fourth Bosnian banovina, comprising western Bosnia, enjoyed a Bosnian Serb majority. Thus, in three of these four new banovinas, Serbs were in the majority; in the fourth, Croats were in the majority; the Muslims were reduced to a minority in all four. Yet the JMO and Muslims remained unbroken.

The period of King Aleksandar's dictatorship, 1929-1934, was a period of Bosnian Serb ascendancy in Bosnia. But it ended in 1934 when the king was assassinated, and the following year, a new prime minister of Yugoslavia, Milan Stojadinović, assumed office and reversed Aleksandar and Srškić's anti-Muslim policy. Stojadinović allied with the JMO and, in return for its participation in his government, granted it renewed hegemony over the Serbs in Bosnia, much to the fury of the Bosnian Serb nationalists. But fortunes changed again in 1939, when Yugoslavia's regent, Prince Pavle, dismissed Stojadinović and appointed a government committed to reaching an agreement with the Croats at the expense of the Muslims. That year, Croatia was established as an autonomous banovina within Yugoslavia, while Bosnia was effectively partitioned between Croatia and Serbia. The Muslims responded by mobilising in the Muslim Movement for the Autonomy of Bosnia-Hercegovina, which demanded that Bosnia, like Croatia, be established as an autonomous banovina. Bosnian Serbs responded by mobilising in a counter-movement called Serbs Assemble!, opposed to any such Bosnian autonomy, which they feared would separate them from Serbia. Serbs Assemble! was closely linked to the Serb Cultural Club, a group of extreme nationalists in Serbia from the ranks of the elite, which sought Yugoslavia's reordering on a basis more favourable to Serbian nationalist goals. Bosnian Serbs resident in Serbia featured prominently in the Serb Cultural Club, which was particularly concerned to ensure exclusive Serb possession of Bosnia. The Croat leadership, meanwhile, was largely happy with the 1939 partition of Bosnia, though it sought additional Bosnian territories for the Croatian banovina. But a radical minority of

Croats – the fascist Ustashas – rejected the partition of Bosnia and claimed the whole of it for Croat nationhood.

Thus, on the eve of the Axis invasion of Yugoslavia, Bosnia's peoples were bitterly divided over whom it belonged to or what its constitutional status should be, and had splintered into rival political movements to ensure the resolution of the question in the way they respectively wanted. In these circumstances, the occupation of Yugoslavia and Bosnia in April 1941 by the German Nazis and Italian Fascists – moral nihilists who systematically promoted and exploited ethno-national and other divisions in the lands they occupied – was a recipe for bloodshed and disaster. Hitler and Mussolini dismembered Yugoslavia and grouped the larger part of Croatia and all of Bosnia-Hercegovina into a puppet state, the 'Independent State of Croatia' (NDH), under the Ustashas. The establishment of this state is sometimes portrayed by Serb nationalists as reflective of some supposed special German support for or interest in Croatia, but the truth was the opposite: it was intended as a condominium and buffer zone between the German and Italian empires in what was a strategic backwater – in contrast to Serbia, in which the Germans were much more interested and where they established a tighter and more exclusive control. The NDH was divided into German and Italian zones of influence, with the Germans getting the lion's share: the Croatian capital of Zagreb and the key Bosnian cities of Sarajevo, Banja Luka and Tuzla; the Italians received less politically and economically important parts of Croatia and Bosnia that nonetheless included the Croatian coast and Mostar, capital of the region of Hercegovina.

The Ustashas were extreme even by the standards of 1940s fascists, and embarked on a policy of genocide with the Serb, Jewish and Gypsy populations of their puppet state. Formally, in line with traditional Croat national ideology, they claimed the Muslims as Croats of the Islamic faith and sought to assimilate them into Croat nationhood. But under their ramshackle, heavily factionalised administration, Ustasha relations with the Muslims varied greatly according to locality. Losses resulting from Yugoslavia's agrarian reform led some Muslims to support the Ustasha regime, and in some localities, some Muslims participated in the genocide of Serbs. But in some localities, the Ustashas were Catholic-sectarian and anti-Muslim, and there were cases of Catholic Croat Ustashas wearing fezzes while massacring Serbs, to implicate falsely the Muslims in the genocide and incite Serb retaliation against them, thereby to divide the Muslims and Serbs against each other. Since Serbs made up nearly a third of the population of the Ustasha puppet-state, and the state was anyway based on weak institutional foundations and very limited popular support, the policy of genocide was self-destructive: it incited a popular Serb rebellion that the Ustasha regime was wholly incapable of suppressing. Given the history of polarisation in the interwar period between Serbs on the one hand and Croats and particularly Muslims on the other, the Serb rebellion involved large scale retaliation against, and massacres of, Muslim and Croat civilians.

However, in addition to their history of conflict, there was also a strong countervailing tradition of cooperation between Bosnia-Hercegovina's peoples. In 1941, this tradition was upheld by the Communist Party of Yugoslavia. Its organisation in Bosnia had grown out of the Bosnian Social Democratic Party and labour movement, which had upheld the solidarity of Serb, Croat, Muslim, and other workers against the bourgeoisie of all nations. Furthermore, the Communists subscribed to a Marxist-Leninist belief in the right of nations to self-determination, which they interpreted to include Bosnia. They had opposed the 1939 partition of Bosnia between Serbia and Croatia. Although they only began actively to fight the fascist occupiers from 22 June 1941, when Germany invaded the Soviet Union, they had already begun laying the organisational basis for the resistance from the start of the occupation in April. They had structural roots in the Bosnian countryside, where most of the Bosnian population lived: seasonal workers migrated from the countryside to the cities and towns for work, where they were recruited into the Communist movement and carried it back to their villages. And many village schoolteachers were Communist supporters or sympathisers, forming another bridgehead for the movement in the countryside. The Communists therefore formed a natural leadership for the resistance to the Ustasha genocide of the desperate Serb peasants. They built a movement in Yugoslavia that, under the leadership of Josip Broz Tito, would grow into the most successful resistance force in Nazi-occupied Europe. And in Bosnia, they did so under the banner of a free, unified and self-governing Bosnia-Hercegovina as the common homeland of Serbs, Croats, and Muslims.

Although in some cases Communists in Bosnia accepted or collaborated in Serb rebel massacres of Muslims and Croats, the tendency of their movement was ultimately to restrain and prevent them, and to build a joint resistance encompassing all Bosnia-Hercegovina's peoples: the People's Liberation Movement or 'Partisans', which laid the foundations for an eventual Bosnian state. But this Communist policy of Bosnian state-building and multinational cooperation between Serbs, Muslims, and Croats engendered resistance from Serb chauvinist elements among the rebels that favoured developing the resistance in the opposite direction: the destruction of the Muslims and Croats in Bosnia-Hercegovina to ensure exclusive Serb possession of the territory and its incorporation into an expanded or 'Great' Serbia. This tendency gradually took shape as the Chetnik movement. Whereas the Communists sought to unite Serbs, Croats and Muslims in a joint liberation movement against the occupiers, the Chetniks sought the opposite: to collaborate with the occupiers and, under their umbrella, to kill, expel or forcibly assimilate the Muslims and Croats. In Serbia, the Chetnik movement emerged under the leadership of Colonel Draža Mihailović, representing army officers, politicians, and other notables previously largely associated with the Serb Cultural Club and its circle, who had opposed the pre-1941 Yugoslav regime and rejected formal capitulation to the German invaders. But they quickly moved toward collaboration with the Germans against what they perceived as the greater threat: the Communists and Partisans. The Chetniks attempted to build a movement across Yugoslavia, whose ultimate goal was a restored Yugoslavia based upon the hegemony of an ethnically homogenous Great Serbia that would include Bosnia-Hercegovina and much of Croatia.

The Bosnian wing of the Chetnik movement was spearheaded by former supporters of the old League of Farmers, and increasingly challenged the Communists for leadership of the Serb rebellion. The Communist policy of mobilising Muslims and Croats into the Partisans threatened to reduce the Chetniks, who relied almost entirely on Serbs alone, to a secondary place in the rebellion, while the Communist building of a Bosnian state threatened to erect an insuperable barrier to the Chetnik goal of a Great Serbia. The Chetniks' genocide was therefore catalysed by their rivalry with the Partisans. An opportunity presented itself to them in late August 1941, when the Italians used the NDH's inability to suppress the Serb rebellion to force it to agree to their reoccupation of their zone of the Ustasha puppet-state, so as to extend their power in the region in competition with the Germans and pave the way for their eventual annexation of more South Slavic territory. Although the Italians had previously used the Ustasha movement in their imperialist plans against Yugoslavia, they now cynically switched to a pro-Serb, anti-Croat and anti-Muslim policy as the best way of realising their ambitions. This meant collaborating with the Chetnik movement against both Partisans and Ustashas.

An early example of the atrocities that would flower into full-blown genocide was the massacre at the village of Kulen Vakuf on 5-8 September 1941. Although the village's Muslims had mostly refused to participate in Ustasha crimes against Serbs, when Serb rebels captured it, they proceeded to massacre them indiscriminately. Three local Muslim Communists set up a tribunal at the nearby village of Martin Brod, to determine which of a group of around 400-420 Muslim prisoners was guilty of participation in Ustasha crimes, and it sentenced eleven of the them to death. But Pero Đilas, a rebel commander oriented toward the embryonic Chetnik movement, ordered that they all be killed; all 400-420 of them, along with the three Muslim Communists themselves, were consequently butchered. Meanwhile, other Chetnik-oriented Serb rebel commanders reached an agreement with the Italians not to resist their reoccupation of the area. Thus betrayed, the principal Partisan stronghold in southwest Bosnia, Drvar, fell to the Italians on 25 September. The collaborationist Serb rebels thereupon coalesced as the Chetnik movement under Italian military protection. But it was in East Bosnia that the Chetnik genocide assumed its fullest proportion. Apologists for the Chetnik movement claim that Chetnik massacres were simply retaliation for Ustasha massacres of Serbs. Yet the geographic pattern of the massacres does not support this contention: whereas the epicentre of the Ustasha genocide was in central Croatia (Lika, Kordun, Banija), western Bosnia and Hercegovina; the Chetnik genocide was concentrated in East Bosnia, where the Ustasha massacres generally occurred later and on a smaller scale; and in Sanjak, which was not under Ustasha rule. East Bosnia was closer to the Chetnik movement's heartland in Serbia and Montenegro, and Chetnik officers from these countries were centrally involved in the genocide.

A key Bosnian Serb ideologue behind the Chetnik genocide was Stevan Moljević, formerly a leading member of Serbs Assemble! and the Serb Cultural Club. Following the German invasion, he drew up a plan for 'a homogenous Serbia that must encompass the entire ethnic territory on which the Serbs live', which was to be made homogeneously Serb through the 'resettlement and exchange of population, especially Croats from the Serbian territories and Serbs from the Croatian territories', and in which the whole of Bosnia-Hercegovina, much of Croatia and parts of Hungary, Romania, Bulgaria, and Albania were to be included. Moljević joined the Chetniks' Central National Committee in August 1941. He wrote, in February 1942, that 'the cleansing of the country of all non-Serb elements should be carried out. The miscreants should be punished on the spot, and for the remainder the road should be opened: for the Croats to Croatia and for the Muslims to Turkey (or to Albania)'. This goal was shared by the overall Chetnik leader Draža Mihailović, who in this period wrote in his diary: 'The Muslim population has through its behaviour arrived at the situation where our people no longer wish to have them in our midst. It is necessary already now to prepare their exodus to Turkey or anywhere else outside our borders'.

The Chetniks' genocide unfolded in tandem with their conflict with the Partisans. From the first months of the uprising, Mihailović's Chetnik leadership in Serbia exported its agents to East Bosnia, to exert influence over the Serb rebellion there. In particular, these were Major Boško Todorović, commander of the Chetnik Operational Units in Eastern Bosnia-Hercegovina and the most senior Chetnik officer in the region, and Major Jezdimir Dangić, commander of the Mountain Staff of the Bosnian Chetnik Detachments with immediate jurisdiction over East Bosnia. Dangić, a former supporter of the League of Farmers, was particularly extreme in his hatred of the Muslims of the region, of whom he allegedly said 'I want to kill them all'. These agents stirred the local Bosnian Chetniks against the Partisans.

The Italians expelled NDH forces from the East Bosnian towns of Višegrad, Foča, and Goražde and the surrounding area and, following talks with Todorović, permitted the Chetniks to establish a 'Provisional Administration for East Bosnia' in the region, which they did through persecution, plunder, and massacres of the non-Serb population. The

Chetniks took over Goražde from the Italians on 29 November and began a massacre of NDH soldiers and officials that grew into the systematic slaughter of the Muslim civilian population of the town, claiming several hundred lives. Muslim corpses were left hanging in the town or thrown into the River Drina. The Italians handed over Foča to the Chetniks on 5 December along with a huge quantity of weapons, and the Chetnik administration immediately enacted discriminatory laws against the Muslim and Croat population of the town, according to which: 1) all Muslim businessmen had to turn over the keys to their shops to the authorities; 2) all Muslim and Croat houses had to remain open and unlocked, day and night; 3) all Muslims and Croats aged sixteen to sixty had to report to the Chetnik military command; and 4) Muslim women in the street were not allowed to wear the veil. Muslims were not permitted to leave their homes without permission and, as a Home Guard report noted, 'those Muslims who are permitted to go out must wear a badge similar to the Jewish badge'. All imprisoned NDH soldiers and gendarmes, including several dozen who had been turned over to the Chetniks by the Italians, were executed. Muslim shops and businesses were thoroughly looted. Around five hundred Muslims were massacred in Foča at this time.

The Chetniks entered Višegrad at about the same time, having plundered and burned their way through the surrounding villages. In the reign of terror that followed in Višegrad, the desperate surviving Muslims sent petitions to the NDH leadership, relating how

> without any kind of protection, the Muslim and Catholic element is suffering indescribable violence - deaths are reaching into the thousands. Villages are totally burned and plundered... the town is still surviving, but is on the verge of expiring in agony - hunger is already reigning and the poor are dying in the streets.

The pattern of massacres continued throughout the region in the months that followed. About three hundred were killed at the village of Žepa alone in late 1941. In early January, the Chetniks assembled fifty-four Muslims at the village of Čelebić and massacred them before burning down the village. In the village of Drakan the Chetniks burned forty-two Muslim villagers to death on 3 March. In the town of Srebrenica, which the Chetniks occupied on 18 August 1941, they beat and plundered Muslims, killed their cattle, and destroyed property they were unable to steal, before descending into an orgy of killing in which about a thousand Muslims were murdered.

Although the Chetnik genocide targeted Muslims above all, it also targeted Croats, particularly in Hercegovina. Petar Baćović, who succeeded Todorović as commander of the Chetnik Operational Units in Eastern Bosnia-Hercegovina, reported in September 1942:

> I should add, in reference to our retributive expeditions in [the predominantly Croat areas of] Ljubuški and Imotski, that our Chetniks - greatly embittered by the misdeeds committed by the Ustashas against the Serbs - skinned alive three Catholic priests between Ljubinje and Vrgorac. Our Chetniks have killed all men aged fifteen years or above. They did not kill women or children aged under fifteen years. Seventeen villages were entirely burned... We shall soon, God willing, attack Fazlagić Kula, the last Muslim stronghold in Hercegovina. After that in Hercegovina there will not remain a single Muslim in the villages.

Chetnik propaganda denounced the Partisans as anti-Serb and ethnically alien, pointing to the presence of Croats, Muslims, and Jews in their ranks. Mihailović assured the Germans in November 1941 that 'I have never made a genuine agreement with the Communists, for they do not care about the people. They are led by foreigners who are not Serbs: the Bulgarian Janković, the Jew Lindmajer, the Magyar Borota, two Muslims whose names I do not know and the Ustasha Major Boganić'. A Chetnik pamphlet endorsed by Todorović from late 1941 promised:

> When it achieves freedom, a golden Serb freedom, then the Serb nation will - freely and without bloodshed, by means of the free elections which we are accustomed to in the Serbia of King Peter I - take its destiny into its own hands and freely say, whether it loves more its independent Great Serbia, cleansed of Turks [i.e. Muslims] and other non-Serbs, or some other state in which Turks and Jews will once again be ministers, commissars, officers and 'comrades'.

Dangić's staff denounced the Partisan detachments,

> which are led by the KIKE Moše Pijade, the TURK Safet Mujić, the MAGYAR Franjo Vajnert and that so-and-so Petar Ilić whose real name nobody knows... the Partisans and Ustashas have the same goal: TO BREAK UP AND DESTROY SERBDOM. That, and that alone !" (capital letters in original)

Tito's Partisan leadership had by the end of 1941 been defeated in Serbia by the Germans assisted by the Chetniks, and driven into East Bosnia. There, in the spring of 1942, the Chetniks, agitating on an anti-Communist, anti-Muslim, anti-Croat, and anti-Semitic basis succeeded in subverting much of the Partisan forces, turning their Serb peasant soldiers against their own Partisan commanders and political commissars, and seizing control of them. Under the impact of this political offensive and of the military assaults of the occupiers, Ustashas and Chetniks, the Partisan movement in East Bosnia mostly collapsed. One Muslim Partisan returned to the formerly Partisan-held area of Zvijezda after a stay away, unaware that a Chetnik putsch had taken place. He was caught by former Partisans turned Chetnik and impaled alive on a stake. Tito's Partisan leadership was forced to abandon East Bosnia as it had Serbia and embarked on its 'long march' to western Bosnia, eventually establishing the capital of its movement in the mostly Muslim town of Bihać.

As the Germans, Italians, and Ustashas moved in the early months of 1943 to destroy the Partisan movement in its bastion of western Bosnia and central Croatia, Mihailović mobilised his Chetniks to participate in this, through a 'March on Bosnia'. In this period, the Chetnik genocide of Muslims, above all in East Bosnia and the neighbouring region of Sanjak, assumed its greatest extent. Pavle Đurišić, the Montenegrin commander of the Lim-Sanjak Chetnik Detachment, reported to Mihailović on 13 February the results of the Chetnik actions in the Pljevlja, Foča, and Čajniče districts: 'All Muslim villages in the three mentioned districts were totally burned so that not a single home remained in one piece. All property was destroyed except cattle, corn, and senna'. Furthermore: 'During the operation the total destruction of the Muslim inhabitants was carried out regardless of sex and age'. In this operation, 'our total losses were 22 dead, of which 2 through accidents, and 32 wounded. Among the Muslims, around 1,200 fighters and up to 8,000 other victims: women, old people and children'. The remaining Muslim population fled, and Đurišić reported that action had been taken to prevent its return. These losses inflicted on the Muslims were in addition to the approximately one thousand women and children massacred by Đurišić's forces in the same area in early January. In March, according to Ustasha intelligence, the Chetniks massacred about five hundred Muslims in the Goražde district, 'mostly children, women and old people', and raped many women. In the village of Moćevići, they built a lavatory out of Muslim corpses and wrote on the entrance 'Muslim mosque'.

There are no precise figures for the numbers of Bosnian Muslims and Croats killed in the Chetnik genocide. The two leading demographic studies of World War II losses in Yugoslavia suggest that in Bosnia-Hercegovina alone around 170,000-209,000 Serbs, 66,000-79,000 Croats, and 75,000–78,000 Muslims perished in the war – significantly greater losses among all three nationalities than perished in the 1990s war and genocide. Yet the Chetnik genocide failed to achieve its goal. It succeeded in mobilising the Muslim and Croat population against it, large numbers of whom joined the Partisans, giving them a decisive edge in their conflict with the Chetniks and in their struggle for mastery in Yugoslavia as a whole. Italy's capitulation to the Allies in August 1943 deprived the Chetniks of their protector, and increasing German collaboration with the Chetniks, and rumours that Hitler was planning to turn East Bosnia over to the quisling regime in Serbia, prompted the Muslims in the region to join the Partisans en masse. The Partisan victory in the war against the Chetniks, Ustashas, and foreign occupiers, completed by 1945, resulted in the establishment of a new, federal Yugoslavia, one of whose six republics was the People's Republic of Bosnia-Hercegovina, billed by the Communists as the common homeland of Serbs, Croats, and Muslims.

Yet the 'Bosnian question' was not thereby resolved. Half a century later, the heirs of the Chetniks repeated their genocidal experiment.

HINDUTVA

Sufyan Hatia

For most of the world, India conjures the image of Gandhi's *Satyagraha* (non-violent resistance) and a pluralist state fondly labelled the 'world's biggest democracy' under the inclusive tricolour. Yet, in barely a generation, the centre of gravity has thrust a secular promise into a toxic majoritarianism called *Hindutva*—literally 'Hindu-ness', as a political test of belonging. Hindutva was propagated by the fascist paramilitary organisation, *Rashtriya Swayamsevak Sangh* (RSS), in the 1920s and has been normalised through its electoral arm, the *Bharatiya Janata Party* (BJP). Founded in 1980, the BJP initially floundered electorally but gained public attention by reframing communal violence as moments of national redemption while providing an emotional fix for genuine socio-economic grievance. Supporting this rise was the *Sangh Parivar* network—youth, militant, student, labour, tribal, and religious wings—transforming everyday discontent into disciplined electoral capital. Hindutva bridged caste fault lines by offering lower-caste Hindus symbolic belonging and scapegoats, while selectively elevating Dalit and Other Backward Class (OBC) figures to maintain broad appeal. Unlike the British policy of 'divide and rule', Hindutva aims to 'expand and rule', twisting Hinduism to forge a broad voter base primed for violence.

Hindutva offers a fusion of mythic nostalgia tied to a unique form of nationalism epitomised by victimhood and hatred of the 'Muslim Other'. Its mythical origins trace a linear past towards a misty future: India, once a pristine, advanced Hindu civilisation, was crushed by an alien Muslim faith arriving as desecrators; only an awakened Hindu majority can restore its lost glory and remove the cancer of the alien once and for all.

The rousing narrative is elastic enough to justify nearly any measure. Textbooks are rewritten, distorting established history. Mosques are demolished, vigilantes are deputised, and houses are bulldozed, all as acts of 'historic correction'. All the while, corporate oligarchs bankroll the mortifying spectacle in exchange for deregulation, while social media 'IT cells' convert baseless conspiracy into clickbait for an Islamophobic audience. Abroad, the project borrows from a global constellation of far-right, fascistic, and Islamophobic allies—from American proponents of authoritarianism to hard-line Zionists bent on the genocide of the Palestinians.

To legitimise Hindu supremacy, Hindutva rewrites India's past as a binary play with two characters: the pure Hindu civilisation in defence against a parade of foreign humiliators. In this tampered description, the Hindu Vedic 'golden age' met its end when Muslims, Christians, and later secularists contaminated the soul of Bharat. All that is authentically Indian is declared Hindu, while everything non-Hindu is cast as an intrusion. There is rampant textbook revisionism. State-level BJP governments have cleansed school syllabi of Muslim contributions while inflating Hindu exploits—especially those of the Mughal Empire. Entire chapters are shrunk or vanish; syncretic saints (such as Dara Shikoh) disappear, and pseudo-archaeology is taught as fact. Fabricated mythos such as Vedic aircraft, millennia-old nuclear science, and Sanskrit as the 'mother of all languages' are treated as settled history. Any academic who challenges this pseudo-historical view is barraged with toxicity and violent threats, often sexual in nature—such as the esteemed scholar Audrey Truschke. Muslim rulers are cast as national villains— chiefly Aurangzeb—and any attempt to nuance his record is branded as excusing the Hindutva avatar of Satan. The goal is not empirical history but emotional pedagogy: students must affirm that Hindus alone built civilisation and invaders merely squatted on its glory.

No symbol better distils this mythology than the sixteenth-century Babri Masjid. RSS pamphlets long parroted the claim that the mosque stood atop Ram's exact birthplace and was erected only after the original temple was destroyed by the Mughal emperor Babur. This allegation galvanised a mass movement, though archaeological proof was thin. In December 1992, mobs chanting *'Mandir wahin banayenge'* ('We'll build the temple right here') smashed the mosque to rubble while politicians merely watched. The act was celebrated as 'historic correction'. By stamping on Islamic worship, Hindus wiped away centuries of humiliation. When Prime Minister Modi laid the foundation of a new Ram temple in 2020, Hindutva leaders hailed it as fulfilment of 'national destiny'—Hindu resurgence rising from Islamic ruins.

Hindutva storytellers portray Indian Muslims as loyal to the Muslim *Ummah* (community) and Christians as willing slaves to British rule. Secularism is derided as a colonial imposition that sustains perceived minority 'supremacy'. In the Hindu Rashtra, minorities have a place only by acknowledging Hindu supremacy or converting to Hinduism, echoing twentieth-century fascist ethno-states such as Nazi Germany and Fascist Italy. The irony is stark: Hindutva cloaks itself in anti-colonial rhetoric yet recycles colonial myth. British administrators once exaggerated Hindu–Muslim hostility through 'divide and rule', painting Muslim rulers as despots and themselves as civilised liberators. Contemporary Hindu nationalists and pseudo-historians parrot the same Orientalist clichés, only now to prove Muslims permanent outsiders. The goal is to transform a diverse, centuries-old Muslim presence into a caricature that justifies repression today.

These invented memories are not academic curiosities but political fuel. Once a community is recast as an eternal, barbarous invader bent on destroying 'us', murder becomes self-defence and violence a righteous correction. The golden-age narrative thus underwrites modern policy. From historic revisionism to lynch mobs, Hindutva persuades the majority that reclaiming the past demands revenge, discipline, and the erasure of the 'other'. To this end, it must define the enemy internally and externally.

The first enemy is the state of Pakistan, or the 'original sin'. Hindutva rhetoric treats the 1947 Partition as the unforgivable proof of Muslim duplicity. Pakistan's very existence is branded like a weapon. If Muslims 'seized' an integral part of our homeland once, they must secretly nurse plans to establish more. National disputes such as border shelling and cricket matches trigger televised loyalty tests for Indian Muslims. 'Go to Pakistan' remains a common slogan in street scuffles, and prominent Muslim legislators like Asaduddin Owaisi are heckled with *'Jai Shri Ram'* (Victory to Lord Ram) in state assemblies. The insinuation is that Muslims possess a 'second home' and can never be truly Indian. Finishing the 'incomplete Partition' ultimately means pressuring Muslims to swear deeper fealty, become Hindu, leave, or be faced with death.

The second enemy is more insidious, relying on the trope of 'population jihad' to justify cruelty against Hindutva's internal enemy—the Indian Muslim. The fifth-column trope runs side by side with an insidious demographic horror story. Social-media sites are weaponised to proclaim that Muslims, constituting fourteen percent of the population, will soon outnumber Hindus. In reality, the Muslim fertility rate has fallen steeply compared with the Hindu rate for two decades. Instead, Hindutva's propaganda arm parrots the false notion of 'demographic war' and invokes conspiracy theories such as 'population jihad'. Inter-faith couples are maligned as cases of 'love jihad', in which Muslim men supposedly seduce and target Hindu women to surge the Muslim population. Nine BJP-ruled states have passed stringent anti-conversion or 'anti-love-jihad' laws that criminalise mixed marriage and employ misogyny—describing Hindu women as morally lacking.

Birth-control policy has been exploited to target Muslim communities. Two-child rules are floated in Uttar Pradesh and Assam with thinly veiled Muslim targets, while Hindutva monks push Hindu women to bear 'four sons for the nation'. Muslim women's fertility is recast as a threat, teetering into genocidal logic. Once a community's mere reproduction is framed as aggression, coercive sterilisation or worse is viewed as defensive. Consequently, Hindutva discourse promotes the *'Bhagwa Love Trap'*, inciting Hindu men to marry Muslim women to increase the Hindu population and bring 'dishonour' to the Muslim community. In both cases, women are stripped of their agency and become battlegrounds for demographic shift and 'honour'.

The final enemy is Kashmir—India's only Muslim-majority region—which doubles as a warning and an experiment. The valley's very demography brands it disloyal. The Kashmiri insurgency that began in 1989 is weaponised to portray Muslims as 'terrorists' hell-bent on Hindu genocide, with the most frequently cited example being the Pandit expulsion in the early 1990s. On 5 August 2019, the BJP government revoked Article 370, dissolving the state's special status, arresting thousands and enforcing a media blackout. Yet for three decades prior, Kashmiris suffered under the Armed Forces Special Powers Act (AFSPA), granting soldiers effectively total impunity. The result is the weaponisation of rape as a tool of terror, pellet shotguns with the aim of causing blindness, enforced disappearance and collective punishment.

Hindutva narratives frame this repression as proof that a muscular state can tame the 'Muslim savage'. Following the revocation of Article 370, real-estate adverts tout 'buy land in Kashmir', and political commentators call for an 'Israeli-like solution' to the Kashmir problem. The valley thus becomes trophy evidence of Hindu resolve, yet continued Kashmiri resistance lingers as evidence that more should be done.

The three myths—Pakistan betrayal, demographic siege, Kashmiri treason—interact to create a climate where Muslim visibility triggers rage. Friday prayers overflow into a park? 'Land jihad'. An Eid goat market? 'Hurt sentiments'. Islamic missionary gatherings? 'Corona jihad'. Whenever riots flare, Hindutva spokesmen insist Hindus are engaging in 'self-defence', regardless of the fact that Muslims statistically die in far greater numbers. The constant is the logic: if Muslims are an existential threat, extraordinary measures become patriotic acts of self-preservation. This mindset supersedes any single policy and cements Muslims as a permanent enemy to saffron fiction, thus justifying violence as 'historical correction'.

Hindutva's victim narrative transcends mere rhetoric and is translated into horrific bloodshed. What distinguishes Hindutva violence is not only its scale but the moral stance on which it is based. Every pogrom, lynching, demolition—even rape—is framed as redressing ancient humiliation. Three emblematic fronts—Gujarat 2002, vigilante lynchings, and 'bulldozer justice'—illustrate how brutality is sold as patriotic duty.

On 27 February 2002, a coach of Hindu pilgrims caught fire at Godhra station, killing fifty-nine. While the blaze's cause remains disputed, state leaders instantly blamed Muslims. Within hours, organised mobs—often wielding voter lists and escorted by police—swarmed Muslim neighbourhoods across Gujarat: Entire families were burned alive; women and girls suffered gang-rape before murder. Mosques and bazaars were systematically torched; upward of 1,000 died (independent tallies run higher). Tens of thousands fled to relief camps—later mocked by Chief Minister Narendra Modi as 'baby-making factories'.

Investigations found that senior officials obstructed rescue calls. Internationally, Modi was black listed by the US, yet inside Hindutva circles the massacre was hailed as a righteous crusade. The pogrom forged

Modi's image as an ally of the Hindutva cause and helped propel him to hard-line voters, contributing to his premiership in 2014 and proving that mass violence can become electoral strategy.

Next is the 'cult of the cow'. Since 2015, mob attacks by self-styled *gau rakshaks* (cow guardians) have been normalised, patrolling highways and accusing Muslims on flimsy evidence. For example, Pehlu Khan (Rajasthan, 2017) was dragged from his truck and beaten to death on video; courts later acquitted the accused. Junaid Khan (Haryana, 2017), aged fifteen, was stabbed on a commuter train after rumours he carried beef. Violence is not exclusive to Muslims. Dalit leatherworkers, Christian butchers— even Hindu cattle traders—have been attacked, yet political condemnation is rare. Lynch videos circulate with the chant *'Jai Shri Ram',* transforming a devotional cry into a murderous slogan. Cabinet ministers have publicly praised convicts, justifying vigilante murders as community service. The dead are criminalised as blasphemers, while the mobs are lauded as guardians of Hindu honour.

From 2020 onwards, BJP-ruled states began using bulldozers as a blunt instrument to flatten Muslim homes and shops as punishment for protest or minor clashes. The formula is consistent: Unrest erupts—often after a derogatory remark or communal scuffle. District officials declare targeted buildings 'illegal encroachments'. Excavators arrive with armed police; families watch livelihoods crumble, paperwork unheard. Some notable anecdotes include Prayagraj (2022), when student leader Afreen Fatima's house was razed after protests against anti-Prophet slurs. In Madhya Pradesh, entire Muslim rows were demolished overnight following stone-throwing allegations during a Hindu procession. Delhi's Jahangirpuri witnessed bulldozers even after a court stay order, signalling impunity. The bulldozer has become an election mascot—a promise to 'level' troublemakers. Because comparable tactics are not applied to Hindu rioters, the practice functions as collective punishment. Recently, it has been abused to clear Muslims from contested zones to ensure Hindu majorities.

Whether orchestrated pogroms, cow vigilantism, or demolition, it is evident that violence is employed as corrective therapy. Public discourse rarely mourns Muslim victims; pundits instead ask what they 'must have done', tantamount to victim-blaming. A discriminatory court system and police countersuits mean legal justice is rare. Each atrocity sets a precedent for the next and affirms a culture of impunity. Apologists paint critics as 'anti-Hindu' or invoke whataboutery, yet casualty charts tell a one-sided story, while the state's selective wrath proves intent. The decentralised nature of brutality is what makes the project uniquely dangerous: ordinary citizens are converted into noble executioners, and state machinery is used as cover-up, ensuring blame cannot be pinpointed precisely on BJP.

Hindutva sells itself as a civilisational awakening but its political success is founded on a toxic fusion of identity passion, an unsatisfactory status quo, and class interests. Like earlier fascisms, it rose amid an exhausted establishment and mass disillusionment, eventually forging a pact with big business that channels frustrations away from wealth towards scapegoats.

By the late 1980s, India's Congress Party—previously the architect of secular nationalism—had become synonymous with corruption and inertia. During the 1980s and 1990s, it faced the Bofors scandal, which even implicated the then Prime Minister, Rajiv Gandhi, in receiving 'kickbacks' from a weapons contract between India and Sweden. Then, with the Congress's wavering positions on Muslim personal law, an impression was created that 'secularism' privileged minorities while ignoring the majority. Amid looming globalisation and persistent Hindu caste issues, discontent grew. The RSS–BJP combine filled this vacuum. The economic reforms of the 1990s and 2000s generated growth but widened inequality. The BJP offered a partitioned promise: investors received deregulation and pro-corporate governance, while the under-employed were fed muscular cultural nationalism. Discontent over jobs and debt was deflected into conspiracy and hatred centred on Muslim 'terror', beef consumption, and imagined enemies on university campuses.

By the 2010s, big capital had decisively embraced Hindutva governance. Modi's blueprint of low regulation, cheap land, and flexible labour cemented his pro-business image. After 2014, instruments such as electoral bonds enabled opaque funding streams, and nearly ninety percent of corporate bond donations now flow to the BJP. Concessions in mining, airports, and telecoms clustered around a few conglomerates, notably Adani and Ambani. This alliance, dubbed 'crony Hindu capitalism', fuses economic power with majoritarian ideology: tycoons fund the party; the state rewards them with contracts; and culture war keeps the public distracted.

When economic woes threaten the government—be they farm protests, fuel-price spikes, or joblessness—the Hindutva apparatus pivots to identity politics. In 2020–2021, Sikh farmers protesting agricultural liberalisation were smeared as separatists and *'Khalistanis'*. Similar diversions recur with hijab bans, temple inaugurations, 'love jihad', and periodic Pakistan scares, dominating the news cycle and diverting attention from crumbling institutions, corruption, and rising living costs. This strategy is enforced with growing authoritarianism. Journalists, students, and activists who critique economic injustice are branded anti-Hindu or Pakistani agents. Sedition charges, tax raids, and digital censorship narrow public discourse to two routes: Hindu patriot or national traitor. Despite surging inequality, endemic corruption, and institutional decay, the BJP continues to win elections, proving that sectarian culture-war rage and media control can override economic discontent. Prominent economist Prabhat Patnaik warns that this fusion of monopoly capital and militant nationalism recalls Europe in the 1930s, where oligarchs used identity politics to crush dissent and consolidate power. The Hindutva-corporate alliance now poses a double threat: to India's pluralist democracy and to meaningful socio-economic development for over a billion Indians.

Hindutva is no longer a narrow Indian current. It has fused into a transnational archipelago of right-wing populism fuelled by diaspora networks and global lobbying. A distinguishing marker is its fondness for digital propaganda. Unlike traditional bot farms that defend a nation-state, India's disinformation network primarily promotes direct hatred of Islam and Muslims, often superseding the promotion of Hindu nationalism. Hindutva, through the BJP, leverages India's international standing to align with kindred far-right movements. The most high-profile convergence came at Houston's 2019 'Howdy Modi' rally, where Narendra Modi implicitly endorsed Donald Trump's re-election. Both leaders draw power from ethno-religious majorities—Hindus for Modi and white evangelicals for Trump—and cast Muslim immigrants as threats. White-nationalist pundits in the United States even praised Modi as someone who 'gets Islam'.

A parallel bond links Hindutva and Israel's far right: the BJP and Netanyahu's Likud routinely exchange rhetoric about 'fighting Islamic terror'. Indian security forces adopt Israeli crowd-control gear tested in the West Bank, while Indian social media glorifies Israeli policy as a template for the 'Kashmir problem'. In Europe, figures such as Geert Wilders laud India and defend Islamophobic remarks by BJP leaders, and far-right European parliamentarians are overtly courted. In November 2019, the BJP—working with two think tanks—invited twenty-seven Members of the European Parliament to Kashmir, most from anti-immigration parties including Marine Le Pen's National Rally, Alternative for Germany (AfD), and the Brexit Party. Hindutva affinities, once fringe, now shape policy thinking from Berlin to Jerusalem.

Indian-origin communities in the United States and United Kingdom serve as ideological conduits and lobbying tools. Groups such as the Hindu American Foundation brand themselves as civil-rights NGOs while pressuring textbook boards to sanitise caste and reframe Indian history, often labelling critics 'Hinduphobic'. In 2021, when US academics hosted a conference on Hindutva, diaspora activists launched harassment campaigns that forced universities to increase security. BJP overseas wings stage Modi rallies in packed arenas abroad, which are then rebroadcast in India as proof of global reverence.

Hindutva's lobbying reach is extensive and strategic. Political action committees use the allure of investment to woo Western lawmakers while downplaying human-rights abuses. Investigations have traced funds from RSS-affiliated charities to Western public-relations firms. During the 2022 Leicester riots in the UK, local Hindu nationalist organisations stoked tensions via WhatsApp, framing Muslims as aggressors. Indian embassies quietly brief diaspora leaders to counter negative narratives on Kashmir or citizenship laws, casting any critique as 'Hinduphobia' orchestrated by perfidious Islamists or naïve leftists. This ecosystem manufactures consent for Hindutva not only in India but also in liberal democracies abroad.

Hindutva-aligned networks have also emerged as significant contributors to digital Islamophobia and white-supremacist discourse online. Studies show that Indian-based accounts weaponise slurs and hashtags to inflate anti-Muslim content. Platforms such as Twitter have seen an overwhelming proportion of anti-Muslim hate speech originating from India. They often use Western far-right profiles in an attempt to further their agenda. This strategic mimicry is tactical, as Indian-based impersonations attempt to clear India's name, presenting it as an equal partner in the war against Islam. For example, it has been established that disinformation spread by Indian accounts played an important part in the 2022 unrest in Leicester. False statistics and clips were intentionally disseminated to slander the British Muslim community in an attempt to paint British-Hindus as the 'good guys' in comparison to the racialised caricature of the barbaric Muslim.

Hindutva's global alliances provide three key advantages: legitimacy, technology, and cover. If the world's largest democracy can privilege one faith, others feel licensed to do the same. Technologies of repression—from Israeli policing hardware to US-style disinformation strategies—amplify the BJP's reach. Diaspora influencers and corporate lobbies help deflect Western criticism, likening Muslim persecution to standard counter-terrorism. The result is a replicable model: marry Islamophobia with nationalist myths, mobilise an emotive diaspora, and weaponise social media to deflect scrutiny. Hindutva's international popularity—evident in investor confidence, diplomatic passivity, and crowds from Times Square to Tel Aviv—makes it not merely a domestic project but a template for twenty-first-century authoritarianism everywhere.

Ultimately, Hindutva advertises itself as a liberation movement, draped in symbols of India's mythical heritage and promising grand rebirth after more than a millennium of subjugation. In practice, it replicates the very systems it claims to resist. Like the British Raj, it divides India into two camps, marked by the dehumanisation of the 'other', and justifies coercion as salvation. Under BJP–RSS rule, India's democratic institutions have been hollowed out: courts serve ideology, the press is forced to assimilate, and dissenters are jailed. Empowerment of the Hindu majority is preached, yet the instruments used are classic authoritarian ones. Suppression of speech, demolition of homes, and impunity for lynch mobs are the new political norms. There is nothing patriotic about beating unarmed men to death or sexually assaulting defenceless women, yet such acts are recast as a warrior's pride. Any 'restoration' of Hindu honour demands fresh spectacles of Muslim humiliation.

Psychologically, Hindutva pays its majority in the 'salary of supremacy'. Much as Jim Crow America gave poor whites the comfort of racial superiority, Hindutva offers the disillusioned Hindu a thrill of dominance, providing symbolic dividends to distract from unemployment, rising prices, and shrinking freedoms. For India's 200 million Muslims, the project is existential. Everyday Islamic practice can trigger state-sanctioned assault. Ruling-party figures openly fantasise about genocide, while saffron-robed monks complain that current oppression is too soft. A permanent guillotine hangs over the second-largest Indian community—one that helped build and uphold the republic's plural fabric.

To confront Hindutva is not to oppose Hinduism in India. It is to defend India's proclaimed ethos and redeem the plight of its Muslim victims. For those who claim universal humanity, and for the Muslim ummah, it is time to name the project for what it is: fascism robed in saffron. Recognising the warning light now is the only way to avoid paying the full, tragic price later.

LUTON'S FEAR OF FREEDOM

Ghazal Tipu

Disturbingly, and yet without doubt, fascism has made a home in our contemporary politics. Authoritarian leadership, political gains by far-right groups, white supremacy, the crushing of dissent and rising Islamophobia have become hallmark features of western politics. We live in a state of in-betweenness – what has been called postnormal times – between the old and new world orders, an age of great divides: late-stage capitalism, precarious employment, toxic masculinity, the effects of Big Tech, austerity, and weakened community ties are macro factors bearing upon our sense of our collective security and identities. What is going on in our individual and collective inner lives that would make us acquiesce to creeping fascism, though we said, 'never again'? What of this new fascism? From where and whom does it come?

In *The Fear of Freedom*, Erich Fromm constructed a psychoanalytic and psychosocial theory about the origins and devotion to fascism in twentieth century Europe. Fromm claims that modern man finds freedom in capitalist society to be a great burden, due to the precariousness of the market and the loss of identity and community. Man therefore has developed authoritarianism and corresponding destructive and conforming behaviours that help him to alleviate his anxiety and create a sense of control.

Fromm's perspective tells us a great deal about our current state of affairs in the UK. But why understand fascism in the UK from a psychosocial perspective? Aren't authoritarian leaders and their stooges just plain 'evil'? It could be argued that there is value in humanising the souls who've turned towards fascism. Admittedly, some fascists have wilfully chosen a misguided path, and one thinks of the those the Qur'an describes as 'wilfully deaf, dumb and blind, so they will never return to the Right Path' (2:18).

Fascist leaders and their adherents develop their mentality from a dynamic combination of individual psyches and groupthink, as well as social, political, and economic factors. It is too easy to think in a binary 'good or evil' way and write off adherents of far-right groups as 'fascist scum'. Instead, we could see them as products of social processes. Philosophically, we wish to believe that our thoughts and actions are actualised from our own volition. More realistically, we are products of the attitudes and beliefs we absorb from our peers, leaders, and mass media.

Fromm understood the dynamic interplay between psychology and social factors. He posits that our human nature is not biologically fixed but is in dynamic interplay with social forces. 'The most beautiful as well as the most ugly inclinations of man are not part of a fixed and biologically given human nature but result from the social process which creates man', he says. Each epoch is marked by different passions, strivings, and anxieties. Man's inner nature and history are in a kind of symbiotic interplay for 'man is not only made by history – history is made by man'.

In *Alt-Reich*, Nafeez Ahmed theorises that far-right views never went away in twentieth-century western thought but continuously simmered away under the surface. But despite the continuity of far-right ideas, Brexit in 2016 marked a major historical turning point, when fascist and xenophobic ideas moved from the sidelines to the mainstream, and were legitimised as the supposed views of the common man. This is why we should be cautious in using the term 'fascist' at counter demonstrations in support of refugees and asylum seekers, given that far-right protestors don't consider themselves fascist when mainstream politicians legitimise their views. However, this is a very curious phenomenon. Are a cohort of Britons collectively in denial about who they have become?

Applying Fromm's observation, Brexit has shaped our collective inner lives – our attitudes, prejudices, and biases. It has legitimised isolationist and parochial views that already existed but has also catalysed them further, and it has brought the simmering far-right ideas up to the surface. In 2018, the UN's Special Rapporteur for racism said that Brexit had contributed to a growth in 'explicit racial, ethnic and religious intolerance'. With Brexit, gone was the post-WWII spirit of cooperation. Covid-19 also arguably weakened community ties, compounding the effects of Brexit. As a nation, our collective identities were no longer European, co-operating in a spirit of togetherness. Now we were English, Welsh, Scottish, and Northern Irish, operating separately from Europe.

Fromm suggests that each epoch is marked by 'different passions, strivings and anxieties'. It would be fair to say this is the epoch of Brexit. It has firmly altered the landscape of the UK and fundamentally affected the tone of politics and the media. In 2024, the Reform Party – that is, the successor to the UK Independence Party, or UKIP, which agitated for Brexit – was further legitimised, winning seats in both national and local elections. This marked a key success for the far right, after decades in which it only represented the fringes.

The Labour Party, meanwhile, far distant from its working-class roots, now panders to right-wing voters deploying right-wing rhetoric and policies that continue those of its Conservative predecessors. Keir Starmer's recent 'island of strangers' speech eerily echoed Enoch Powell's 'Rivers of Blood' speech.

Fromm indicts modern capitalism and how it affects the human condition, rendering the average individual powerless in the face of changing market forces. Capitalism is unable to meet our basic human need for security. This is what authoritarian leaders take advantage of, particularly during times of economic precarity. Germany's eventual submission to the Nazis was not solely due to obvious political factors such as propaganda but also because at a subconscious level people were eager to escape their 'freedom' in capitalist society. Fromm argues that submission to an authoritarian leader provided Germans with a sense of security and a feeling of power following the collapse of the Weimar Republic. It gave them purpose and national identity.

According to Fromm, man in modern capitalist society feels the need to be part of something greater than himself in order to feel secure. In contrast, feudal mediaeval society, he argues, gave people a sense of security and belonging. Man felt at one with nature, and was integrated in Christianity. This period is seen as lacking individual freedom; man was 'chained' to his role in the social order. But our modern notion of freedom is based on unrestrained individualism. As Fromm notes, 'mediaeval society did not deprive the individual of his freedom, because the individual did not yet exist; man was related to the world by primary ties.'

This sense of knowing one's place in life changed with the arrival of capitalism. The new system provided freedom for individuals but not a sense of security. It created a change in the personality structure of man.

This new economic system 'freed the individual and allowed him to stand on his own feet and try his luck.' But this new freedom came with new conditions: 'the individual stands alone and faces the world – a stranger thrown into a limitless and threatening world.' Fromm argues that the middle classes, then and even now, felt, 'threatened by the power of monopolies and the superior strength of capital, and this threat had an important effect on the spirit and ideology of the threatened sector of society by enhancing the individual's feeling of aloneness and insignificance.'

An individual must try to alleviate his feelings of aloneness if he is to function successfully. One mechanism for escaping freedom is authoritarianism. This involves the individual either submitting to or dominating others in order to escape feelings of insignificance, and to provide a sense of control. Fromm describes authoritarianism as, 'the tendency to give up the independence of one's own individual self to somebody or something outside oneself in order to acquire the strength which the individual self is lacking.' Sadistic (dominating) and masochistic (submissive) behaviours are present in both normal and neurotic people.

From Fromm's perspective, it is possible to argue that the political behaviours we are seeing today are concerned with acquiring strength through psychological 'authoritarianism' in response to the socio-economic circumstances we find ourselves in. In the UK, the horizon looks bleak, marking a clear change from the prosperous post-WWII years. Cuts to public services, a struggling NHS, stagnation of wages, and welfare reforms have greatly impacted living conditions. A recent report by *Hope not Hate* found that 75 percent of British people think things are worse now than they were ten years ago, and 52 percent of people think things will be worse in ten years' time. The report also found a relationship between economic insecurity, democratic distrust, a lack of social connectedness, and feelings of anger, pessimism, fear and hatred.

As such, there is a disenfranchisement of working-class people in particular in post-industrial Britain. Known as the 'left behind communities', they feel invisible and insecure in the face of changing market circumstances. Many members of white working-class communities are responding to this feeling in specific ways, notably by scapegoating migrants and people of colour for societal ills. These attitudes have been hardened and inflamed by Brexit, the right-wing media, and much of the Establishment. With society dividing along ethnic lines, joining far-right movements provides members of white working-class communities with a sense of security and belonging. The aggression we are witnessing by far-right groups like the English Defence League (EDL), Voice of Wales, Britain First, Patriotic Alternative and others are arguably expressions of authoritarianism in order to alleviate feelings of psychological 'aloneness' and disenfranchisement.

The English Defence League (now disbanded) emerged from Luton, a town with population of 325,300. Its diverse communities come from white English, Irish, Caribbean, Pakistani, and Bangladeshi backgrounds. Luton paints a picture of disenfranchisement and economic uncertainty, like communities in pre-WWII Germany, but it also tells a story of how the War on Terror and British foreign policy have directly affected working-class communities and fostered division. The EDL erupted onto the streets of Luton in 2009 following anger against Islamist demonstrations, and soon grew, recruiting as many as 35,000 supporters.

Luton fits easily into the narrative of being a 'left behind' community. Luton Council estimates that 7.2 percent of the population lives in destitution, while around half of the population lives below the Financial Quality of Life band. In other words, Luton suffers a socio-economic scenario in which traditional white-working communities feel both dissatisfied with their lives and overlooked by traditional left-wing politics. This is particularly the case for young people; most of the adherents of the EDL are white, male, and under thirty years old.

This is backed up by *Angry White People* in which the writer Hsiao-Hung Pai looks at the lives of white working-class people in Luton. She paints a picture of disillusionment. Alfredo, an EDL supporter who used to support Labour tell her that he has become 'increasingly frustrated' with mainstream politics. Pai reports that many on the Farley Hill estate, where the EDL originated, have expressed difficulty finding employment. Darren, a middled-aged painter and decorator and former member of the EDL, talks of many people wishing to work but who cannot find employment. 'The young on this estate are just feeling lost,' he says. He complains that there are no longer jobs at the Vauxhall factory, and describes those joining a demonstration in Birmingham as 'crying for help'. The Vauxhall factory once provided as many as 37,000 jobs in Luton, but the car plant shed 1,900 jobs in 2000. General Motors, the parent company, blamed the closure on changing market conditions in Europe. More jobs were cut in 2009, and in 2025 the plant has fully closed, leading to 1,100 further jobs lost. Now the main sources of local employment are Luton Airport and a retail park.

Rohima Anwar*, a forty-something charity worker from Luton whose father once worked for the Vauxhall factory, shares with me the impact of the 1998 closure on Luton's communities. 'There was a lot of depression when it closed. People thought "what are we going to do next?" A lot of Asians went into taxi jobs, and the white people went on the dole. The white people didn't learn a trade. There were a lot of divorces and single parent families'. Anwar complains that her school offered 'zero aspiration' for young people. 'The white boys didn't have a lot of aspiration,' she tells me. 'There was a lot of pregnancy, they didn't dream of going to university, or plan to do A-Levels. You didn't hear people say "I want to be a doctor". And people fell into gangs.' Anwar continues, 'It wasn't cool to be good at school. There was a cycle of going on benefits.' She contrasts this with her own and other Asian families who expected their children to go to university.

The EDL can also be understood as an anti-Islamist movement. The tensions experienced in communities across the UK at this current fascist moment simply cannot be understood without recognising the effects of British foreign policy. The politicisation of different communities in Luton in different ways can be traced back to the 1991 Gulf War, 9/11, and the 2003 invasion of Iraq. A particular turning point in the relations between the Muslim community and the white working class seemed to occur when a demonstration took place against a British army parade in 2009. This eventually led to the founding of the EDL. A man called Derek tells Pai, 'I was so angry how those Muslims could disrespect our soldiers.' Anwar tells me, 'After the Iraq war, the Asian people started becoming more political. The Asians would join these groups. The army came parading in Luton and the Asian kids got really annoyed.'

The EDL has now disbanded, following its leader Tommy Robinson's withdrawal. The centrality of the leader marks the group as potentially

* Rohima Anwar's name has been changed.

'authoritarian' in Fromm's terms. Robinson fuelled the EDL as a street movement, and provided his followers with something to follow and submit to that gave them a sense of security and belonging.

Thankfully, Anwar and other residents suggests that Luton's communities have managed to move beyond recent tensions via the community's concerted efforts to build bridges. 'The kids are now good here, and they're educated. Some of them did go to university. EDL members have been in prison'. The radical Muslim group Al-Muhajioroun has been banned. Muslims have embraced Sufism. 'We're a lot more clued up', says one resident. 'In the dark days of 2005–2006, Islamophobia was high. We don't want to repeat it. People have learnt to soften'.

Anwar speaks in increasingly positive terms, pointing to the capacity of British towns and cities to dynamically counter the far right. 'In 2010, we started learning more about Islam. The white kids now have better understanding of Asian culture. They have social gatherings together. White people say "as-salaamulaykum" and "insh'Allah". We have a sense of home and we welcome everyone. We don't have hatred towards them, and we have moved on. The older English people are kind'. During Eid, I am old, Muslims invite their white neighbours to parties. There is less tension and more communalism. The Asians have really worked hard to change the narrative. 'They don't see us as the enemy, says Anwar. 'In 2005 there was Islamophobia, and now there is less. Even if the EDL came now, the English people wouldn't welcome them.'

Alongside authoritarianism as a defence mechanism, Fromm also talks about the destructiveness as a response to the anxiety provoked by modern freedom. Rather than confronting their anxiety directly, some people may turn either to self-destructive behaviours or to externalizing their anger by attacking others. This serves as a defence mechanism to eliminate perceived threats and the sense of powerlessness; the destruction or self-destruction is carried out unconsciously, and it is rationalised without realising its underlying unconscious motives.

The violent race riots of summer 2024 and the ongoing ire towards asylum seekers in the summer of 2025 can be considered examples of this destructive behaviour. Vehicles were set on fire, shops were looted opportunistically, and people were injured. In Southport, rioters targeted a mosque, throwing bricks at the building. In Rotherham and Tamworth, attempts were made to barricade and set fire to hotels with asylum seekers were still inside. Hate crimes were committed across towns and cities nationwide, targeting Muslims, immigrants, asylum seekers, and people of colour.

One of the often cited motivations for joining a far-right demonstration is to protect women and children, yet those same demonstrators would never join any initiatives opposing violence against women. The *Guardian* found that two out of every five people arrested after participating in last summer's riots had been previously reported to the police for domestic abuse, while for those arrested by one police force in particular, this figure was as high as 68 percent. The most violent protestors could therefore be viewed as using angry demonstrations or riots as a means of unleashing their personal anger, arguably arising from toxic masculinity as much as from the anxiety provoked by economic precarity.

What can we say from this about the future of the UK? It is important that we maintain hope and encourage the strengthening of community bonds. According to Fromm, it is certainly possible to enjoy the fruits of freedom in a positive and constructive way. It is necessary to make ourselves busy in a 'spontaneity of love and productive work'. Fromm also suggests that being part of a community is a positive force. 'The identity with nature, clan, religion, gives the individual security. He belongs to, he is rooted in, a structuralised whole in which he has a place.'

We must continue to believe that human beings have the capacity to change their views. Darren has now left the EDL, after stating that being called racist by counter demonstrators made him think twice about his actions. Some parts of the far right, like the EDL, can potentially be seen as a zealous youth movement. This means that the potential exists for young people to soften their views as they mature and see more of the world. We need to focus on community grassroots work and foster dialogue between different ethnic groups. Getting to truly know one another remains as vital and urgent as ever. As the Qur'an tells us:

O humanity! Indeed, We created you from a male and a female and made you into peoples and tribes so that you may 'get to' know one another. Surely the most noble of you in the sight of Allah is the most righteous among you. Allah is truly All-Knowing, All-Aware (49:13).

FRIENDLY FAR RIGHT?

Sean Goodman

In the summer of 2012, I was sitting in my friend's living room. He was in barber college and offered me a free haircut. I had just come back from a three-week educational trip to Israel, the West Bank, and Jordan. I, along with about twenty-five other university students, met with several activists, experts, and politicians who gave us conflicting accounts regarding what caused the violence between Israelis and Palestinians, and how peace can be achieved. I was excited to share my experience with anyone who would listen. This included my friend who was cutting my hair, and his mother. Then his father walked in, and the mother introduced me.

'This is Sean', my friend's mother said. 'He just got back from the Middle East, and he was learning about peace building in Israel and Palestine'.

My friend's father scoffed, 'Well, there's a conflict you'll never solve', he said as he grabbed something out of the refrigerator, barely acknowledging my presence.

'I don't know', I said, 'People were saying the same thing about Northern Ireland fifteen years ago and look at how that turned out'.

'No. This is different, and I'll explain why', he said.

Given my recent experience, I was expecting a nuanced take. Perhaps he thought a peace agreement couldn't be reached because of the multiple state actors involved. Or perhaps Israel's expansion of settlements in the West Bank shattered any hopes of a two-state solution.

'It's different because Jews are the chosen people of God, and the Arabs hate them for that. Did you know that they fire rockets from Palestine into Israel every day? The only realistic solution is for Israel to *nuke Palestine*'.

'Dad!' my friend said while trying to keep his composure as he was cutting my hair.

I sat there taken aback. Knowing that he didn't value Palestinian life, I said what I thought would appeal to his senses.

'You'd kill a lot of Jews in the process if you did that'.

'Doesn't matter, it's what needs to be done', he said, and walked out of the room.

Before this interaction, I had met with Israeli settlers who proudly displayed handguns at their hips. I also met with active members of the right-wing Likud party, human rights organisations, and Palestinians protesting the destruction of their villages. None of them said anything as extreme as what this man said to me. His genocidal proclamation, said with as much nonchalance as if he were to say he was leaving to fill up his car, made me question his alleged Christian faith. It was also the first time in my adult life that I had interacted with someone who, if asked, would have likely identified as a Christian Zionist.

For the next eight years, I continued to engage with peace building and interfaith initiatives. Given the nature of this work, I have been exposed to a plethora of opinions well before 7 October 2023, and well after. After the Hamas-led attack against Israel, I was not surprised by Israel's brutal response. I was not surprised, though abhorred, when I heard Senator Lindsey Graham say he wanted Israel to 'level' Gaza just days after the attack. I was not surprised when Max Blumenthal, Jackson Hinkle, Abby Martin, and Rania Khalek criticised Western media outlets for parroting Israeli state talking points, despite building so much of their careers on parroting Assad-regime talking points. What did surprise me was seeing so many of my progressive friends and colleagues suddenly platform far-right pundits like Tucker Carlson and Candace Owens. I was even more surprised once I started to see lesser-known figures associated with the far right show up in my social media feed: Individuals like Holocaust deniers Lucas Gage and Nick Fuentes, and misogynists like Andrew Tate and Jake Shields. All these individuals were platformed under the assumption that they were engaging in sincere solidarity with the Palestinians within Gaza and the West Bank. This has become a growing concern of mine. If we are to effectively confront anti-Arab racism and Islamophobia, then we must not only ignore these individuals, but call them out when we see in every instance. The 'anti-Zionists' of the far right are no more concerned with Palestinian liberation than the average Christian Zionist is with anything remotely resembling liberal democracy in Israel. To recognise it, we must dissect the history of both Christian Zionism and anti-Zionism within the far right and where they both stand today.

Although Democrats and Republicans in the United States have remained steadfast in their commitment to the state of Israel since its inception in 1948 due to a geopolitical ideology shaped by the Cold War, the Republican Party embraced a Christian Zionist ideology around 1980. Although Christian Zionism has manifested differently throughout the centuries, today it is mostly associated with a specific fundamentalist, evangelical Christian interpretation of biblical end times prophecy. Writing for Political Research Associates, Aidan Orly describes this particular belief is one 'which builds Christian political power that supports expansionist, authoritarian policies by Israel, and is justified by beliefs in the Jewish State's role in Christian Prophecy'. Unlike their Roman Catholic and Eastern Orthodox contemporaries, most Christian Zionists believe that the Second Coming will occur only after multiple nations attack Israel. For this prophecy to be fulfilled, Jews will need to control Israel, the Palestinian territories, Jordan, Syria, Lebanon, and Egypt. Jerry Falwell, an American evangelical pastor who founded the influential Christian political lobbying group the Moral Majority, was the man who, many scholars note, was responsible for ushering Christian Zionism into mainstream American politics.

It is difficult to gauge how many Christians in America support Israel for geopolitical reasons over religious ones today, but statistics reveal Christian Zionism's influence. There are over 70 million evangelical Christians in the United States, and over 80 percent of them support Israel. Christians United for Israel, or CUFI, is the largest Zionist organisation in the world, and claims to have over 10 million members, which is 2.5 million more people than there are Jews living in the US. Moreover, American evangelicals make up 40 percent of tourism to Israel each year, and third-party investigations into CUFI revealed that the organisation financially contributes to settlement projects in the West Bank.

Christian Zionism presents an obvious problem to non-evangelical supporters of Israel. Although proponents might identify as philosemitic (that is, having a deep love for Jewish people), a core component of its theology is deeply antisemitic. Upon Christ's return, over two-thirds of

Israel's population will die, and unless they engage in mass conversion, millions of Jews will be damned alongside all other non-believers. Another problematic component of Christian Zionism is that any time violence flares up in Israel, there seems to be little concern for the massive loss of life. Instead, it is one step closer to their end times prophecy being fulfilled. While Israel and Iran exchanged rocket fire in June 2025, and Iranians fled to neighbouring Armenia in fear for their lives, and Israelis hid in bomb shelters, the former Republican congresswoman and Christian Zionist Michelle Bachman expressed excitement over the possibility of a mass casualty event. She said, 'We are living in the times that the Bible said that the prophets longed to see', because 'God gave a special purpose to the Jewish people'. The Zionism that Christian Zionists celebrate is not rooted in the inherent need for a Jewish state, but the need for a Jewish state to exist so that they will be able to witness the first phase of the Apocalypse. As the Jewish writer Talia Lavin puts it, 'Christian Zionists love Jews like a hungry man loves a chicken wing;...'

Not every evangelical Christian endorses Christian Zionism, least of all evangelical Palestinian Christians. One of the more prominent Palestinian evangelical voices is Munther Isaac, a Palestinian Lutheran pastor residing in Bethlehem. For the past seven years, Isaac has hosted the 'Christ at the Checkpoint' conference, which invites evangelical Christians from all over the world to raise awareness about the reality of Israeli apartheid. Isaac, along with several other Arab evangelical leaders, signed off on a letter in August 2024 titled 'A Collective Call to the Global Church from Middle East Evangelical Leaders'. Part of the letter reads,

> We assert that the conflicts in the Middle East, including the Israeli-Palestinian conflict, are not manifestations of spiritual warfare but are instead rooted in complex socio-political dynamics that demand nuanced understanding and strategic response ... We lament the silence and at times support of some church leaders within the Western Church regarding the actions in Gaza— actions that have been labelled as plausible genocide by the International Criminal Court, human rights groups, and an increasing number of nations. We urge accountability and call for an immediate ceasefire, the release of all hostages, and the unrestrained flow of aid into Gaza.

Another voice is Fares Abram, founder of the Palestinian Christian organisation Levant Ministries, based out of Florida. Days after 7 October 2023, he wrote,

> As for those now suffering in Gaza, I believe without a doubt that Jesus, if he were today present in the region, would be going to Gaza. He would be pulling men, women, and children out from underneath the ruins of their decimated homes who were brutally killed for no reason. He would be helping the more than 2 million innocent civilians find safety, passage, and shelter. Jesus would be visiting the remaining Christians in Gaza who have taken refuge in churches to pray for protection and call upon God for deliverance from death.

There are, of course, non-evangelical Palestinian Christians speaking out against Christian Zionism. One such group is Friends of Sabeel North America, or FOSNA. On their website, they describe their organisation as 'an unapologetic Christian Voice for Palestine' that stands in solidarity with all Palestinians, aims to raise awareness about Israeli apartheid to an American audience, and labels Christian Zionism as a 'false theology'. They also support the Boycott, Divestment, and Sanctions movement.

While CUFI issued a statement regarding the need to protect Palestinian Christians, it was not over a concern of Israeli bombs in Gaza or settler violence in the West Bank, but rather, a condemnation of Hamas and the Palestinian Authority. The Trump administration also seems to ignore the pleas of Palestinian Christians with its foreign policy regarding Israel. Whether it was moving the American embassy to Jerusalem, to appointing Mike Huckabee, a Christian Zionist, as the US Ambassador to Israel, or most recently, attempting to revoke the legal status of graduate students speaking out in support of Palestine.

Like his predecessors, President Trump continues to provide military and financial aid to Israel. Unlike his predecessors, Trump associates with infamous antisemites, and has personally promoted antisemitic conspiracy theories in social media posts. This apparent contradiction reveals two facts about the history of the American Right and Israel. The first is the most obvious: One can shield themselves against accusations of antisemitism by claiming their support for a Jewish state. The second revelation is less obvious but just as concrete: The strain of so-called anti-Zionism that exists within the far right.

When Tucker Carlson and Candace Owens began to speak out against Israeli aggression shortly after it began its aerial assault on Gaza, they broke away from a pro-Israel narrative that appeared to unify the Republican Party and dominate the conservative narrative for well over forty years. However, anti-Zionism, like Christian Zionism, has also existed within the American Right and dates as far back as the interwar period. In *Taking America Back: The Conservative Movement and the Far Right*, the historian David Austin Walsh writes that anti-interventionists, particularly members of the America First Committee, feared that a Jewish state would be a 'Zionist-Marxist' project in the Middle East, with a high probability of becoming another Soviet republic. Walsh explains that this type of anti-Zionism was 'not rooted in any particular concern for the Arab population of Palestine, but rather a fear that the international Judeo-Bolshevik-Zionist conspiracy would embroil America in a war, weakening the US and allowing for the victory of international Jewish communism'. While scholars of American conservatism have previously described this antisemitic 'anti-Zionist' attitude within conservatism as part of the 'lunatic fringe' far right, new historiographies like Walsh's reveal that mainstream conservatives have historically tolerated far-right figures within their movement. When Christian Zionism became more popular within the Republican Party, the antisemitic 'anti-Zionist' faction survived in far-right circles.

Given this background, it should not surprise anyone that more recently, far-right individuals, whether they be anti-Black KKK leaders or anti-Semitic neo-Nazis, have rebranded themselves as advocates for Palestine. These far-right figures appear to often contradict their views and have the ability to ebb and flow between viewpoints with ease. For example, former KKK leader David Duke, who has a warm relationship with 'pro-Palestinian' influencer Jake Shield and activist Kenneth O'Keefe, has called Israel an apartheid state but has also defended South African apartheid. Tucker Carlson has expressed disgust over Israel's treatment of Palestinian Christians but often peddles the racist 'Great Replacement' conspiracy theory. This is the same conspiracy theory invoked by Brenton Tarrant, the white supremacist terrorist who murdered over fifty Muslim worshipers in Christchurch, New Zealand. In addition to racist anti-immigrant rhetoric, Tarrant wrote in his manifesto that Candace Owens was one of his biggest inspirations. Although this was likely a form of internet trolling, Owens's response to the accusation that she inspired the mass murderer was no less bothersome. Rather than condemning the connection, she responded to the accusation on Twitter with a laughing emoji and claimed she had never created Islamophobic content (despite previous tweets implying that Muslims are taking over Europe). On the day Kabul fell to the Taliban, she responded to a tweet that criticised then President Joe Biden with, 'You think this is bad? He's just getting started. Wait until they start demanding that we now open our borders to Afghan refugees'. Neither Carlson nor Owens has taken back their years of vitriol toward various Muslim populations. Considering that most Palestinians living in the West Bank and Gaza are Muslim, you would think they would include this in their most recent criticisms towards Israel. Instead, it just reeks of insincerity.

Other groups and ideologies within the far right, such as adherents to the Christian Identity theology and neo-Nazi accelerationists, do not see a political solution. Instead, they seek to achieve their goals via revolutionary violence. Of these two, the historian Stuart Wexler writes that Christian Identity has 'directly or indirectly spired generations of white supremacists to acts of terrorism'. While membership has been small compared to other groups in the American Right, its influence is far-reaching and long-lasting. Throughout the decades, several adherents to Christian Identity committed violent acts, from strong-armed robbery to mass murder.

Unlike Christian Zionists, who believe that the end times will begin in Israel, members of Christian Identity believe that the apocalypse will occur in the United States, the true 'Promised Land'. This is because, contrary to what both Jews and Christians believed for millennia, Christian Identity argues that the true Israelis are Euro-American Christians. Today, William Finck, a Christian Identity writer, operates Christogenea.org, one of the most popular Christian Identity websites. In a blog post titled, 'What is Christian Identity?' he writes that Judaism is a 'perversion of Christianity' and that the ADL and other Jewish organisations are 'forever the enemies of Christ'. Whereas Christian Zionists view Jews as assets in their apocalyptic theology, believers in Christian Identity view Jews as their archenemy. This is rooted in what Christian Identity calls the 'two-seed' or 'serpent seed' doctrine, which suggests that Jews are descendants of an unholy union between Eve and Satan after she fornicated with the serpent in the Garden of Eden. The doctrine, which undoubtedly dehumanises Jews (and other non-White people), allows a justification for any form of violence inflicted upon them.

Finck also shows no love for Islam. In another post he writes, 'When some Jew prints a cartoon depicting Mohammed in a newspaper, the Muslims go berserk and start slaughtering Christians in the streets, while the Jewish-controlled media finds a way to put even the blame for that upon Christians'. It is the Jew, he asserts, that is 'flooding Christian lands with Muslims' to destroy Christianity. Although he suggests that Jews weaponise Muslims in Europe but demonise them in Palestine, adherents to Christian Identity clearly do not support anything resembling Palestinian liberation. In an article titled, 'The Arab Question' Finck writes that although some Christian Identity writers suggest they should empathise with Arabs, he goes into a tangential biblical argument for why they should not. He then explains:

> In truth, the Arabs have forever been in league with the Jews, and for many centuries the Jews have used the Arab races as cannon fodder in their wars against Christendom, for which reason certain Jews had also contrived the so-called religion known as Mohammedanism, or Islam, in the first place... Identity Christians should have no open displays of empathy or support for either Arab or Turk, or, for that matter, for anyone of any other race.

Christian Identity's hatred for Islam and Arabs begs the question: Why do non-Identity figures like David Duke continue to have a relationship with Christian Identity members? Indeed, why do the likes of him and so many others in the far right weaponise anti-Zionism and portray themselves as having solidarity with Palestinians? There are multiple reasons, but I offer two: recruitment via entryism and accelerationism. Talia Lavin writes that far-right activists are 'trying to manipulate movements through 'entryist' tactics, which are attempts by fascists to enter left-wing movements and corrupt of recruit from them'. This is not unique to Israel and Palestine, but it is an ideal situation for leaders of the far right to offer people a path towards their hate-filled ideology. It is made all the easier with the gruesome images of carnage coming out of Gaza because of Israel's genocidal bombardment. This provides fertile ground for an extremist to spark up a conversation with someone disgusted by these images and ask them, 'They lied about 40 beheaded babies, what makes you think they wouldn't lie about the Holocaust??' Indeed, this is not an obscure strategy. In one correspondence with the neo-Nazi accelerationist leader James Mason, a neo-Nazi wrote, 'Wear the swastika on the heart, not on the arm'.

Another reason is offered by Bruce Hoffman and Jacob Ware. In their book *Gods, Guns, and Sedition,* they write 'Extremist movements that cannot broaden their appeal and tap into new sources of recruits and support risk both their continued relevance and very existence. One of the noteworthy features of American white supremacism has been its capacity for reinvention'. This idea is further corroborated by a recent report released by the Institute for Strategic Dialogue, which reveals that extremists on Telegram are flooding the social media platform with gory imagery to radicalise individuals and have them commit violent acts against Jews. ISD notes in their report that these same extremists also employed Islamophobic content.

The tactic of recruitment has been previously attempted in environmentalist spaces, Occupy Wall Street, and the broader anti-war movement. In their article, 'Why Does the US Far Right Love Bashar Al-Assad?' Leila Al-Shami and Shon Meckfessel write that one member of the 'Hands Off Syria' coalition in Australia was outed as a Nazi who posted on the popular hate message board Stormfront. The 'Hands Off Syria' movement was also a space in which anti-Semitic conspiracy theories could thrive. Since Israel had been formally at war with Syria, far-right Assad supporters could claim that the Jews were the ones orchestrating calls for regime change. Even before the Syrian Civil War, there was at least one US white supremacist who showed admiration for Bashar Al-Assad. In 2006, David Duke visited Syria and praised the now-deposed dictator for fighting 'Zionist occupation', which, he alleged, his own government was under.

Before 7 October 2023, I had never seen so many people, especially those who share progressive and leftist opinions, unquestioningly platform outspoken white supremacists, Islamophobes, and misogynists. When I messaged my friends and colleagues and informed them on who they were platforming, I was met with two reactions: admitted ignorance of who these people were, followed by them immediately removing the content, or, feigned shock, followed by them saying something along the lines of, 'I don't like what they stand for, but they make great points about Israel so it's worth sharing!' The latter response sometimes makes me question why I messaged them at all. It sometimes makes me question why I should even bother writing about this in the first place.

The French Psychiatrist Frantz Fanon once wrote about one of his philosophy teachers telling him, 'When you hear someone insulting the Jews, pay attention; he's talking about you'. There might be no better way to articulate this message than by describing the white supremacist violence that has been rampaging across North America and Europe for the past two decades. In 2014, a seventy-three-year-old white supremacist, who was once associated with Christian Identity, opened fire on a Jewish Community centre in Overland Park, Kansas. The attack left three dead, including a fourteen-year-old boy. Ironically, none of the victims were Jewish, but Christian. Another mass shooter, John Earnest, believed that Jews were orchestrating the 'Great Replacement' of white Americans. In 2019, he walked into a Synagogue in Poway, California, and murdered one worshipper while injuring three. A month before he committed this terrorist attack, he tried to set fire to a Mosque in the neighbouring city of Escondido, just days after Brenton Tarrant committed his attack. More recently, seventy-one-year-old Joseph Czuba stabbed Palestinian American Wadee Alfayoumi days after the Hamas attack in 2023. Wadee was just six years old. Czuba stabbed him twenty-six times. It is hard to imagine that these men consumed a healthy media diet and suddenly woke up one day and decided to murder innocent people. It is far easier to imagine they inundated themselves with antisemitic and Islamophobic media and then chose to act upon the lies they bought into.

Antisemitism and Islamophobia are intimately linked, and by further analyzing this linkage, we can find a way to confront both. In their book, *Safety Through Solidarity: A Radical Guide to Confronting Antisemitism*, authors Shane Burley and Ben Lorber view the fight against antisemitism and justice for Palestinians as the same struggle. Therefore, it is paramount to form 'alliances across differences, building bridges not walls, and striving alongside others for a future free from inequality, exploitation, and oppression in all its forms'. Both authors are Jewish, and both emphasise the importance of holding oppressive governments accountable without delving into harmful stereotypes. For example, they argue that it is entirely valid to call out the Chinese government's treatment of its Uyghur population. What is not valid is peddling Sinophobic talking points when that callout happens. I would go one step further and say that we should be calling out ideas, and not identities. For example, the current US Director of National Intelligence, Tulsi Gabbard, is a transphobic, Islamophobic, Assadist shill. There is no justification for spewing misogynistic talking points to address my absolute disgust with her actions and views.

I have encountered some cynical attitudes towards Israel and Palestine over the years. It comes from neither the left nor the right, but often from the 'enlightened' centrist. I have often heard them say that the violence is 'too complicated for us to understand', and how 'if you are not stakeholders then your opinion is invalid', or perhaps the worst one of all, 'this conflict is unsolvable because the hatred had lasted for centuries'. I contend that if you are not a stakeholder, then on some level, practising solidarity is of utmost importance. As one podcaster I listen to said, and it is something I say to myself every day, 'Solidarity is a responsibility you have, not an aesthetic you put on'.

One of the ways I have been practising solidarity is directly combating antisemitism and Islamophobia whenever they arise, either in person or through the written word. Over ten years ago, I published a blog about how going to the Middle East, specifically the Palestinian territories, destroyed my previously held Islamophobic convictions. I shared that blog post with my friend's dad, the one who advocated for the annihilation of over 2 million people. It didn't change his mind. If anything, his response showed me how deeply-seated his hatred towards Palestinians, Arabs, and Muslims was. Since I wrote that initial post about addressing my Islamophobia, I've tried to do what's in my power to ensure that harm doesn't come to any marginalised group, especially those who bear the brunt of anti-Arab, Islamophobic, and antisemitic narratives. I counter these narratives through writing and presenting ideas to people who might be susceptible to believing in harmful falsehoods. Essays like this one are one way I can accomplish this. I suspect that many people will ignore the words that I write. I will write them all the same.

GODS, MONSTERS AND ERNST JÜNGER

Boyd Tonkin

A man can harmonise with the powers of his time or he can stand against them. This is secondary. At every point he has the opportunity to show how he has grown.

Ernst Jünger, preface to the 1972 edition of *On the Marble Cliffs*

Some people had dirty hands, some people had clean hands, but Jünger had no hands.

Jean Cocteau

I

On 22 July 1942, a German writer called on Pablo Picasso at the artist's studio in Paris. There, on the rue des Grands-Augustins, the visitor 'had the impression that I was looking at a magician'. Picasso's magic cast a strong spell over the German, who wrote that the artist's 'alchemical experiments' were 'essentially showing things as yet unseen and unborn'. The pair chatted amiably about art, and current affairs, before the entranced author departed.

This cosy rendezvous, recounted by Ernst Jünger in his published diaries, practises a sort of magic of its own, a trick made up of concealment and misdirection. Jünger, then aged forty-seven, visited as a distinguished creator of novels, memoirs, treatises, and essays in Germany. His sensational front-line memoir of trench warfare on the Western Front, *Storm of Steel*, had established the multiply-decorated veteran as a literary firebrand in the early 1920s. A maverick standard-bearer for the 'Conservative Revolution' in Germany, he had turned prophet of the technological future in his tract-manifesto *The Worker* (1932).

Then, on the eve of the Second World War, he had published an eerie fantasy novel – *On the Marble Cliffs* – that many readers took as a forensic allegory of Nazi rule. But on that day in Paris, as he did from 1939 until 1944, he wore the uniform of a captain in the Wehrmacht. He worked as a military censor, comfily billeted in one luxury hotel (the Raphael) with an office next door in another (the Majestic). There he enjoyed the company of discreetly Nazi-averse colleagues: they agreed not to use the 'German greeting' – the Hitler salute – at work.

Jünger had promptly re-enlisted on the outbreak of war and, for a year already, had served in the army of occupation that controlled Paris after the fall of France in June 1940. He would remain an officer of the Third Reich until his dishonourable discharge in October 1944, (rightly) suspected of association with the senior officers who attempted to kill Adolf Hitler that July. But at this point, with France humiliated and its German overlords eager to recruit high-status cultural collaborators, the painter of *Guernica* could – whatever his private opinions – scarcely have refused to talk to this courtly invader.

The background to this agreeable *tête-à-tête* had darkened by the day. A week prior to Jünger's meeting with Picasso, French police had – at the occupiers' behest – rounded up more than 13,000 Jews in Paris. After deportation, most would perish in Auschwitz. In France, the bureaucratic machinery of the Holocaust had started to hum loudly. As for the lesser crimes of the occupation, Picasso himself was not untouched. Five days later, on 27 July, some of his works would feed a huge bonfire of 'degenerate art' (in reality, looted pieces that their Nazi plunderers had failed to sell) at the Jeu de Paume museum. In Jünger's dairies, he nonetheless claims that when he and the artist discussed the war, Picasso told him that 'Both of us sitting here together would be able to negotiate peace over the course of this afternoon.'

Aesthete and warrior, dandy and hero, visionary and functionary, Jünger over the course of an epically long life (1895-1998) cultivated a unique ability to wear the uniform, even to fight in the front rank, and yet to stand above the fray. Critics, and admirers, had noticed this 'Olympian' detachment even when the be-medalled soldier (wounded fourteen times) published the original version of *Storm of Steel* in 1920. As a raw infantry recruit in 1915, Jünger had found the tumult of the battlefield 'as distant

and peculiar to me as events on another planet'. He adds, crucially, that
'This meant that I was unafraid.' In a chilling passage from the Paris diaries,
Captain Jünger delivers a meticulous second-by-second account of the
execution by firing-squad of a deserter in a wood outside Paris, up to the
moment when the dying man's face expresses an 'extraordinary surprise'
as the salvo 'produced five little dark holes in the cardboard' fixed to his
chest. Jünger insists that 'I want to look away, but I force myself to watch'.
The stance – or mask, or pose – of the clear-eyed extraterrestrial observer
scarcely slipped until his death, aged 102, in 1998.

Jünger scrutinised, and dissected, the monsters and monstrosities of
twentieth-century history as closely as this keen entomologist studied his
beloved beetles. Arguably, no writer of genuine talent has made himself
so thoroughly 'embedded' in the darkest forces, and ideas, of their age.
Yet he seemed to move through them as if encased in an invisible armour
woven of irony, disdain, aristocratic snobbery and scientific curiosity.
Neither neutral nor indifferent, he remained profoundly *uninvolved*. As the
writer Jean Cocteau (who met him often in Paris) memorably quipped,
'Some people had dirty hands, some people had clean hands, but Jünger
had no hands'. Thomas Mann, one of Jünger's sworn enemies from liberal
Germany, indicted him as the 'ice-hearted playboy of barbarism'.

However, Bertolt Brecht (a drinking chum from Weimar-era Berlin)
stoutly defended him. His later champions included pillars of the post war
literary left such as Heiner Müller and Hans-Magnus Enzensberger. Jünger
himself knew how to swim in many seas of thought, without ever getting
soaked. His affections and affinities crossed clear lines. He found in the
Nazi-supporting legal theorist Carl Schmitt – now frequently seen as an
ideological forefather of the Trump administration – a close friend and
intellectual soulmate: 'Of all the minds I have ever met, Carl Schmitt is
the one who defines things best.' Yet he could also call the revolutionary
anarchist and satirist Erich Mühsam – tortured and murdered by the Nazis
in 1934 – 'one of the best and most good-natured people I have ever met'.

All the same, Ernst Jünger surely belongs in the domain of Fascist
literature. That judgment can withstand his decisive rejection of the
National Socialist party; his vehement contempt for anti-Semitism and
racial ideology; his absolute detestation of Hitler and the 'satanic'
genocidal course of the Second World War; even his deep sympathy for

the ecological consciousness that would later fuel green movements. Although their Nazi exponents disgusted him, he believed in war, nation, power, rank, and hierarchy as the perpetual mainsprings of human society. Masculine will and strength should supply the dynamo that drove an order built on force, authority and obedience.

With Jünger, this Fascist imagination climbed higher and dug deeper than the fetishism of ritual, uniform and sado-masochistic style associated with the idea since Susan Sontag's incisive, but limited, analysis of 'Fascinating Fascism'. Neither did he care exclusively about the 'aestheticizing of politics' identified by Walter Benjamin in his landmark essay on 'The Work of Art in the Age of Mechanical Reproduction'. Rather, he envisaged – though fitfully and waywardly – a totalised society of warriors and workers united in a national 'great community of fate'. Accordingly, he scorned the tenets of liberal democracy and individual rights. Modern technology, which he loved and loathed, had bred a class of omnipotent 'technicians' – in politics as much as engineering – who would oversee a future automated state peopled by willing drones.

All these ingredients, along with Jünger's signature detachment, blended into a modernistic aesthetics of violence and unreason all the more hypnotic for its distance from vulgar adherents of the same creed. In his diaries, Jünger writes of the ideas he cherished that 'the Munich version [ie, the Nazi version] – the shallowest of them all – has now succeeded, and it has done so in the shoddiest possible way.' Not the most savage or tyrannical, but the 'shoddiest'.

The vast arc of Jünger's career, from the birth-pangs of the Weimar Republic to the aftermath of German reunification in 1991, offers a singular example of a Fascist ethos and aesthetic unbendingly pursued alongside a consistent revulsion from Fascist politics in practice. That this vision of blood and steel comes from a writer of multiple gifts who despised hatred, cruelty and prejudice in everyday life only makes the Jünger case – *der Fall Jünger*, as German pundits avidly discuss it – all the more compelling. His moral compass worked perfectly well. He simply declined to follow where its needle pointed.

By late 1942, Jünger has picked up hideous rumours of Jews carried by trains into 'poison gas tunnels'. He knows that, in Eastern Europe, 'extermination is certainly occurring on a huge scale'. Faced with such horror, 'I am overcome by a loathing for the uniforms, the epaulettes, the medals, the weapons, all the glamour I have loved so much. Ancient chivalry is dead; wars are waged by technicians.' Still, Jünger went on wearing his uniform – and performing his duties – for almost two more years.

II

Many of the writers who, between the two world wars, fell prey to the temptations of Fascism were dilettantes, dupes, poseurs, casualties, or (rarely) outright fanatics. Derailed by the trauma that industrialised slaughter had imposed on combatants and civilians, post-1918 rebels might look for relief in any cause that promised redemption through upheaval. From Wyndham Lewis to Ezra Pound and Henry Williamson, several English-language authors and artists proved as susceptible as their Continental counterparts to the allure of (at first) Mussolini's regime in Italy, then Hitler's ascent in Germany. Most, however, proved to be short-term hangers-on, thrill-seekers, and ideological tourists.

For the minority who stayed, as with the nature-writer Henry Williamson, a warped idealism bred from wartime suffering gave their allegiance roots. Naked opportunists also hitched a ride on Fascist barbarism. So the brilliant, conscience-free Curzio Malaparte converted his proximity to Mussolini's inner circle into a pair of incandescent non-fiction novels that reported from the depths of the wartime inferno, *The Skin* and *Kaputt*. Malaparte believed in very little and, after the war, pretended to be a sort of Maoist. Vanishingly few authors of genuine ability did share the murderous racial hatred that defined Fascism in its National Socialist form. Among them was the French doctor-novelist Louis-Ferdinand Céline: not only the author of *Journey to the End of the Night* – the definitive modernist urban nightmare – but a fanatical anti-Semite. Jünger encountered him socially in Paris. In December 1941, Céline shocks Jünger with a tirade in which he regrets that 'we soldiers were not shooting, hanging, and exterminating the Jews'. Inwardly aghast, the officer privately notes that people like Céline 'radiated the immense power of nihilism'. But he gives no hint that he ever pushed back against this toxic rant.

For furious, confused survivors of the First World War, the new planet of Fascism could exert a gravitational pull as strong as its Bolshevik rival. Still,

Jünger remains a special – and unsettling – case. He didn't rashly jump on an authoritarian bandwagon that took him to a sinister place; he had helped to build and drive the vehicle himself. His daredevil exploits at the front – where he led bands of 'storm troopers' in perilous, even suicidal raids on French and British trenches – had earned him the *Pour le mérite award*: the German army's highest, and almost never bestowed on an infantryman.

Storm of Steel, adapted from his journals and obsessively revised over many years, made this celebrity veteran of the 73rd Hannover regiment a poster-boy for the disappointed ex-soldiers who thronged radical-right parties in Germany after the humiliation of the 1919 Versailles treaty. Yet the memoir hardly ever indulges in jingoism: Jünger excised outbursts of tub-thumping nationalism during his revisions. It does capture, and celebrate, the reckless spirit of a generation of young warriors 'yearning for danger' and 'enraptured by war'.

Despite the horrors that *Storm of Steel* evokes as well (or better) than any other Great War testament, that thrill of exhilarating comradeship persists. Jünger lauds 'the aristocrat of the trench' who meets his counterpart in knightly duels, fearless seekers of their chosen fate. In this idealised combat among a chivalrous elite, terror and carnage fill the pages, but not personal or national hatred. In one episode, Jünger's unit captures trenches held by a Highland regiment in a gory showdown at Vraucourt near Arras. The revised edition of *Storm of Steel* tells us that one of the Scotsmen he had shot wrote Jünger 'a nice letter from Glasgow' (presumably in response to the first version), 'with an exact description of the location where he got his wound'.

On Jünger's battlefields, described in graphic detail, mud-caked bodies are roasted, ripped, shredded, speared, shattered and pulverised by high-explosive shells, fizzing grenades, bullets and bayonets. No matter: this grotesque delirium must later be recalled in friendly exchanges of 'nice letters' between Glasgow and Hannover. Extreme violence and decorous gentility intertwine. The succession of bloodbaths in which Jünger's company stormed the British lines left them 'pleasantly impressed with their [opponents'] bravery and manliness'.

Few veterans could boast the fourteen wounds and chest stacked with decorations that supported Jünger's faith in this code of chivalry. His record, and his fame, equipped him to emerge in the early Weimar

Republic years as a tribune of the soldiers and a militaristic apostle of national renewal. Unlike many literary survivors, he did not find a refuge in pacifism. Quite the opposite. His 1922 tract *Battle as Inner Experience* looks back to Nietzsche – always a looming presence for Jünger – and forwards to Fascist propaganda in its rhapsodic praise of warfare as existential liberation. Its molten prose revels in 'the irrational right of the blood' as the supreme escape from civilised inhibitions, when 'the cave dweller breaks forth in the total release of impulse'.

Battle becomes orgy, and killing the ultimate orgasm. This overheated theoretical fervour, combined with the glacial objectivity evident in Jünger's accounts of his wartime ordeals, makes the reader speculate about the author's state of mind. If we can treat literature as evidence of delayed trauma, then much of Jünger's 1920s work reads like the compulsive exposure of unhealed inner wounds.

Yet this personal psychodrama – sustained in 1925 by another searing front-line memoir, *Copse 125* – made Jünger an uneasy fit with the nationalist politics of those years. He joined the chief veterans' association, the Stahlhelm, and wrote extensively for its press, above all the *Standarte*. He shared the anti-democratic, anti-bourgeois romantic militarism of these circles but – ever the insider-outsider – began to go his own way. An erratic, lyrical streak of anarchism and solipsism (most visible in his almost-surrealist 1929 work, *The Adventurous Heart*) cut across his schemes for submission and solidarity.

Above all, Jünger grew close to the 'National Bolshevist' strand of anti-Weimar ideology, with its populist rejection of capitalist inequalities yoked to calls for patriotic renewal. He contributed to papers edited by the National Bolshevist theorist Ernst Niekisch, whom he doggedly praised for the rest of his life. Niekisch haunts Jünger's Paris journals as the lost saviour, one who could have been 'a significant force in German history', and whose leadership would have avoided both ruinous war with Russia and the 'atrocities perpetrated against the Jews, which enrage the cosmos against us'.

Glance at the career of Jünger's political lodestar, and you glimpse the confused tangle of motive and affiliation that marks this age. Niekisch had chaired the executive of the revolutionary Bavarian Soviet Republic in 1919. He had no time for the Nazis and admired Stalin rather than Hitler as an icon of the 'Führer principle' he promoted. In 1939, the Third Reich sentenced him to life imprisonment for 'literary high treason'. He almost went blind in Hitler's jails but emerged to opt for East Germany, and to lecture on Marxism in East Berlin. Yet he left for the West after Stalin's tanks crushed the workers' uprising of 1953. Jünger – never a Nazi in any meaningful sense, but a committed National Bolshevist for several years – would recruit a surprisingly wide fan-base in the post-war GDR.

As for the National Socialist party itself, Jünger kept it at a long arm's length. He did pen two nebulous articles for the party daily, the *Völkische Beobachter*, but in 1927 refused permission for reprints. Adolf Hitler (whom he never met) had, like many embittered veterans, venerated *Storm of Steel* and its author. Also in 1927, the Nazis offered Jünger a Reichstag parliamentary seat. He turned them down. Josef Goebbels, who had flirted with National Bolshevism, wanted to find a use for Jünger's 'sharp pen' but was rebuffed by its wielder. In his diary, Goebbels voices his disappointment that Jünger has forsaken national uplift for aesthetic experiments, 'just ink, literature'. The two met again at a first night in 1933, with Goebbels freshly installed in office. 'What do you say now?' crowed the Minister for Propaganda. Hitler himself seems to have retained an awed respect for the valiant hero of the Flanders trenches. Some sources claim that when the question of his potential disloyalty was raised, the Führer insisted: 'Nothing will happen to Jünger'.

III

After the Nazis' rise to power, Jünger embarked on a period of 'inner emigration' during which he shunned all appeals for political engagement. In 1932 he had published his futuristic treatise *The Worker*, in which modern technology functions as the implacable generator of a totalitarian worker-soldier society which will exert complete control over its hyper-regulated subjects. *The Worker* swings erratically between utopia and dystopia. Jünger, 'Olympian' as always, heralds the triumph of the beehive state with equal measures of glee and horror. Rather than offering a social planners' blueprint, it belongs with near-contemporary visions such as Fritz Lang's film *Metropolis* and Aldous Huxley's *Brave New World*. In *Storm of Steel*, Jünger had experienced technologically-enhanced warfare not merely as the relentless mincing-up of men by machines, but the transformation of the soldier into a machine himself. That insight never left him.

Jünger might dread the advent of this robotic, war-driven tyranny, but he depicts it with a mesmeric power. Elements of Fascist aesthetics ignited his imagination even if their political corollaries appalled him. Pointedly, *The Worker* makes clear that 'race and the biological conception of race' play no role in the state it foresees. This hi-tech future will offer equal-opportunity servitude.

Some factions of the left and right acclaimed *The Worker*; others from both camps denounced it. When, in 1931, Jünger had published a related tract called *Total Mobilisation*, the Nazis had purloined the title as a slogan although the work itself stands, typically, loftily above the quarrels of ideology. Technology, it argues, is digging the grave of every outworn creed, as armed nationalism and socialism – those 'two great millstones' of modernity – implacably grind each other into (human) dust.

War-hungry, ultra-masculine, order-seeking, enamoured of the ideal state as a machine-made work of art: Jünger the Weimar polemicist cultivates a Fascist sensibility while recoiling in disgust from activists who seek to convert ideas into policies. The Fascist ideal seduces; the Fascist reality nauseates. This paradoxical position reaches its zenith in the book that offers the best, and briefest, introduction to his mind and art. Published in summer 1939, *On the Marble Cliffs* was first translated into English soon after the war's end by the left-wing Scottish scholar-soldier Stuart Hood (he would later become the BBC television controller who commissioned *Doctor Who*). Indeed, extracts first, improbably, appeared in the *Interim British Army of the Rhine Intelligence Review*. Hood's version served a vital purpose at the time, but Tess Lewis's 2022 translation has superseded it. Her rendering of Jünger's refined but macabre parable confirms its curious status as a major anti-Nazi, anti-totalitarian, novel written not by a convinced democrat but by an elitist authoritarian – if you like, by a Fascist.

The story's fantastic, idyllic landscape merges Jünger's home on Lake Constance, the shores of the Mediterranean, and coastal Brazil (where he had travelled). Two erudite brothers study the local flora and fauna from their cliffside home above the lush and civilised lakeside port, 'Marina'. Behind the cliffs stretch the pastoral 'Campagna' and, beyond the plains, dark woods where the 'Head Forester' rules over bands of marauding thugs. Weary of the battles they have fought, the narrator and his brother Otho claim their place in 'the natural aristocracy of this world'. They peaceably study the herbs, flowers, insects and snakes (Jünger had a lifelong snake fixation) around their beautiful abode. However, they live in a decadent era when a revival of raw violence and despotism menaces the 'spiritual detachment' and tranquil superiority they prize.

Bluff, coarse but charismatic, the Head Forester – who much resembles Hermann Göring – extends his sway over the cowed Campagna, raid by raid, ruse by ruse. His 'forest ruffians' arrive under the pretence of upholding the law: 'So terror established its reign behind a mask of order.' Aided by two companions – a frail but brave aristocrat, and a rough, shrewd operator – the narrator uncovers the atrocities that the Forester's henchmen have committed. In a torture-house in a woodland clearing, malign dwarves flay captives and adorn the walls with skulls. (I can't establish whether, at this point, Jünger had encountered Mister Kurtz in Conrad's *Heart of Darkness*. It seems possible.)

The narrator recoils from such 'putrid caves of a gruesome kind in which the depraved rabble regales itself with the violation of human dignity and liberty for all eternity'. But the Head Forester's power grows across the Campagna, then in the urbane Marina itself, while 'humanity threatens to fall completely under the sway of the demonic'. In a Hollywood-horror battle, his slavering hell-hounds tear the feeble forces of resistance to pieces. As an apocalyptic finale, the Marina burns in a 'purple mantle of destruction'. The brothers escape, protected by the lethal but loyal vipers they have domesticated. A rescue boat carries them across the lake towards the happy, peaceful land of Alta Plana.

With its bizarre geography and scrambled chronology (medieval warfare and Renaissance architecture coexist with automobiles), *On the Marble Cliffs* swings closer to the fantasy literature of the twenty-first century than to mainstream political dystopias. Yet Jünger, who wrote the novel during early 1939, soon found that every allegorical hint he had dropped was eagerly picked up. Swiss critics pointed out the Nazi bigwigs lurking under Jünger's Gothic masks; the book sold 14,000 copies within weeks. Fortunate as usual, its author survived. Complaints by party hacks came to nothing. Perhaps Goebbels enjoyed the transparent caricature of his arch-rival Göring, self-appointed 'Chief Forester' of Germany – although the propaganda minister himself lends some traits to the ruthless technocrat Braquemart, a nihilistic 'zealot of power and supremacy' but also an enemy to the Forester.

After the war, this outlandish fantasy began to read like prophecy. Prince Sunmyra, the etiolated nobleman, plans and fails to assassinate the despot – just as a cabal of Prussian aristocrats did in 1943–1944, with Jünger as a sympathetic but sceptical onlooker. Meanwhile, the blaze that incinerates the Marina presages the firestorms that would soon raze the ancient cities of Germany: 'The devastation made the old disputes seem as senseless as a remembered drinking bout. Calamity alone remained.'

Still, the narrator and brother Otho do not waver in their faith in a 'natural aristocracy': an educated elite, hardened by battle, whose benevolent lordship guarantees social and natural harmony. This flame-lit twilight of the gods never challenges the right of gods to rule. Besides, as none other than his National Bolshevist idol Ernst Niekisch wrote, *On the Marble Cliffs* ends not in fight but flight. The brothers flee, just as their creator retreated deep into himself. As he contemplates the severed head of Sunmyra, the narrator vows that 'I would cast my lot with the solitary and free rather than with the triumphant and servile'. But a year after Jünger had written those defiant words, he would ride into subjugated Paris as an officer in Hitler's all-conquering army.

IV

Whether in person, or via his fictional proxies, Jünger wants to exempt himself from choice. He aspires to rise above the terrain where monsters flourish to a level of god-like understanding, and god-like unavailability. There is some evidence that, during his Paris years, Captain Jünger did help Jews by discreetly spreading advance information about planned deportations. Still, he never, as the historical Prince Sunmyras did, put his life on the line. At the Hotel Georges V, he shared anti-Nazi gossip with like-minded Wehrmacht officers such as Hans Speidel (later the West German defence chief who brought the postwar state into NATO). Yet when a fraction of the old Prussian elite – with Erwin Rommel as their inspiration – began to stiffen their distaste for Hitler and his cronies into a specific assassination plot, Jünger faded from view.

He knew of the conspiracy that culminated in Count Stauffenberg's bomb of 20 July 1944 but warned that if 'Kniébolo' (his diary code-word for Hitler) falls, 'the hydra grows a new head'. The plot's failure convinced him that 'assassinations change little and improve nothing' – but the stoic fatalist also argues that 'We are undergoing a test that is justified and necessary; there is no reversing this machinery'. Germany required bitter, utter defeat rather than a titled junta of Prussian nostalgists that would pursue further bloodshed in the East.

In retrospect, Jünger's position shows a degree of wisdom and foresight. It also reflects the untouchable, untraceable detachment – 'no hands', as Cocteau said – that let him surface, and flourish, as bolder spirits sank. Even in the midst of carnage, he seeks the longer view, the bigger picture. Human good and evil, grief and pain, figure simply as minor disturbances of the cosmic design that spans the beetles and the stars. The uniformed officer may fret when a shop assistant gazes at him with 'incredible hatred', and register that such looks 'can bring us only ruin and death'. He may counsel compassion and remind himself that he lives in a snug bubble surrounded by 'unfortunate people who endure the greatest suffering'. Not to worry: all this will pass.

At Père Lachaise cemetery, he muses that 'Life lies in death like a small green island in a dark ocean'. Posted for a while to the mountains of the Caucasus, he regrets that brutal close-quarters skirmishes with the Red Army curb his opportunities to enjoy the magnificent scenery: 'the *Zeitgeist* was trying to extinguish all beauty in us'. Don't blame Hitler (or Stalin, or me); blame the spirit of the age.

Ever the aesthetic voyeur, Jünger loved to watch bombing raids, those modern pageants of annihilation that unite 'great beauty and demonic power'. In a notorious journal entry, for 27 May 1944, he observes the 'stupendous beauty' of Paris under the rain of bombs from a sunset perch on the roof of the Raphael, while holding 'a glass of burgundy with strawberries floating in it'. No sentence has done more to brand, and damn, Jünger as a decadent Fascist dandy. But the raids on Paris that day had finished in the morning. He probably made up the scene, though not the sentiment. His posturing included a dash of self-caricature that could (as he hoped) fool simple-minded moralists.

Though the shadows of genocidal war thicken around him, Paris still offers pleasurable hunts for antiquarian books or rare insects, good food and wine, and rejuvenating encounters with spirited women. Sophie Ravoux, the French paediatrician with whom he conducted a long affair, was Jewish. Another intimate friend, the Azeri author Banine (Umm-el-Banine Asadullayeva), came from a Muslim family. He disdained Nazi racial dogma in practice as much as theory. All the same, he persisted in viewing the criminal machine he minded as the manifestation of impersonal destiny rather than the sum of human acts and decisions. About Hitler, he confessed that he had 'the impression that the world spirit has chosen him in a subtle way'.

Along with this serene fatalism went the notion of equal victimhood: that the carnage inflicted by Allied area bombing made innocent Germans as much the casualties of Nazism as all those the regime had killed. That became a commonplace of postwar rightist politics. Monstrously, Jünger writes in spring 1945 that 'the situation of the German is now like what the Jews experienced inside Germany'. However, unlike the neo-Nazis to come, he admits that such abjection 'is still better than seeing the Germans with their illegitimate power'.

Master of the distant view and the elevated panorama, Jünger had plenty of time to watch the postwar world evolve from his eagle's nest near Stuttgart (he was gifted this house by a relative of Count Stauffenberg). Characteristically, he refused even to submit himself to denazification procedures by the Allied forces, and so suffered a four-year publication ban. But he wrote prolifically, spoke far and wide, and started to win German honours again (ultimately, the prestigious Goethe Prize in 1982). His later science-fiction novels – *The Glass Bees*, *Heliopolis*, and *Eumeswil* – score some uncanny future-spotting hits. Citizens in the dystopian *Heliopolis* (1949), for instance, carry all-purpose smartphones known as Phonophors. The rebel protagonist dubs this 'universal communicator' device a 'machine for the destruction of solitude'.

Now, the remote superior being who recurs throughout Jünger's work retires completely into private life. In fiction and essays, he sketched the figure of the 'Anarch'. This proud loner never yearns to shake up society but relishes liberty alone, preferably deep in the German woods. In *Eumeswil* (1977), we learn that the Anarch 'doesn't want to be a great man or a free spirit... freedom is not his goal: it is his property'. This fresh spin on the virtues of an alien-like detachment failed to stop Jünger from busily defending his pre-war and wartime conduct in interviews and articles. From the late 1960s, he became a semi-reluctant icon for 'new right' journalists and ideologists in Germany and France – but also attracted interest from dissident leftists. They found in his corrosive critique of liberal capitalism a heterodox relief from the stifling conformity of the Federal Republic.

The former flag-bearer for a 'Conservative Revolution' against Weimar democracy now edged closer to environmental politics. Meanwhile, his 1948 tract *The Peace* had made him a pioneer champion of a reunited Europe, with Franco-German friendship at its heart: no surprise that François Mitterrand, the Socialist president of France who had worked under the collaborationist Vichy regime, was an ardent Jünger fan. Always curious about altered mental states, this lifelong hunter of exotic perceptions also dropped acid with Albert Hofmann, the Swiss biochemist who first synthesised LSD.

As a writer and thinker, Jünger indubitably stands on Planet Fascism. His aristocratic, even anarchic, individualism meshes with the cult of military violence engendered by the Great War and the feverish vision of a managed, tech-driven society governed by an enlightened super-class. So far, so canonical, according to the standard profile of inter-war intellectual Fascism in Italy, Germany and France. Yet he hovered above the surface of that planet, at ever-varying altitudes, and never truly breathed its emotional atmosphere.

The racism, savagery and escalating genocidal frenzy of the Third Reich whose army's uniform he wore repelled him. Hitler's mind, he justly said, was 'bent on the most comprehensive homicide possible'; he wanted to create 'a world of corpses'. Advocates and detractors will continue to debate whether this lordly distance increases or diminishes his responsibility. Jünger was not a true believer, nor a deluded dreamer, nor a witless dupe. He came, he saw, he understood, he recoiled in horror – and still he served the conquerors. Others with a fraction of his talent exhibited far more courage when the fate that he liked to invoke came knocking for them.

These true resisters included his own son. As a teenage naval cadet, Ernstel Jünger was arrested for having joked about Hitler and German defeat. The report on his first trial stated that 'during the proceeding he showed no remorse'. Wearing all his medals, his father pleaded for him. But Ernstel was sentenced to a kind of high-risk front-line service that meant almost certain death. He duly died at Carrara in Italy in November 1944 – uncannily, in a fabled place of marble cliffs. Jünger believed that the SS, rather than any enemy, had murdered him. On this occasion, the diary thaws: 'Ever since childhood, he strove to emulate his father. Now he has done so on his first try, and truly surpassed him.' For once, the man with no hands did have a heart.

EXCAVATING THE
WARSAW GHETTO

Martin Smith

Every year I take a group of my students on a tour of the site of the Jewish Ghetto in Warsaw, Poland. It was the largest Nazi ghetto and at its height nearly half a million Jewish people were imprisoned there. We assemble at the Umschlagplatz monument, the site where Jewish people were forced to assemble before being deported by train to the death camp at Treblinka, in Eastern Poland. From the Umschlagplatz monument we take the symbolic 'from death to life' route, looking at some of the most important Jewish historical sites, ending at Tłomackie Street.

Tłomackie street was once the religious heart of Jewish Warsaw, it was the site of the Great Synagogue, the largest in Europe. Photographs show this beautiful place of worship that made it a symbol of Jewish pride. It was demolished by the Nazis on 16 May 1943. Today on Tłomackie Street you will find the Jewish Historical Institute (Żydowski Instytut Historyczny). The institute houses the Ringelblum Archive, an unparalleled collection of testimonies, documents, and photographs of Jewish life and culture in the Ghetto.

I must confess, I never intended to become a Holocaust lecturer; my PhD focused on contemporary fascism, and my plan was to pursue an academic career in that field. However, by pure coincidence, to help pay for my studies I was offered a part time post working as a historian and researcher at the site of the Treblinka extermination camp. So, instead of teaching about the rise of the new far right, I now lecture on the crimes of the Nazis.

The mass extermination of Jewish people in Europe began during the Nazi invasion of Russia on 22 June 1941. In the wake of advancing Axis armies, Nazi paramilitary death squads (the *Einsatzgruppen*), murdered over a million Jews, as well as communist officials, and Roma people. At his trial in Nuremberg, Rudolf Höss (a German SS Officer and commandant of the Auschwitz Concentration camp), acknowledged that the shooting of women and children 'placed too heavy a burden on my SS men'. It was this 'mental toll', the financial cost of using bullets, and the failure of these death squads to systematically wipe out European Jewry that persuaded the Nazis to find new methods of mass extermination.

In January 1942 at Wannsee, a suburb of Berlin, Reinhard Heydrich and leading Nazi officials planned the extermination of Europe's 11 million Jews. Heydrich concluded that the deportation of Jews to killing centres where gassing was seen as the most 'efficient' way to achieve the Final Solution.

All the Nazi death camps were built in Poland, the first was constructed in Chełmno (1941). The three Operation Reinhard Death Camps were built in Belzac (March 1942), Sobibor (April 1942) and the largest Treblinka in May 1942. Over two million Jews would perish at these centres. Two further death camps were constructed at Majdanek and Auschwitz II-Birkenau, both also served as labour camps.

Unlike Auschwitz, if you visit Treblinka you will not see gas chambers, electrified wire fences, or rows of prison huts. Instead, in a remote clearance in a forest, you see two concrete blocks, they represent the camp gates. Treblinka's borders are marked by large stones and concrete representations of railway sleepers and an unloading railway platform leads onto a paved road. As you look up the paved road you see a monument built of blocks of granite. This monument is topped with a stone carving of a menorah on one side and anguished human figures on the other. Around the monument are hundreds of smaller memorial stones with the names of every town or city from which Jews were deported to Treblinka. The cremation pit is memorialised by a rectangular hollow, filled with black basalt rocks. The only visible traces of the nearly one million people murdered at Treblinka are the tiny fragments of cremated human bone that occasionally come to the surface, especially when it rains.

Despite only operating for thirteen months (23 July 1942 - 19 October 1943) around 900,000 Jews and an unknown number of Roma people were murdered at Treblinka. These statistics are numbing and incomprehensible. The Nazis made every effort to ensure that the world would not know what happened there. After a revolt by Jewish inmates in the camp on 2 August 1943, the Nazis used Jewish prisoners to demolish the camp, wiping out any trace of it. The site was then covered in a thick layer of sandy soil and pine trees were planted. To further hide the true purpose of the site the Nazis arranged for a former Ukrainian German camp guard, named Strebe, to build a farmhouse on the site of the camp bakery. We now know that the bricks used to build his farmhouse came from the gas chambers at Treblinka.

One of the few survivors of Treblinka was Samuel Willenberg. He describes one soul-destroying conversation he had with an SS guard at the camp: 'what goes on here will be unmanageable to most people...even if a Jew survived the world would not believe him'.

Another Holocaust survivor, Primo Levi, in his book *The Drowned and the Saved*, describes a similar conversation he had with a guard at Auschwitz:

> However, this war may end we have won the war against you; none of you will be left to bear witness, but even if some were to survive, the world would not believe him. There will perhaps be suppressions, discussions, research by historians, but there will be no certainties, because we will destroy the evidence together with you. And even if some proof should remain and some of you survive, people will say that the events you describe are too monstrous to be believed, they will say that they are exaggerations of Allied propaganda and will believe us. We will be the ones to dictate the history of the lagers.

The lack of visual evidence of an extermination camp at Treblinka has made it a target for modern day Holocaust deniers. In the documentary film *The Meaning of Hitler*, Holocaust denier, David Irving, is seen taking a group of 'tourists' around Treblinka. Irving alludes, that Treblinka was a work camp and not a killing centre. He mocks the victims claiming, 'Jewish prisoners died because they were not used to doing hard work'. Another infamous Holocaust denier Friedrich Berg also refutes the idea that there were gas chambers at Treblinka. Lesser known, but equally foul Holocaust deniers post videos on social media sites, spewing out the same lies – where is the evidence of the camp and where are the gas chambers they ask.

I spent three summers at Treblinka writing a history of the extermination site. The first report from Treblinka, I came across, was written by the Russian novelist and journalist Vassily Grossman who visited the camp shortly after it was discovered by Soviet troops at the end of 1944.

Gathering a small number of eyewitness testimonies, Grossman wrote, *The Treblinka Hell*. It is a damning indictment of the inhumanity that occurred there and provides important insights into the extermination process. However, it is limited in scope and overestimates the number of victims. Notwithstanding this criticism the passage below should be the mantra of all students and academics studying genocide today, 'it is the writer's duty to tell the terrible truth, and it is a reader's civic duty to learn this truth. To turn away, to close one's eyes and walk past is to insult the memory of those who have perished.'

Grossman and later Soviet historians believed that the camp had been completely erased by the Nazis. A chance to test their theory presented itself in 2007. Caroline Sturdy Coles and her team of archaeologists from Staffordshire University were given a licence to conduct a forensic archaeological survey of Treblinka I (a Nazi work camp about a mile from the extermination centre) and Treblinka II. The team used non-invasive methods – arial photographs, GPS technology, ground penetrating radar, and laser-scanning technology to map out an accurate picture of the camp. These surveys located large burial pits used to intern cremated remains. In 2013, Coles and her team were granted permission to carry out the first ever archaeological excavations at a Nazi killing centre. Four small excavation trenches were opened, the first two found little of significance. However, trenches three and four produced many finds – building materials, personal belongings (false teeth, coins, jewellery), and functional items (glass, scissors, bullets). Trench four was the most significant, it contained a number of broken red tiles embossed with a Star of David and brick foundations were revealed. These were the remnants of a gas chambers.

While researching the red tiles, I read testimony of two Jewish survivors of Treblinka, Abraham Krzepicki and Samiel Willenberg. Both stated that the floor of the gas chamber was made of red tiles with a Star of David embossed on them. Willenberg's testimony is of great importance, he was one of the Jewish prisoners forced to build one of the gas chambers. These little red tiles have played a small part in revealing the hidden secrets of Treblinka.

According to historian Martin Gilbert, only forty prisoners from Treblinka survived the war. The lack of eyewitnesses makes the testimonies of camp inmates all the more important. In 2013, I was able to interview

Treblinka camp survivor Samuel Willenberg. Samuel was born in Czestochowa, Poland in 1923. At the age of sixteen, he ran away from home to join the Polish army and was badly wounded and captured fighting the Soviet army in 1939. While recovering in hospital he escaped and made his way to his family home in a suburb of Warsaw. He was imprisoned in the Opatów Ghetto. Samuel described the Ghetto's liquidation on 20 October 1942:

> What happened to the Jews of Opatów was unimaginable. Thousands of us were made to march the 18 km to the railway junction at Jasice. Dogs and guards with whips tormented our every strep. Of course, the old, infirm and mothers with young children could not keep up and fell further and further towards the back of the column. Then we heard rifle shots, the butchers were killing the stragglers… When we arrived at the railway junction, we were herded into railway cattle trucks. It is just 300 km from Jasice to Treblinka, but we spent three days and nights in those stinking cattle trucks, no food, no water, and no sanitation. Hundreds died…. those who survived the journey went straight to the gas chamber.

Samuel was the only known survivor of the Opatów Ghetto. He was only saved from being gassed at Treblinka because a Jewish prisoner told him to tell a Nazi guard that he was a builder by trade. In the interview he recounted in graphic detail the workings of the camp and the roles he carried out as a Sonderkommando (a Jewish slave labourer).

Treblinka was divided into two sections – the upper and lower camps. In the upper camp (Todeslager) the Sonderkommandos were given the grislily task of emptying the gas chambers and the disposing of the bodies. Samuel worked in the lower camp, they were responsible for emptying the train wagons, supervising the undressing of victims, and sorting their belongings. During our interview I only saw tears well up in Samuel's eyes once, it was when he talked about his sisters:

> My first day in the sorting hut I was instructed to bundle together some coats. On the floor I recognised a brown coat, it had belonged to my little sister Tamra, next to it was a skirt worn by my older sister Itta. At that terrible moment I knew that my sisters had been killed, a silent rage and anguish engulfed my body… I vividly remember looking outside the sorting shed, the factory of murder continued working as normal.

Later Samuel joined the Tarnungskommando, they chopped down pine trees from nearby forests to camouflage the camp. The entire camp was run by deception, every effort was made to pacify those going to their deaths. The unloading ramp was made to look like a railway station, the infirmary (the Lazarett) was a place of execution for those too weak to walk to the gas chambers and the concealed tunnel (Schlauch) that led to the gas chambers was euphemistically called the 'road to heaven'.

In the spring of 1943, the Nazis attempted to remove any traces of those murdered. This task became even more urgent when decomposing bodies buried in the camps pits began to rise to surface emitting the foul stench of death. The Nazis forced the Sonderkommandos to dig up all the decomposing bodies and cremate them on grills made of railway girders, unlike Auschwitz, no crematoria were built at Treblinka.

Yet, ever since the Russian troops discovered the demolished camp at Treblinka, bodies have been discovered all around its perimeters. My hypothesis was that this was a conscious effort by the prisoners to ensure that the world would know what happened there. This theory has been challenged by some historians, who claim that the bodies were left uncremated by mistake or in the rush to dismantle the camp. I discussed this with Samuel, and I believe his response gives some credibility to my hypothesis:

The prisoners in Treblinka were always worried that the world would not know what happened there. In the sorting hut we would leave notes in trouser pockets in the hope that those receiving them would know where they came from. This was a risky thing to do, if we were caught, we would be sent straight to the Lazarett. I had little communication with those in the upper camp, so I cannot say for certain, but it is possible, I would even say likely that prisoners would secretly hide bodies in the hope that they would be found by future generations.

I recently re-read testimony from another survivor, Chil Rajchman, who worked in the upper camp and was part of the team that exhumed the bodies. I missed this passage first time round, but he also states, that 'the Jewish workers who were employed in the emptying of pits, nevertheless used every opportunity to leave behind in the earth some remains of human bone.'

Survivors' accounts of the uprising at Treblinka on 2 August 1943 are clear that by early 1943 the murderous operations were near to completion and any potential witnesses would be murdered. A group of prisoners set up a resistance committee, although we know most of their names none survived the revolt. In the run up to 2 August wire cutters, money and weapons were procured and hidden. The planned breakout was partially discovered just thirty minutes before it was set to begin. Nonetheless around 800 Sonderkommandos took part in a desperate break out. As many as six guards were killed, the camp was set ablaze, and hundreds of prisoners stormed the gates of the camp. Around 300 escaped, of those only forty survived the war.

Samuel, the last survivor of the uprising at Treblinka, provided me with an account of the revolt. He believed that the Jewish Ghetto Uprising in Warsaw on 19 April 1943 was a motivating factor. The inmates found out about the Uprising from victims coming to the camp on transports from Warsaw. He recalled how on one transport train from Warsaw a man pulled out a grenade and threw it, injuring several camp inmates. But it was the SS guard's reaction that surprised Samuel: they 'ran away like snivelling dogs, they were scared, and we knew it'. He also explained that any injured member of the Sonderkommando would immediately be sent of the Lazarett and executed. When the SS guards returned, they instructed several inmates to take the wounded to the Lazarett, without saying anything the prisoners defied the order and instead took the injured to the Jewish camp doctor. This act of defiance would normally have meant the immediate execution of those disobeying orders, but this time the SS guards turned a blind eye. Samuel noted, 'the dynamic between the guards and the camp inmates had ever so slightly shifted, they no longer seemed invincible'.

Samuel talked about the Uprising as a triumph of the human spirit and a unified act of defiance. But he also described some opposition to the revolt among the inmates:

> Even as the revolt neared there were those amongst us who said it was not the right time, for these people the time would never be right. The will of those who wanted a mass breakout had to be imposed. And of course, we had our fair share of Jewish informers who would tell the Germans about any resistance group just to save their own skins. There were also Kapo's [Jewish inmates

responsible who supervised work details] who were sadists. Wherever possible they were dispatched.

After Samuel escaped Treblinka, he miraculously made his way back to Warsaw and became a member of the underground resistance. During the Warsaw Uprising in 1944 he joined the Home Army and fought in Śródmieście area of Warsaw, just a few kms from the burnt-out streets of the Jewish Ghetto.

Samuel died on 19 February 2016. He led an extraordinary life; he both witnessed and gave testimony to the horrors of the Holocaust. And he resisted the Nazis with every fibre in his body.

The Warsaw Ghetto was the largest Nazi ghetto and was established in November 1940. It was separated from the rest of Warsaw by a two-metre-high wall. More than 460,000 Jewish people lived in an area just under three and half square kilometre. The Ghetto was created to isolate and dehumanise Jewish people, and ultimately make it easier to transport them to the extermination camps. Life in the Ghetto was unbearable, it was overcrowded (an average of ten people per room) and inhabitants were given below subsistence food rations (180 calories per person). There were severe shortages of medicines and diseases like typhus and tuberculosis were rampant. Around 92,000 inhabitants perished in the Ghetto. Any attempts by Jewish people to escape the Ghetto or obtain food and medicine from the Polish side were fraught with danger, an official Nazi proclamation displayed on both sides of the Ghetto wall read: 'Jews who leave the quarter without permission are liable to the death penalty. The same penalty awaits any person who knowingly gives shelter to such Jews.'

Our understanding of life in the Warsaw Ghetto is due in large part to Emanuel Ringelblum. He was a historian and a member of Poale Zion, a socialist Zionist organisation. Ringelblum and his family lived in the Warsaw Ghetto and it was there that he set up the underground organisation Oneg Shabbat. The express purpose of Oneg Shabbat was to set up an archive and document life in the Ghetto. This group of historians, scientists and writers collected documents, diaries, underground newspapers and Nazi decrees. The archive also obtained first-hand reports from the death camps at Chełmno and Treblinka. Found in the archive was the following statement from the organisation: 'it must be recorded with not a single fact omitted. And when the time comes – as it surely will – let the world read and know what the murderous have done.'

To ensure that the world did know, in the spring of 1943, the archive was stored in metal boxes and large milk churns and buried in the Ghetto. After the war, part of the archive was found in the Ghetto ruins and a further section was recovered in 1950. Sadly, the final part of the archive is yet to be found. Containing over 25,000 documents the Ringelblum archive is an unparalleled and unique resource for historians. Much of my research centres on the archive at the Żydowski Instytut Historyczny in Warsaw.

Historians estimate that between 15,000 and 20,000 Jews lived in hiding in the Polish area of Warsaw. A small number were able to obtain forged documents that enabled them to live as so-called 'Aryans'. They faced the constant fear of being discovered by the Nazis or blackmailed by those who knew their secret. The historian Richard Lukas estimates that several thousand Poles were executed for aiding Jews.

One of the Jewish survivors of the Ghetto I interviewed was Ada Willenberg, she was born in Warsaw in 1929. Her father was killed fighting for the Soviet Army in 1941 and her mother was deported to Treblinka in 1942. A few months before the Ghetto Uprising, she and her grandmother escaped from the Ghetto and were given shelter by a Polish women named Helena Majewsky. Part of her interview covered Polish–Jewish relations. She told me:

> Yes, there were Poles who would denounce a Jew for a few Młynark [The Polish currency during the war]. But we also had traitors, Jewish spies, and informers and the cursed Group 13. If it was not for the Polish family that hid me and the Polish man who supplied me with a new ID card, I would not be here to tell you, my story.

Ada described how a complex network of support groups helped find safe shelter, food and clothing for the 15,000-plus Jews in hiding. A list of these organisations can be found in the archives. The most famous was Zegota, the Council to Aid Jews, dedicated solely to saving Jews. Other groups helping to protect Warsaw's Jews included the Catholic Church, the Jewish National Committee, Zionist political groups, the socialist and anti-Zionist Jewish party the Bund, the Polish Socialist Party, and the Communist Party.

At the bottom of this list of organisations is an intriguing entry: the Association of Tatar-Muslims. Looking at the archive papers was the first time I had ever heard of this group or its role. The Tatar Muslim community – sometimes called Lipka Tatars – are a little-known but long-established community that has lived in Poland for more than six hundred years. The community was centred in the northeast of the country, near modern Lithuania. It was one of the last to surrender when the Nazis invaded Poland and its officers were held in concentration camps throughout the rest of the war.

The role of the Association of Tatar-Muslims has gone unnoticed by history. They were a relatively small group, with at most a couple of hundred Tatars living in Warsaw. The Tatars provided over 3000 Jewish people with false documents – 'Aryan' papers. This was invaluable, especially for young Jewish boys, as it provided them with an explanation for why they were circumcised.

Another Ghetto survivor I have interviewed was Estelle Glaser Laughlin (who sadly died in 2024). Estelle was born in Warsaw in 1929 and lived with her family in the Ghetto. In our interview she recounted the brutality of Ghetto life – the death, disease, and hunger. Her own family survived because of the black market. She stated:

> It was the brave young children who sneaked out of the Ghetto at night to beg, steal, or barter for food that kept our family alive. So many of these poor children were captured and killed by the Ghetto guards…Yet in this inferno, people found heroic ways to resist. The Jewish community formed its own self-help centres to feed the poor. We even had theatres, imagine that theatre when there was no bread?

The Grossaktion Warsaw was the Nazi codename for the mass deportation of Jews from the Warsaw Ghetto to Treblinka which began on 23 July 1942 and by the end, 21 September 1942, the Nazis had deported over 260,000 men women and children to their deaths. Only 60,000 Jewish people remained in the Ghetto, it was now obvious to all that only death awaited those sent on the transports from the Umschlagplatz.

By September 1942, the resistance movements had become the de-facto leaders of the Ghetto. There were two Jewish resistance groups, the left-wing Jewish Combat Organisation (ZOB) and the ultra-right-wing Jewish Military Union (ŻZW). ZOB was comprised of young members of the Bund, left Zionist groups (Hashomer Hatzair, Poale Right Zion, Poale Left Zion, and Dror) and the Communist Party. By October 1942, ZOB was led by Mordechai Anielewicz. This poorly armed resistance movement consisting of no more than thousand fighters between them. They knew that victory was impossible and survival unlikely. Marek Edelman wrote 'that our inspiration to fight was not to allow the Germans alone to pick the time and place of our deaths'. When the Nazis launched a further round up of Jews for deportation in January 1943, the resistance movement struck, after a brief skirmish, the Nazis fled the Ghetto. They returned on the 19 April 1943 with the intention of smashing the resistance and deporting the remaining inhabitants to the death camps. During the Uprising, Estelle and her family hid in an underground bunker. She told me:

> While we hid in the bunker fighting erupted in our street. Against tanks and aeroplanes our brave fighters battled longer than it took Poland to capitulate... One day there was a huge explosion, and our trap door was blown out. Within an instant the barbarians were upon us. My father was a member of the resistance, he helped build the bunkers, but we had no weapons. Our resistance was to hide for as long as we could and show the Nazis that the Jews of Warsaw would resist them in any way they could.

For nearly a month the inhabitants resisted. The Nazis had to use tanks and artillery, but the fighters went into the underground bunkers and engaged in hit-and-run attacks during the night. In the end, the Nazis used flamethrowers, poison gas, and dynamite to destroy the Ghetto. Over 13,000 Jewish people lost their lives in the Uprising and nearly 50,000 captured inhabitants were deported to Treblinka and Majdanek. A handful of Ghetto fighters, including Marek did escape through the sewers and continued their struggle.

In his report, SS commander Jürgen Stroop claimed that the German's suffered 110 casualties, including seventeen killed. It was the largest revolt by Jewish people during World War Two. Stroop announced that the resistance was defeated on 16 May 1943 and celebrated by blowing up the Great Synagogue on Tłomackie Street. However, there were still sporadic gun battles between Jewish fighters and the Nazis in the Ghetto as late as July 1943.

What does the Warsaw Ghetto Uprising teach us? The question was answered at the twenty-fifth-memorial meeting of the Uprising in Warsaw. In attendance were a number of survivors including Yitzhak 'Antek' Zuckerman, a key organiser of ZOB. Referring to how the Uprising might be analysed in the future, he said:

> I don't think there's any real need to analyse the Uprising in military terms. This was a war of less than a thousand people against a mighty army, and no one doubted how it was likely to turn out. This isn't a subject for study in a military school. Not the weapons, not the operations, not the tactics. If there's a school to study the human spirit, there it should be a major subject. The really important things were inherent in the force shown by Jewish youth, after years of degradation, to rise up against their destroyers, and determine what death they would choose: Treblinka or Uprising. I don't know if there's a standard to measure that.

RETURN TO SYRIA

Robin Yassin-Kassab

This was a journey that I didn't expect to make. I had reconciled myself to never seeing Syria again. I had reconciled myself too to my children never knowing it. They had visited a few times, but only in their unmemorised infancy. Similarly, I had reconciled myself to not seeing my father again. He died in Damascus five years ago in the absence of his children. In our last telephone conversation he'd made statements such as 'A bird flew over last night'. This was code for a missile passing by, or artillery fire. Then I stopped phoning in case our communication landed him in trouble. It wasn't unusual for the Assad regime's goons to beat up the elderly parents of Syrians abroad who spoke or wrote against them. In his final years my father was struck by dementia, and then he died, almost alone, with his country burning. I didn't see him in his last days, and I was sure I'd never visit his grave. I lost faith. The fascists had won.

A critical mass of those inside the country didn't lose faith. Those in Idlib province in particular, both original Idlibis and those driven from every other province into a besieged and bombarded strip of land of a similar size to Gaza – those people kept believing, and building, and struggling. And the Best of Planners planned, using various instruments to hollow out the regime and weaken its foreign protectors, and to increase the revolution's fighters in wisdom, until in 11 remarkable days revolutionary fighters surged out from Idlib and took Aleppo, then Hama, Homs and Damascus. Suddenly Syria could be a home again, for me, and more importantly for the millions in the camps and slums of exile.

Syria had been the victim of a myriad forms of fascism. Now, for the moment at least, it was free of them, though still beset on all sides, though the vultures still circled. Navigating between these vultures and various offensive military birds, a plane brought my wife and I in to land at Beirut airport. This was late March, late Ramadan, but we'd bought the tickets

in January when there was only one flight into Damascus – from Istanbul
– and that was prohibitively expensive. So we took the Beirut route, and
the next day a taxi to Syria.

Outside the airport we came into contact with one of those forms of
fascism. The airport is in the *dahiyeh*, the southern suburbs which are a
Hizbullah stronghold. A banner pinned high showed a portrait of Hassan
Nasrallah, killed by an Israeli bunker-busting strike a few months earlier.
Nasrallah was grinning in this portrait. The words on the banner
proclaimed: 'We are Not Defeated!' The correct translation of the slogan
is of course: 'We are Certainly Defeated!' Otherwise, why the need to
pretend that Hizbullah wasn't, after the elimination of its upper and
middle leadership, and its weapon stores, and the Shia villages of southern
Lebanon?

The reader may at this point cry out for me to hold on a moment and
define my terms. Because, this reader may say, Hizbullah isn't a fascist
group but a resistance movement. To which I, and the vast majority of
Syrians, would respond that Hizbullah was once a resistance movement
but that it destroyed itself by assisting the Assad regime in Syria on Iranian
orders, at which point it transformed into a fascist group, or at least a tool
of fascism, demonising a weaker population in order to erase it. Hizbullah
had certainly been a resistance movement in the late 1990s when it
resisted Israeli troops in South Lebanon, and in the year 2000 when it
managed to push the 22-year occupation out of the country. It was still a
resistance movement in 2006, when it fought Israel to a standstill in
renewed hostilities. By then the Sunnis of the region loved Hizbullah as
defenders of the Arabs and Muslims in general, especially the Syrian
Sunnis, who welcomed refugees from Zionist bombing in their schools,
mosques and homes. Not only did Hizbullah enjoy widespread popular
adulation, its security procedures were water tight. The Israelis couldn't
penetrate its communications or anticipate its movements.

Once the Syrian Revolution broke out in 2011, Hizbullah's focus shifted
from the defense of south Lebanon to the repression of those who
threatened Iran's allies. It deployed various excuses – from defending
Lebanese border villages to protecting Shia shrines – but in reality it
terrorised Syrian civilians across the country, many miles from the border
or from the shrines. And it did so with gusto, imposing starvation sieges,

reducing towns to rubble, waving sectarian flags and screaming sectarian slogans as its men burnt, tortured and raped. It played a leading role in the mass expulsion and slaughter of Syrian Sunnis. And its undisciplined interactions with the notoriously corrupt Assad regime allowed it to be thoroughly penetrated by Israeli intelligence, rendering it useless as a resistance movement. During the war catalysed by the Hamas attacks of October 7, 2023, the Israelis had already been able to plant explosives in the militia's pagers and walkie-talkies, and they knew exactly where militia leaders were at any moment. Hence Nasrallah's death, and the militia's defeat, and the banner outside the airport claiming otherwise.

Fascism requires a victim complex. Hizbullah bought into the originally western war-on-terror rhetoric which Assad used to demonise the Syrian people. According to the story, Sunnis were a fanatical and dangerous mass, a majority which had continuously oppressed minorities, like the Alawite minority from which Assad emerged, or the Shia minority which Hizbullah claimed to defend. Since Alawites and Shia were victims, every crime which the defenders of these victims committed was justified, because it was always an act of self-defence.

In Lebanon you can tell the sectarian make-up of an area by the banners hanging on the buildings. A few minutes after the Nasrallah banner we passed a similarly enormous picture of Kamal Jumblatt. Three single-word sentences accompanied the image: 'We Were Patient. We Were Steadfast. We Were Victorious.'

Kamal Jumblatt was the founder of the Progressive Socialist Party, and more to the point the leader of the Druze during the 1975-90 Lebanese Civil War. He was the prime mover of the Druze-Muslim-Palestinian-Leftist axis which opposed the mainly-Maronite Christian Phalange. The Phalange was fairly open in its fascism, modeling itself on Hitler, Mussolini and Franco's parties. Jumblatt's politics were more liberatory, but his Druze militants did murder civilians based on the religion listed on their ID cards.

In March 1977, Jumblatt was assassinated on Syrian dictator Hafez al-Assad's orders, allegedly at the hands of Syrian intelligence officer Ibrahim Huweija. In March 2025, Ibrahim Huweija was arrested by the new Syrian leadership. Kamal Jumblatt's son Walid, inheritor of both the PSP and the Lebanese Druze community leadership, responded to the news of the arrest on Twitter with 'Allahu Akbar'. And this is the meaning of the Kamal Jumblatt banner: Jumblatt's supporters waited patiently and steadfastly for justice, and were victorious in concert with the Syrian Revolution.

That victory towards which we were headed. We spent a night in Beirut, then took a private taxi to Damascus. Half an hour after we left Beirut, the driver, in consultation with his phone, informed us that the city had been bombed by the Israelis, the very masters of aggressive 'self-defence', who had been 'defending themselves' continuously since their original capture of Palestine in 1948, who had first invaded Lebanon in 'self-defence' in 1978, before Hizbullah was invented.

Up we drove through tower blocks and fluttering, contradictory banners into the mountains, and down into the broad agricultural Beqaa Valley, then up again into rocky heights. Shortly before the border post we passed a really desperate-looking refugee camp. It looked like a crash space for the urban homeless rather than a camp. There were no proper tents but only boxes and plastic sheets held down by rocks. Formal refugee camps are not permitted in Lebanon, therefore international bodies like the UN won't assist in setting up basic services. Whether in these makeshift shelters or in city slums, the refugees have a hard time here. A compound of class prejudice and sectarian disdain has united a wide range of Lebanese in hatred of Syrians. That hatred has been a key marker of nationalist discourse here as much as in Turkey, though Lebanese and Syrians are almost the same people, speaking almost the same dialect of Arabic, eating almost the same food.

Then the Lebanese border post. Then the Syrian.

At these borders every local had felt a plunge of the heart. What bribe might it be necessary to pay? What insult might it be compulsory to stomach with a smile? What if their name had been added to a list, and in a few moments, they'd be heading for the abyss? That went for both sides of the border, because both Lebanon and Syria were run by the Assad regime and its allies.

The Lebanese border post was easy enough, but crowded and smoky. The officials were as sullen as one would expect. We queued for our exit stamps, received them, and drove on. The Syrian border post, on the other hand, was friendlier and faster than expected. 'Ahlan wa-sahlan,' they smiled. 'Welcome home!'

And we were in Syria. My wife hadn't been here since 2006, when she was ordered to leave, and when her colleagues in the human rights organisation for which she worked, not lucky enough to possess foreign passports, were imprisoned. I hadn't been in Syria since 2013, when I made two quick visits to a liberated but bombarded and very violent Idlib. My last visit to Damascus was in 2009. I hadn't actually lived in Damascus since 1999.

As the taxi rushed down through dry yellow hills towards the city, wide grins plastered themselves across our faces. Images of the unsmiling faces of Hafez al-Assad and his sons were still painted on the blocks of officers' housing, and 'Our Leader for Eternity' was still spelled out on the hillside in whitewashed rocks. But the flag of the revolution was everywhere. Eternity was over at last.

And so we arrived into Damascus, which can't be eternal, for only God is eternal, but is one of the oldest and still one of the greatest of cities. Its diesel-fume infused yellow-dust air is still sweetened by jasmine and spiced by cardamom coffee. It's full of delicate pigeons and messy elegant cats, as it always was. There are car horns blaring and men calling their wares. And still the mountains sit, on whose edge the city grows, ochre, white in the midday glare, almost pink at dawn and dusk.

Twenty-six years ago my son was born here. Most of my extended family lived here then, though they originated from Latakia. I had dozens of friends and hundreds of neighbours and acquaintances in the city. Now everybody I knew then had moved to another country, or had died, or had disappeared. There are suburbs where I'd spent time then which don't actually exist anymore. But in the city centre it was easy to ignore the changes.

The city centre was a time capsule. Almost everything was exactly the same – the same restaurants, shops, residential blocks – only with a thicker layer of grime on the surfaces. I walked towards the flat I'd lived in that had felt most like home. My way was lined by the same shops selling more or less the same items. The same restaurant opened its doors on the alleyway corner. And there was our balcony. It looked exactly the same, except someone new was sitting on it.

How did I know that a quarter century had passed? Some of the city trees had been cut down. Others had grown from saplings to adults, altering the atmosphere. And I knew that time had passed because people told me so. When people bumped into me or asked a question, they often addressed me as 'uncle' or 'hajji', which they didn't do last time, when I still had hair.

In addition, of course, the statues had been toppled. Everybody had their least favourite statue, and mine — because it was the nearest to my home — was the clumsy concrete rendering of a scowling Hafez al-Assad raising a tyrannous arm across Arnous Square. Now that one has been replaced by a sculpture in colour of the revolutionary flag. In unintended illustration of the transition, the colours of two flags are painted ubiquitously throughout the city. These are the new flag, with its bands of black, white and green, and three red stars, which is in fact the old flag, the flag of the independence movement against the French occupation; and the Baathist flag, with bands of black, white and red, with two stars, which interrupted the country for several decades. On shop front shutters stencils of Bashar's face are still visible in between the flags, but they have been crossed out and embellished with horns.

As well as the long-suffering constant residents, Damascus was crowded with newcomers. Some of these were people fled from elsewhere in the country over the last 14 years. Instead of clustering in the outskirts, as new arrivals did before, they have crammed into abandoned buildings in the centre. Many others are Syrians back from outside, some just for Eid, some like me for a few weeks, some for a few months, to see what happens, and some — especially those who have been living in the utmost precarity in camps — forever. I read that at least 1.5 million had returned already.

In the space of a few days I ran into a British Syrian friend, and a Syrian American friend, and Syrian activists who live in Germany and France. In the airport — we left by air — I met the amazing Dr. Zaher Sahloul, founder of the Syrian American Medical Society (Zaher was with a couple of white American doctors who had worked with him in besieged Aleppo as well as in Gaza and Ukraine.) This was one reason I immediately felt at home, despite the passage of a quarter century since the city actually was home. I met more friends in an average day than I do where I live in Scotland.

One type of newcomer was newly gone entirely. That is, the Iranian occupiers and their hangers-on, the officers, militia men, tourists and pilgrims. For years these people had taken over parts of the city centre to perform their mourning ceremonies with chanting, amplified anthems, and self-flagellation. Syrians generally felt about it as Palestinians feel when they see Jews performing their rituals in Jerusalem and the West Bank. I had felt that way too. I feel no animus when I see pictures of Shia rituals in Mashhad, Najaf or Kerbala, just as I feel no animus when I see Jewish celebrations in Brooklyn or Golders Green. But in Damascus, the overwhelmingly Sunni capital of a country whose Sunnis have been expelled in their millions by Shia militia, the foreign Shia presence was a violation. Militiamen would curse and rave at the graves of certain of the Prophet's companions, striking the graves with shoes.

Now the shoe is on the other foot. The empty Iranian embassy has been moderately vandalised. Someone has painted 'Life, Woman, Freedom' on its walls in English and Farsi. The streets surrounding the Sitt Ruqiya shrine and mosque in the Old City used to be controlled by Iranian security, in part because Iranian officials and their allied militia leaders used to frequent the shrine precincts. Now only Syrian Shia and a few non-militant visitors were present. This made life easier for the locals. I visited what used to be the Algerian emir Abdulqader al-Jazairi's home, right across the alley from Sitt Ruqiya. Half of this palatial abode is owned by the Russian ambassador (who was as absent as the Iranians), and half by a member of the Jazairi family. None of it is open to the public. I was invited by a Jazairi. We sat under leaves in the mosaic-tiled courtyard and wandered the crumbling ornate rooms. Then we climbed to the roof for a stirring view of Sitt Ruqiya, the Umawi Mosque, and the spires of the Old City churches. For years the owners had been forbidden from visiting their own roof, because Iranian snipers had been stationed there.

The Russian cultural centre on 29 May Street is likewise closed off with metal sheets, plus defended by bollards. There are still some Russians in the Hmeimim airbase on the coast, but they have to ask permission before they leave its perimeter. It would have been more emotionally satisfying if these imperialists had been rewarded for their destruction of Syrian cities with an immediate, humiliating expulsion, but the transitional president is playing a probably necessary game. If the Americans refuse to lift sanctions, and the Europeans refuse to restrain their Zionist ally, then Syria must demonstrate that it has other options… (In May, President Trump would announce the lifting of sanctions.)

The city center cafés and restaurants were surprisingly full. Surprising because this is a country where the economy has collapsed so absolutely that at least 90 percent of the population suffer below the poverty line. Perhaps some of the patrons were nursing a single glass of tea for as long as they possibly could. But plenty of others were sitting around tables covered with what is still the best food in the world. Where did the money come from? I think a lot of it, like ours, had recently been brought from outside, either carried in by those like us who had just arrived or sent by relatives working abroad. All the Damascenes I know are living off foreign remittances. And then there is the criminal money made by war profiteers, and the drug money made from the captagon trade. The authorities are arresting some of those guilty of the worst crimes, but they have also granted a general amnesty. This policy has both benefits and drawbacks. One of the benefits is that some of the Assad-associated rich are still in Syria, still spending money.

Even so, and even though Syrians manage to not only survive but also keep up appearances in a way that westerners would surely find impossible, there are plenty of signs of poverty. When I looked closely enough I realised that many people were wearing clothes and shoes that were threadbare. A taxi driver stopped his vehicle close to a petrol station, apologised, and ran over to fill half a small water bottle with petrol, which he then poured into the tank. Clearly he was living from fare to fare, and never had enough to actually fill the tank. There were queues for bread, and long queues outside the banks as a result of the liquidity crisis. The electricity came on for between two and five hours a day, depending where in the city centre you were. Food poisoning is common because of intermittent refrigeration. Water was available only rarely and in small quantities, so luxuriating in the shower was impossible.

That was the city centre. The suburbs which actually make most of the city, or used to, were far, far worse.

The old frontline was just after Abbassiyeen Square, which is really quite central, not far from Bab Touma in the Old City, and next to the upmarket, mainly Christian, Qusoor area. There's the Abbassiyeen Stadium, which the Assad regime at one point used as a detention and torture centre. Just a couple of hundred metres further on the rubble begins.

This area is Jobar, held by the rebels for years and therefore bombed for years by Assad, the Iranian militias, and Russia. (Although the Syrian conflict is called a civil war, and in many respects was a civil war – or a series of civil wars – it was very one-sided. Any area which has not been destroyed by bombing is an area that never slipped regime control.) I visited Jobar during Eid, when local people were returning to the ruins to attend their relatives' graves. They picked between shattered and overturned gravestones which were surrounded by shattered and overturned buildings. It was necessary to watch where we stepped very carefully, not only for the risk of unexploded ordinance, or to avoid stumbling on the broken breezeblocks, but because every so often a deep shaft opened in the ground. These were signs of the tunnel system built by the rebels which had allowed them to hold out for so long.

The rubble stretched for mile after mile. We drove on over pulverised dust to what had once been the suburb of Harasta. My cousin Mustafa had built a home and a dental clinic in Harasta. He now lives precariously – without permanent residence – in Germany, having fled Syria after arrest and extreme torture. The home and the clinic were as impossible to find as the past.

Opposite the flat in central Damascus that I'd lived in twenty-five years ago, there was a working man's restaurant called at-Tayabat. In those days I would sometimes call down and across the narrow alley from my tiny kitchen balcony for a meal. 'Ya Muhammad! Send me some fried liver, please!' Muhammad was the owner, a hardworking, gentle-eyed, softly-smiling man who performed his prayers behind the restaurant counter and invited me for tea and cigarettes after closing time. Once he knew me well enough, he told jokes mocking Hafez al-Assad. Muhammad had commuted to work from his home in Harasta. I checked for the restaurant when I looked for my old flat. No sign of it remained.

And no sign of anything in Harasta, save the relics of a previous existence. The rusted shells of vehicles were three quarters buried in the earth. And young fig trees emerging from the cracks. If the place were left as it is for another decade or so, it would turn into a forest of figs.

These destroyed suburbs are in the Ghouta region which not so long ago was mainly green, a great stretch of orchards and streams fanning out from the mountains before they dried up in the *badia*, the rocky Syrian Desert that extends to the Euphrates. This is the Ghouta whose villages rose fiercely against the French occupation in the 1920s, and whose towns rose fiercely against the Assad tyranny from 2011 on.

There is a story that the Prophet – who came to Syria as a caravan trader before his prophetic mission began – refused to enter Damascus for fear that he would commit the sin of thinking himself in paradise before he actually arrived there. The story refers to the fabled beauty of the Ghouta which surrounded and penetrated the city. It had already lost most of its greenery before 2011. Urban sprawl combined with corruption meant that much of the designated green belt was concreted over. Summertime temperatures increased as a result. But the counter-revolutionary war brought a higher order of vandalism. The area suffered day after day of barrel bombs, for years, along with heavy artillery shelling, cruise missiles, and incendiary weapons including white phosphorus and thermite. The people here were subjected to starvation sieges, and ended up eating dandelion leaves and dogs and cats to survive.

We continued through crumpled residential blocks and flat rubble fields to the next ex-settlement, Irbeen. Some of these areas had been destroyed by bombing. Others had been destroyed first by bombs, and then bulldozed to make it entirely impossible for anyone to return. But someone had painted on an intact bit of wall the words *Eid bil-eid n'amara min jadeed* or 'Hand in Hand We'll Build it Anew'.

There was almost nobody in these ruins. That explained further the crammed busyness of the city centre – the restaurants were full there because there were no restaurants out here. We drove on to Douma, another hard-hit Ghouta town, where the buildings were more often semi-intact, if scarred, and where more people were living. But the people were war-blasted. Men missing legs were propped on broken wheelchairs at roadside.

On another day we visited Yarmouk Camp, which fifteen years ago housed the biggest Palestinian community anywhere outside of Palestine. In the 1950s it was a field of tents, but over the decades canvas was replaced by brick, people added storeys to their houses as their families grew, and the camp became an inner city neighbourhood. Twenty five years ago I'd had friends here and knew the place well, but that made no difference now. It was unrecognisable, and not only to me. My brother-in-law's aunt also couldn't find her way around, though she had lived in Yarmouk for most of her life.

What was very obvious in the remains of Yarmouk was the organised looting practiced by the regime. Once the residents had been bombed and starved out, regime operatives arrived in trucks to strip the ruins of everything that could possibly be taken: soft furnishings, sink units, copper pipes, electrical cables, bathroom tiles. Former urban areas were cannibalised as effectively as the economy. Plenty of planning went into this process. It was a master-class in de-development. Or more than that, because the regime didn't just wish to erase the progress that had been made, it wished to erase the entire population that had lived here. It was fully annihilationist. And it nearly succeeded.

On one floor of one of the hollowed-out, monochrome, skeleton buildings of Yarmouk, someone has fitted new windows. In a few other buildings, families have claimed a space by pinning a sheet across a blown-out wall. People are returning. A million and a half so far, and more every day.

The hall and courtyard of the Umayyad Mosque were brimming full for Friday prayers. The Umayyad – or Umawi – Mosque is one of the oldest in Islam, and is in fact much older than Islam. Before mosque it was cathedral, before cathedral it was a temple to the Roman god Jupiter, and before that a temple to the Aramean god Haddad. The head of John the Baptist is allegedly buried in a chamber within the mosque, which is why Pope John-Paul II once visited the place. It's at the centre of the city and always has been, a place where God has been worshipped, according to different cultural understandings, for thousands of years continuously. The outer walls are decorated in gold and green mosaic crafted by mainly Christian craftsmen of the Umayyad city in continuity from Byzantine styles. The work is representational, illustrating the orchards and streams that had so impressed the Prophet, and the stately mansions of the ancient city.

We paid my father's widow a visit. She lives in what used to be a family home, but now the children are all abroad and the father is dead. It's an apartment in a block just off Mezzeh Autostrade, behind the Iranian embassy. I remember looking down from the salon window at a prickly pear plantation covering the ground between Mezzeh and Kafr Souseh, but today the ground is all churned up for the Marota City building project. That was overseen by Asma Akhras, the dictator's rapacious wife, and was supposed to recreate a bit of Dubai in Damascus. A few of the sci-fi skyscrapers for the global elite were half built before the funds were diverted or the regime fell, whichever came first.

Iranian officials and officers favoured Mezzeh — a fairly upscale neighbourhood — which made it a target for Israeli missiles. It's difficult to find a Syrian who was upset by the Iranians being killed; even the regime was resentful of the power the Iranians exerted as payback for saving it, and many believe that regime insiders were helping Israel with its targeting. But ordinary Syrians were upset when ordinary Syrians were hurt, or when their property was destroyed, because of the rivalry of the occupiers. If my father's widow had been standing in her kitchen on the first of April 2024, when Israel hit the Iranian embassy complex, she would have become one more of the Syrian dead. The windows smashed in the blast, and hot chunks of shrapnel drove through the fridge door and the plastic of the chopping counters. The glass has been replaced and the charred walls and ceiling have been repainted, but there are still deep grooves in the wall.

As we sat in the scratchy red soil garden of my wife's uncle's villa, in what used to be called Quraat al-Assad (Assad Villages) and is now called Quraat ash-Sham (Damascus Villages), we heard Israeli warplanes breaking the sound barrier. And at a restaurant on the mountain side in Barzeh, in the city's north east, looking out on the only partially-illumined blocks and streets below, we heard an enormous, echoing crash. The diners surged toward the windows, not in panic but bright curiosity. That was Israel too, striking the nearby Scientific Research Center, not for the first time, and not because the new government has yet had any time or resources for scientific research, but to make a point, and to prevent Syria from stabilising.

On the day the regime fell, the Israelis began a campaign of hundreds of strikes on Syrian military targets. They had generally left Syrian assets alone in the war years, focusing on the Iranian instead. That arrangement lasted so long as the Israelis understood that the Syrian military was designed to fight only the Syrian people. Now Syria's potential recovery from fascism is terrifying Israel. Perhaps the Syrian army to come will serve a more representative, more accountable government. Perhaps the Syrians will pick themselves up, learn to defend themselves. Perhaps they'll link up with the Turks. Perhaps one day they'll even learn to defend their Palestinian neighbours...

Israel has advanced from the Golan Heights – which it occupied in 1967, when Hafez al-Assad was defence minister – to the snow capped summit of Jebel ash-Shaykh (Mount Hermon) and into parts of Daraa and Quneitra provinces. It currently occupies areas which potentially give it control over water resources of crucial importance to both Syria and Jordan. Every few days during our time in Damascus news arrived of a further outrage. For instance, Zionist troops murdered nine villagers in Nawa, Daraa province, who had resisted their incursion. On 3 April there was an enormous funeral for these martyrs, attended by delegations from across the country. Zionist troops also abducted several farmers from their fields – this resulted in zero outraged articles about cross-border hostage taking in the western press.

On the same night that they bombed near our Barzeh restaurant, the Israelis pummelled airbases in Homs and Hama provinces which the Turks had announced they were planning to develop. The new Syria is being driven by relentless Israeli aggression further into the arms of Turkey than perhaps she would have chosen. People are fervently hoping for Turkey to establish air defence.

Some social media accounts are affronted that the Syrian authorities have not declared war on Israel. They opine as if the authorities, or the Syrian people, are pleased that they are being bombed and insulted and their territory grabbed. This is victim-blaming of the higher order, and a clear case of willfully misunderstanding a situation by seeing it through a fantasy lens. Because there is currently no Syrian army with which to prosecute war. There isn't even a Syrian state. A quarter of the country is ruled over by the Turkish-Kurdish PKK, with US troops backing them up. Even the parts of the country which the map shows as under central control is in fact controlled by a variety of competing militias. Ahmad al-Sharaa does a very good impression of being in charge, but nobody is in charge.

As for the complaint that 'Ahmad al-Sharaa isn't talking about Palestine,' well, six months ago he wasn't talking about Aleppo or Damascus either. He moved when he was able to move, and I'm sure he didn't expect to reach Aleppo, let alone Damascus. The forces of history moved. The best of plotters moved.

But the Syrian people are talking about Palestine. During our time in Damascus, people demonstrated against Israel in the Umawi Mosque, the Hamidiya Market, and the Midan neighbourhood. They demonstrated in Muadamiyeh in the suburbs too. And there were demonstrations in Idlib, Aleppo, Latakia and Tartous. Even this would have been impossible under Assad rule, when any independent initiative, even protesting against those the regime pretended were its enemies, would lead to imprisonment and torture. The spontaneous military responses would have also been impossible. Hundreds of Bedouin fighters of the Aqaidat tribe, for instance, headed to the defence of Daraa. And while I was attending Friday prayers at the Umawi Mosque, an imam in a Hama Mosque gave the *khutba* with a Kalashnikov in his hand. 'Don't put down your weapons,' he said. 'For the confrontation with Israel is inevitable.'

But more often the authorities are trying to persuade the armed men in the country to give up their weapons, or at least to bring them under central control. The old regime surrounded major cities like Damascus and Homs with Alawite colonies inhabited by the families of men who worked in the army and security services. These people were weaponised but were not privileged. The housing in these colonies was unlicensed, and so only avoided demolition because of the regime precarious favour. One day we visited the rickety, steep-laned colony of Ash al-Warwar, at whose entrance stands a checkpoint run by the Public Security. There were three or four men on duty, bearded, long-haired, very young, smiling. Three nights after our visit, old regime 'remnants' emerged from the shadows and shot all the young men dead.

The forces of state repression were far less visible, far less present, than they used to be. The old army and police were not dissolved by the authorities, as in post-Saddam Iraq, but dissolved themselves in the last eleven days of the old regime, as it collapsed. The new army and police were being recruited and trained when I visited, though there was still no money to pay them. They scare many Alawites and some Druze who, understandably, fear the extremists in their midst, or at least those associated with them. Most Syrians, however, refer to the Public Security as heroes. They offer them sweets, and wave and smile as they pass. Amid the gratitude for the liberation, the public imagination has elevated the status of rural Idlibis and the working class.

A shot was fired at a checkpoint in the suburbs just after we'd passed through. 'What's that?' we asked the men in black at the junction, who were peering back down the road. 'It's nothing,' they replied, peering back themselves. And it didn't seem to be anything much, nobody was dead or screaming, it was nothing but a reminder of the ubiquity of weapons. Every night. if there was internet and enough charge on my computer, I looked at the latest haul of rifles, rockets and missile launchers captured, discovered or handed in. Tons of weaponry. And there must be tons which aren't handed in.

One day I went to Sednaya Prison, built in dry hills forty five minutes from the city. Sednaya was also known as Military Prison One. I visited four months after the liberation, but filthy blankets still covered the floors of the group cells in which dozens of men had been crammed. The solitary confinement cells, where the prisoners were starved, naked, their feet in faeces, in absolute darkness, still stank, despite clouds of incense being burnt.

Tens of thousands were murdered in this location only, among them the activist Mazen Hamada, who was killed in the last hours before the regime's final fall. Mazen was first arrested in March 2012, and was tortured terribly. Released in September 2013, he sought refuge in Holland, and from there travelled the world advocating for torture victims. His refugee status didn't allow this travel, so he was hounded by the Dutch authorities, and then lured back to Syria by the regime. He was arrested on his arrival in February 2020, and taken to Sednaya. He languished there until he was murdered. A post-mortem showed nails and screws had been driven into his body.

The sadism is difficult to understand. Like the destruction of the cities, the relentless torture of prisoners took organisation, energy, commitment, hard work. It would have been easier to execute people as they arrived than to murder them over months or years by beatings, starvation, overcrowding, and medical neglect. At least 100,000 were murdered in the most brutal of ways. How to come to terms with all this? How to absorb the fact that, though prisoners were left without water until they drank their own urine, or until they died, in Ramadan the guards entered the group cells and forced the prisoners to drink? How, for that matter, to respond to the massacres of Sunni women and children by regime-enabled Alawite mobs?

One possible response is that enacted by the sectarian atrocities on the coast in March 2025. That episode was provoked by regime remnants launching a coordinated attack on the Public Security and civilians, killing hundreds, but the reaction went far beyond an anti-insurgency operation. Some militias murdered civilians simply for being Alawite. The victims included women and children, and supporters of the revolution against Assad.

The crimes were justified by the usual fascist logic: 'They' injured 'us'; therefore, our crimes are not real crimes. I heard some say it in Damascus: 'They deserve it.' 'It's their turn now.'

Today fascism is rising everywhere, but it's been dominant in the Middle East for a long time already. My visit exposed me to its multiple forms and their shared victimology. Zionist fascism justifies its crimes by reference to the victimisation of the Jewish people. The Maronite, Shia and other forms of Lebanese fascism are built on the notion of their respective communities' historical exclusion and victimisation. ISIS fascism thrived on the victimisation of Iraqi and Syrian Sunnis by Iran's Shia militias. Assadist fascism played on the Alawite sense of victimhood. Syrians were returning to Syria from Turkey, where the racist mobs attacking Arab refugees felt like the victims of Arab betrayal in 1917.

Where does it end? In liberated Syria there is at least the possibility of building a post-fascist politics.

We returned to Douma for the commemoration of the 2018 chlorine attack that had killed between 40 and 50 people and injured hundreds more. That wasn't the worst of Assad's gas attacks. In August 2013, regime forces choked around 1,500 people to death with sarin. In any case, this commemoration mixed sadness and anger with triumph. Raed Salah of the White Helmets – now minister of emergency and disaster management – was there, and so were several revolutionary media figures. A helicopter flew over the crowd and threw down roses rather than gas canisters or explosive barrels. We met several activists, among them Wafa Ali Mustafa, who has campaigned tirelessly for her disappeared father and hundreds of thousands of similar victims.

But we were conscious of who wasn't there, first amongst them the Douma Four – Razan Zeitouneh, Wael Hammada, Samira Khalil, and Nazem Hammadi. These activists were long-term members of the Syrian human rights movement. My wife had worked with them during the first years of Bashar's rule. When the whole team was imprisoned, my wife – thanks to her British passport – was merely deported. Then when the revolution erupted several years later, Razan Zeitouneh was instrumental in setting up the Local Coordination Committees. These bodies organised protests and linked up revolutionaries throughout the country. She set up the Violations Documentation Centre too, which recorded and reported the crimes of the regime and other violent actors. Razan was one of the towering revolutionary leaders, but she, and the other members of the Four, were not killed by Assad. They were detained by Jaish al-Islam, the authoritarian Salafi militia which ruled Douma for most of the war years. Today it is presumed that Jaish al-Islam fighters murdered the four in 2018 before the regime retook the area with the help of the Russian air force.

An entire generation of revolutionary leaders is gone, murdered in Sednaya, or by regime bombs, or by authoritarian militias including the one that now makes the government. We had hoped that these were the people who would inherit Syria. Instead, Ahmad al-Sharaa is in top position – someone I would have considered a type of fascist not very long ago. His organisation – Hayat Tahrir al-Sham (HTS) – evolved from Jabhat al-Nusra, which in turn evolved from the Islamic State in Iraq. The evolution involved a war with ISIS, a split from al-Qaida, and a purge of the extremists in the Nusra-aligned Hurras al-Din. HTS has been on a journey of moderation and diplomatic outreach, including to non-Muslims. If it hadn't made this journey, it wouldn't have been able to win the trust of key Syrian constituencies, and it wouldn't be in government today. Nevertheless, HTS was responsible for closing down women's centres and radio stations and persecuting revolutionary activists in Idlib. When I visited the liberated territories in 2013, I stayed in the home of the activist (and lovely man) Hamoud Jnaid in Kafranbel. Hamoud was assassinated alongside the revolutionary Raed Fares in 2018, presumably by HTS.

Then Ahmad al-Sharaa wore a turban and went by the nom de guerre Abu Muhammad al-Jolani. Today he wears suit and tie, and has given up the alias. Opinion polls suggest that around 80 percent of the population supports him. Syria desperately needs him to succeed, but not too much.

Almost everybody wants al-Sharaa to manage to stabilise the country, to reign in the militias, to provide the necessary atmosphere for return and rebuilding. Almost everybody is very pleasantly surprised that he addresses Syrians as a national leader would, rather than as a Sunni jihadist – though many Alawites and Druze suspect that he remains a Sunni jihadist at heart. Almost everybody agrees – even many of those who don't trust him – that the worst thing that could happen would be for him to be assassinated. This could happen at any moment. Apparently, there have already been several attempts, and the prime suspects are either ISIS or HTS-adjacent extremists who see him shaking hands with western politicians, or who see women in Damascus in sleeveless tops, and decide that the man is a sell-out.

At the same time, those with their eyes open don't want al-Sharaa to succeed so far that he manages to indefinitely keep the power that he's concentrating in his hands. Currently, there is space for movement. Just as there is no army or air force to defend Syria, so there are no intelligence services to oppress the Syrians. That means that Syrians – exhausted as they are, and hemmed in by foreign vultures – have at last the opportunity they fought so hard for. It would be unheard of for a country to transition from 14 years of war and six decades of dictatorship to democracy and social justice, but that's what millions of people want.

To be honest, I'd been reluctant to leave our home in Scotland to travel to Syria. We should have gone in the first days of the liberation, before the sectarian massacres on the coast, when Syrian cities were celebrating their freedom with endless public parties. It hadn't been possible for us to go then, in December and January. By the time we arrived in late March I was wary, a little scared. My mind was full of bad news. But what I hadn't counted on was the enormous enthusiasm of the vast majority for the new stage. Stalls were selling previously banned books. Everybody was fearlessly talking politics. In this enthusiasm I put my faith, despite Israel, despite the weight of the past. I won't lose faith again.

ARTS AND LETTERS

}

GUERNICA: THINGS TO COME

Marjorie Allthorpe-Guyton

On 24 June 1937, a mass meeting was convened by the National Joint Committee for Spanish Relief in aid of refugee Basque children at the Albert Hall, London. Picasso was billed to speak but sent apologies, he was working against the clock painting *Guernica* in response to the brutal Nazi bombing of the Basque town of Guernica on 26 April 1937. The meeting was chaired by the 'Red Duchess', Katherine, Duchess of Atholl, conservative Member of Parliament, author of 1938 book *Searchlight on Spain*. The treasurer was Roland Penrose, artist and patron, the supporters were left leaning politicians and luminaries of the arts and sciences, signatories of an open letter to *The Times* in support of the Spanish Republican government. *Guernica,* the icon of anti-war paintings, and its creator were at the eye of the storm which was the Spanish Civil War 1936–1939. The conflict, loosely between Fascism and Democracy, with political, religious, and class divisions, impacted worldwide. It both divided and galvanised artists. In Britain, the Artists International Association (AIA) founded in 1933, joined the Popular Front of anti-Fascist political forces in the Republican cause and in the attempt to resolve the post war crisis of democracy. To this end Picasso was persuaded to allow *Guernica* to tour to England in 1938–1939. As a major political commission *Guernica* is an exception in his oeuvre, it is also the distillation of his art, a fevered expression of his private demons and pain, fuelled by outrage at human barbarism. As John Berger said, it is a profoundly subjective work. Picasso described it as an allegory. Its chilly grey imagery, cubist surrealist in style, both impressed and mystified the public, and prompted fierce critical controversy – then as now. That it failed to influence events was as much to do the fragility of democracy as it was to the complexities of the work itself.

Guernica's gestation and exhibition are the sum of a complex personal and political history. Picasso travelled freely between Spain and France after he settled in Paris in 1904, but as Fascism took hold in Spain attempts were made to petition him to return. Picasso was flattered by the offer of a retrospective in Madrid, which the Republicans had failed to fund. He attended a dinner at San Sebastian's Café Madrid, a Falangist haunt, charmed by its founder José Antonio Primo de Riviera. But he last set foot in Spain in September 1934. He spent the rest of his long life exiled in France. The cumulative impact of events in Spain had an inevitable and profound impact on Picasso's work long before the tragedy of Guernica. Under pressure from the reactionary factions of Catholics, Fascists, Falangists, and the military, the Spanish Popular Front government just held as the left split into factions. By 1936 the country descended into anarchy and Civil War. Picasso was embroiled in his own private wars, with two mistresses, one, Marie-Thérèse Walter, pregnant, and he was contemplating divorce from his wife. His inner turmoil found expression in his greatest etching *Minotauromachy,* 1935. Evolved from seven plates or states, it is dense with opaque imagery: a Christ like figure, a woman, a monstrous minotaur, horse, a young girl, which confound straightforward interpretation. It is the precursor of *Guernica.*

Appalled by the success of General Franco's Nationalist rebel forces supported by Hitler, Picasso suffered a further blow when his friend the poet Federico Garcia Lorca was executed on 19 August 1936. In January 1937, Picasso met with politicians and members of the Alliance of Anti-Fascist Intellectuals for the Defence of Culture and agreed to paint a large mural for the Spanish Republic's pavilion at the Paris International Exposition opening in May. With the Pavilion commission, Picasso was officially harnessed to the Republican cause. His early design was tentative, *Painter and Model* 19 April 1937 incongruously sports the Communist fist with hammer and sickle. The symbol had first appeared in 1936 in his drop curtain for Romain Roland's play *Le 14 Juillet,* a celebration of the election victory of France's Leon Blum's short-lived Popular Front government. On 27 April 1937 came news of the carpet bombing of Guernica, (Gernika in Basque), by the Nazi German Luftwaffe and the fascist Italian Aviazone Legionaria on behalf of Franco, obliterating the town and killing civilians. It was immediately reported in graphic detail by George Steer in *The Times* which ran the story every day for a week and syndicated it worldwide. In Paris, *L'Humanité* published grim photos of death and devastation. Basque refugees flooded into France and thousands of Basque children were evacuated, many to Britain. The bombing caused widespread panic and fear of what was to come, in Britain as well as Spain. Like Salvador Dali's monstrous work *Soft Construction with Boiled Beans (Premonition of Civil War)* 1936, British surrealist paintings, such as *Pro Patria* 1938 by John Armstrong, designer of the apocalyptic Alexander Korda film *Things to Come* 1936, are suffused with destruction and desolation. The atrocity was thought to be without precedent; the fact that saturation bombing had been used earlier by western colonial powers in the Middle East and Africa was forgotten. Franco's propaganda denied Nationalist involvement. Picasso had his subject. The Socialist politician, later Spain's Prime Minister, Juan Negrin, agreed to fund the project believing that 'the presence of a mural painted by Picasso is the equivalent value in propaganda terms of a victory at the front'. He would be disappointed.

From his rapid first pencil sketch on 1 May 1937, to over thirty studies and several states through to the completed work, Picasso forged and cannibalised images which are at the core of his art: images of primal, often sexual, violence and human suffering. The sacrificial bull, the fallen gored horse, weeping woman and child, the flaring light, the woman with the lamp are constants throughout his work. These have generated myriad interpretations, plumbing Picasso's psyche and personal relationships, Spanish history, religion and culture, art historical and mythological sources. In *Guernica's* female figures the doomed women in his life are clearly recognisable. Importantly, Picasso made no direct literal reference to the bombing, or to contemporary warfare, there is none of the grim hardware of the modern military. The Communist raised clenched fist of the fallen soldier in the first state is erased. Picasso famously said in 1935 'a painting is the sum of its destructions', but there had been early ill-founded rumours of him painting the Soviet leaders which made him then acutely uncomfortable with being associated with Communism.

He was adept at working fast and at scale from his early collaboration with the theatre impresario Diaghilev. *Guernica's* rapid creation, stage by stage, was documented in a sequence of photographs by Picasso's then lover Dora Maar which give unprecedented insight into Picasso's fevered working over five short weeks. Maar's left activism, she was a member of the Contre-Attaque anti-Fascist group and a signatory to their manifesto, and her political conviction and tragic melancholy profoundly impacted Picasso and found expression in his subsequent paintings of suffering and death, weeping women, skulls and still lives. Her brilliance as a photographer undoubtedly influenced Picasso's decision to paint *Guernica* in matt grey monochrome. It is a theatre of pain, of tortured forms, projected, freeze framed on dark voids, its scale and form unlike any other contemporary painting. The work confounded the critics and public alike when the Pavilion finally opened on 12 July. With its uncompromising extreme modernist style, it was in stark contrast to the less challenging or overtly propagandist work in adjoining Pavilions. The British Pavilion, with gentle domestic scale paintings by John Nash and fellow artists was hardly likely to raise the heartbeat, or the political temperature. It was indicative of the ill-judged non-interventionist position of the British Government to the Civil War.

Picasso's work was shown alongside contemporary Spanish artists and photographs presenting graphic images of the war and propaganda of Republican reforms. The most popular work with the Communists was the painting, *Madrid 1937 (Black Aeroplanes),* of bare breasted mothers with babes in arms cowering under falling masonry by the realist Horacio Ferrer de Morgado. *Guernica's* official reception was cool, the Basque President declined Picasso's offer of the work for the Basque people. The Basque painter Jose Maria Ucelay vilified Picasso, declaring the work pornographic; Le Corbusier was dismissive, not a single French newspaper wrote about it. Intellectuals thought it was too sophisticated for the workers who were anyway preoccupied by films, performances and the café nearby. Anthony Blunt, prominent British critic, later infamous Soviet spy, famously denounced it in his *Spectator* review 6 August 1937 as obscure, 'a private brain-storm which gives no evidence that Picasso has realised the political significance of Guernica.' This charge was later to be amplified by a long running public argument in the *Spectator* between Blunt and fellow critic Herbert Read which set the course for *Guernica's* tour of England the following year. This was primarily the initiative, not of the AIA, but of Roland Penrose 'so that the British public might finally be allowed to see for themselves whether Blunt's criticisms amounted to more than Marxist dogma'.

Picasso was persuaded to allow the painting to go to England to support the fundraising of the National Joint Committee for Spanish Relief, he wrote it was 'to draw attention to the horrors of war and it must take its chance'. The Committee and patrons were left wing politicians, scientists, artists and poets, including Penrose, E.L.T. Mesens, Herbert Read, Victor Gollanz,

E.M.Forster, and Virginia Woolf. With the emergence of the British Union of Fascists in 1932 led by Oswald Mosley, the Committee was part of what, following France, became a British Popular Front against Fascism and War led by the Trade Unions, The Independent Labour Party (ILP), the Communist Party, AIA, and other groups which was at odds with the policies of the mainstream parties. In October 1936, the Labour Party conference rejected the affiliation of the Communist Party. The Front held an unprecedented series of anti-Fascist public events and exhibitions through the 1930s to support the Republican cause, to raise arms and to fundraise for food and refugees and to challenge the conservative led British National Government policy of non-intervention. In October 1936, Penrose went to Catalonia and brought posters and legendary photos from the front by the great war photographer Robert Capa for exhibition in aid of Spain. The Front regarded exhibitions as 'demonstrations', interventions for a political and social cause. The AIA's first decades were an unprecedented political project galvanising artists across the board, including architects and commercial artists; modernist artists were a minority, although Picasso and other European artists sent work to AIA exhibitions. The AIA held their exhibition *Artists Against Fascism and War* in Cambridge and London in 1935 when Italy invaded Abyssinia, and followed with the first British Artist Congress 'For Peace, for Democracy, for Cultural Progress' in the radical Conway Hall, London, in 1937. The Association showed work in the Peace Pavilion at the Paris Expo and held an exhibition of Chinese woodcuts in solidarity against the Japanese aggressors in Manchuria. The cartoonists and graphic artists came into their own, producing pamphlets, newsletters, posters and illustrations for the *Left Review* (1934-1938). Intellectual freedom was also at stake and The Association of Writers for Intellectual Liberty was formed in 1936. Writers, including H.G. Wells, T.S. Elliot, Tristan Tzara, and Picasso's friend Pablo Neruda published a pamphlet in June 1937, 'Authors take sides in the Spanish War' posing the question 'Are you for, or against Franco and Fascism?'.

Guernica arrived in London 30 September 1938, the day that British Prime Minister, Neville Chamberlain returned to London declaring 'Peace in Our Time' after signing the perfidious Munich Agreement. In October, *Guernica* was shown at the prestigious New Burlington Gallery, Mayfair, with over sixty preparatory studies alongside Picasso's grief-stricken painting *Weeping Woman,* war planes reflected in her eyes, which Penrose had bought from Picasso after it was completed in October 1937. He considered it 'a postscript to the great mural that contained a cry of agony caused by the fascist government on humanity'. The adjacent gallery was later hired by supporters of Franco who showed a large painting of the Nationalists' defence of the Alcázar of Toledo in 1936 by Franco's favoured academic artist Ignacio Zuloaga. His supporter was Lady Ivy Chamberlain who was awarded the Gold Medal of Merit of Italy by Mussolini. *The Times* and *The Observer* gave *Guernica* poor reviews. *Guernica* attracted just 3000 visitors; Penrose wrote to Picasso of his disappointment, putting the lack of crowds down to 'the crisis and the general demoralisation'.

Guernica's reception also reflected the deepening divisions in British art between the realists and the modernists. Picasso's most overtly political work, two sets of etchings and a poem, *The Dream and Lie of Franco,* was made just after *Guernica* in June 1937 in aid of the Spanish Refugee Relief Fund. In the form of a comic strip, postcard images savagely lampoon the General as a stage strutting, sword brandishing deformity, astride a disembowelled horse, brilliantly evoked by Picasso's poem:

Rage that contorts the drawing
Of a shadow that lashes teeth
Nailed into sand the horse
Ripped open top to bottom
 in the sun...

The work's grotesque excess was denounced by Anthony Blunt in his *Spectator* review of 8 October 'the etchings cannot reach more than a limited coterie of aesthetes'. Blunt, who promoted the Mexican political muralist Diego Rivera, took the realist position of the AIA's influential Marxist intellectual, Francis Klingender. The AIA Newsletter of January 1938 saw 'the bad influence of Expressionism, Surrealism, Futurism and Abstraction.. as fantastic and far less comprehensible than Goya's work in denunciation of war.' Goya's great series of etchings the *Disasters of War* was exhibited that July at the Victoria and Albert Museum, London. Herbert Read argued cogently for Picasso and the revolutionary power of modernism in a letter to the *Spectator* 15 October *1937* where he had described the painting as a 'modern Calvary'. Writing in the *London Bulletin* of October 1938 he saw in *Guernica*'s imagery, not the realism of Goya's *Disasters of War*, but universal symbols 'it is only when the commonplace is inspired with the intensest passion that a great work of art, transcending all schools and categories is born'. Thirty years later, Blunt came round to Read's view. Both critics were pre-empted in their recognition of a masterpiece by the artist Myfanwy Evans, wife of the British artist John Piper who wrote a penetrating analysis in her 1937 collection of essays *The Painter's Object*: 'least of all is it a 'Red Government' poster screaming horrors to a panic-stricken intelligentsia. It is a passionate recognition of the facts, so purged as to become almost detached statement, and ultimately so unrealistic as to be almost as abstract as his most abstract painting. Yet only a Spaniard could have done it...'

From Mayfair *Guernica* moved to the East End of London and to a very different but not uneducated public. In the 1930s, the East End suffered extreme poverty, it was the socialist heartland of London with a population of a quarter of a million people, including anarchists, communists and many immigrants, Huguenots, Irish, Chinese, Jewish, Bangladeshi, Somali. They were victorious at the famous 4 October 1936 Battle of Cable Street, fought against fascist Oswald Mosley's Black Shirts. The Whitechapel Art Gallery, like the New Burlington, was distinct among London cultural venues for its progressive and non-conformist exhibitions. Under its first Director, Charles Aitkins, the programme was eclectic and transnational aiming to serve its local community, promoting knowledge and solidarity. Early shows included modern European art and that of non-western cultures such as the landmark 1908 *Muhammadam Art and Life*. The Gallery was also next-door to the Whitechapel Library, known as The University of the Ghetto. In the 1930s, the Yiddish and Judaica sections were the largest in the country. The Library was a learning and meeting place not only for the East End's many immigrant intellectuals, including Jewish artists Jacob Epstein, Mark Gertler, and David Bomberg, but autodidacts, working people and their children.

Stepney Trades Council East London Aid Spain Committee, a front for the local Communist Party, privately hired the Whitechapel Art Gallery to show *Guernica* from 31 December to January 1939 for their Million Penny Fund. The entrance fee was a pair of serviceable working men's boots. It was a coup, especially as the Gallery's founder Trustee took the view that the Whitechapel people 'have to be delicately led' and that the 'krinks and kranks of modern art movements' were not to be encouraged. The exhibition, attended by the Mayor and the Secretary of the Stepney Trades Council, flanked by members of the International Brigade, was opened by Clement Attlee, a former Mayor of Stepney, MP for Limehouse and Leader of the opposition Labour Party who had served as a Major in the Territorial Army. He had earlier been a volunteer manager of a charitable club for working boys in the borough of Stepney. On 7 January, the *East London Advertiser* reported Attlee's rousing opening speech where he rounded on the Prime Minister 'Mr Chamberlain said he was a realist but he did not show much realism in his dealing with dictators. He told them over and over again that he completely trusted the word of Signor Mussolini.. If once Fascism gets a hold, the people who suffer most will be the young'.

Stepney's Trade Council agenda was entirely political, *Guernica* was to spearhead their propaganda campaign. Communist Party member Norman King left some of the few extant records, including photographs, of the opening of the exhibition in the Whitechapel Gallery archive, donated by his widow in 1998. King lived in Shadwell in the East End, he was a commercial photographer and holder of the Tolpuddle Medal for Trade Union recruitment. He recognised the power of visual images and ran "Propaganda and Art' Courses for trade union activists to teach graphic design skills for placards for anti- Fascist marches and labour causes. An exhibition of work was opened by the Labour politician Herbert Morrison, MP for Hackney South and powerful Leader of the London County Council. *Guernica* received an enthusiastic but cautious welcome as the 'Wonder Picture' in the *The Voice of East London* January 1939: 'Because this picture is so advanced, because it is painted in a peculiarly Spanish way and because the East End of London has had so little opportunity to seeing and becoming accustomed to modern art it is natural that this picture should, at first, be difficult to understand', concluding that the whole was expressing the 'indomitable spirit of the Spanish people'. Films on the Spanish Civil War were screened and talks given by Penrose and other luminaries. The *News Chronicle* of 9 January 1939 reported 15,000 visitors, but *Guernica* raised just £250 for the Million Penny Fund.

Much was expected of *Guernica* and much was at stake. The drawings had been shown at Oxford University, Leeds Art Gallery and again in Oxford for an exhibition organised by the New Oxford Art Society and Denis Healey, future Labour party politician. *Guernica*'s last showing in Britain was from 1-15 February in a car showroom in Manchester in aid of a Food Ship for Spain where the *Manchester Evening News* reported on 31 January, 'people will see it and puzzle over its meaning'.

Expectations of the work to affect change were high, not only in the context of Fascist Spain, but in the growing unease in Britain among the left at the deepening erosion of democratic values. H.G. Wells published *Democracy Under Revision* in 1927, Leonard Woolf article 'Is democracy failing' appeared in the 7 October 1931 edition of *Listener*. Sir Stafford Cripps in 1933 published *Democracy and Dictatorship, The Issue for the Labour Party*, addressing unequivocally the constitutional difficulties of achieving reform of existing 'democratic' institutions. With three million unemployed in 1931, the National government had introduced means testing of benefits which led to the Hunger Marches of 1932. In 1934, the Incitement to Disaffection Bill sought to criminalise any attempt to dissuade members of the armed forces from service and was widely seen as an attack on free speech and civil liberties. It led to the foundation the same year of the National Council for Civil Liberties. Attlee was among the vice-presidents. *Guernica*'s exhibition had the blessing of Cripps, leading spokesman for the left and co-founder of the *Tribune* the oldest democratic socialist paper established in 1937. In its 28 October 1938 edition, *Tribune* published Cripps on imperialism and justice in foreign policy and Jawaharlal Nehru on Britain's waning democracy and imperialism, making an early call for Indian independence: 'Imperialism cannot champion democracy, it cannot fight fascism effectively as at heart it sympathises with it'. The failure of the League of Nations to stem Japanese and Italian aggression, the rise of Fascism in Europe and the Spanish Civil War and the advocacy of Trade Union leaders to support the Spanish Republicans, forced the Parliamentary Labour Party, which had opposed rearmament, to change its defence policy, if not its position on the colonies. Morrison shifted his pacifist position, although others, such as Aneurin Bevan and Stafford Cripps, held to their minority socialist position aligning with the anti-imperialist Popular Front policy then advocated by the Soviet Union.

The Communist Party was held by many then to be anti-Fascist and had strong roots in the founding of the AIA at a time of acute unemployment in Britain. Artists were attracted to work in the USSR which was employing foreign graphic artists for propaganda purposes. Founder member Clifford Rowe came back from Russia after his monumental painting of the Trafalgar Square Hunger March, commissioned by the Red Army, was exhibited in Moscow. He proposed the idea of an 'International Organisation of Artists for Revolutionary Proletarian Art' which became the AIA, recruiting over 1000 members aligned to fight Fascism 'Against Imperialist War on the Soviet Union, Fascism and Colonial Oppression'. The fine artists were trumped by the 'strip cartoonists and the silk screen people'; the cartoons of James Boswell, Ralph Laurier and others produced biting commentary on current events. The AIA painters embraced a new realism, looking back to William Hogarth and Goya, basing their banners and hoardings on Goya for an 'Arms for Spain' demonstration held in Trafalgar Square in February 1939 and for their paintings for an 'Art for the People' exhibition at the Whitechapel Art Gallery. Artist Nan Youngman invited an unemployed man off the street to open the show, it was 'intentionally didactic ...We wanted everyone to use their art, whatever it was, in a political way'.

The Spanish Civil War and the art and visual propaganda it generated harnessed art to activism but the battle was already lost. Guernica's tour and the AIA's valiant project changed nothing. Britain declared war with Germany on 3 September 1939; Franco's dictatorship lasted till his death in 1975. Guernica held no more power to affect events than the AIA's propaganda banners and posters. Its greatest and enduring impact was on artists: from Max Ernst, Henry Moore, John Craxton, Merlyn Evan to Francis Bacon and Jackson Pollock. Most recently, the late British artist Donald Rodney's 2025 exhibition at the Whitechapel included a photograph of his lost work Soweto/Guernica 1988, a collage of Picasso's work and a photograph of the schoolboy, Hector Pieterson, murdered by the South African authorities. Guernica's unique contemporary status as an anti-war icon was built by its subsequent tour and canonisation in the United States. Like Shostakovich's Leningrad Symphony and Britten's War Requiem,

Guernica's latent power is generative. The seminal project of artist Goshka Macuga, *The Nature of the Beast,* at the Whitechapel Art Gallery in 2009 focused on *Guernica's* recent political history and co-option by artist collectives and activists worldwide. The work centred on the tapestry of *Guernica* from the Rockefeller Foundation which has hung since 1985 outside the Security Council Chamber in the UN building in New York. In 2003, when US Secretary of State Colin Powell signalled the invasion of Iraq, the US insisted it was covered with a blue cloth. The *Guernica Remakings* is collective protest project led by artist and designer Nicola Ashmore; its worldwide remakings include 2010 *The Keiskamma Guernica*, a tapestry made by village women in the Eastern Cape of South Africa.

Picasso was a lifelong pacifist. He lived through two World Wars, in France under German occupation, the Holocaust, the Soviet crushing of Hungary and the Prague Spring, the Cuban missile crisis, the collapse of colonial powers, but he did not become a committed political artist. He argued that an artist is responsive to the world and as such is a political being and that 'painting is not done to decorate apartments. It's an instrument of war for attack and defence against the enemy'. But it could not be prescribed. In 1932 he was unequivocal: 'I will never make art with the preconceived idea of serving the interests of the political, religious or military art of any country. I will never fit with the followers of the prophets of Nietzsche's superman'. His work is veiled with metaphor and freighted with sometimes obscure visual references which are not easily read. As his biographer John Richardson said, until the 1930s the nearest he got to any overt political gesture was a red circle he painted on the title page of Stravinsky's *The Volga Boat Song* in 1917. While the maelstrom of horror which gathered in Europe, especially in his homeland Spain, affected him profoundly, he was reluctant to align, he did not join the French Communist Party until 1944, only too aware of internecine factions and threats to individual freedoms, not least his. In the Peace Movement he thought he was among brothers, but he was valued for his celebrity and one drawing, his ubiquitous peace dove, not for his life's work. John Berger even went so far as to suggest that he should have left Europe, that his roots and his work were cross cultural and that he could have 'become the artist of the emerging world, challenging the hegemony of Europe'. But Picasso never really left Spain. He attempted unsuccessfully to negotiate with the Franco regime to try to get his work shown in the Prado, Madrid, alongside his revered Velasquez and Goya. His unwavering core commitment was to his art and to protect his work and his legacy. He would have agreed with Aldous Huxley, writing for the AIA's 'Artist Against Fascism' exhibition 1935: 'the whole activity of the self-disciplined artist is a standing protest against war and dictatorship'.

Postscript

A placard at an anti-Trump demonstration in Los Angeles published in *The Times* on 7 April 2025 cannibalised Goya's terrifying black painting *Saturn devouring his son,* showing Trump as Saturn - and Tyrant. He had earlier made one of his bizarre utterances: 'Republicans Eat Their Young'. It is not hard to see political parallels with the 1930s. In a celebrity and market driven contemporary art world, there is little other sign of the brave militant solidarity among artists which inspired the Artists International Association.

Anti-Trump Demonstrations, Los Angeles. *The Times* 7 April 2025.

Spain and Culture Meeting, Royal Albert Hall 24 June 1938. Leaflet, courtesy Marx Memorial Library.

"GUERNICA" at the Spanish Government Pavilion—International Exhibition, Paris 1937.   (Photo Ramos-Ruan)

Picasso, *Guernica* at the Spanish Government Pavilion, Paris International Exposition 1937. Photograph, courtesy Marx Memorial Library.

Oswald Mosley 1896-1980. Poster, courtesy Tate Archive.

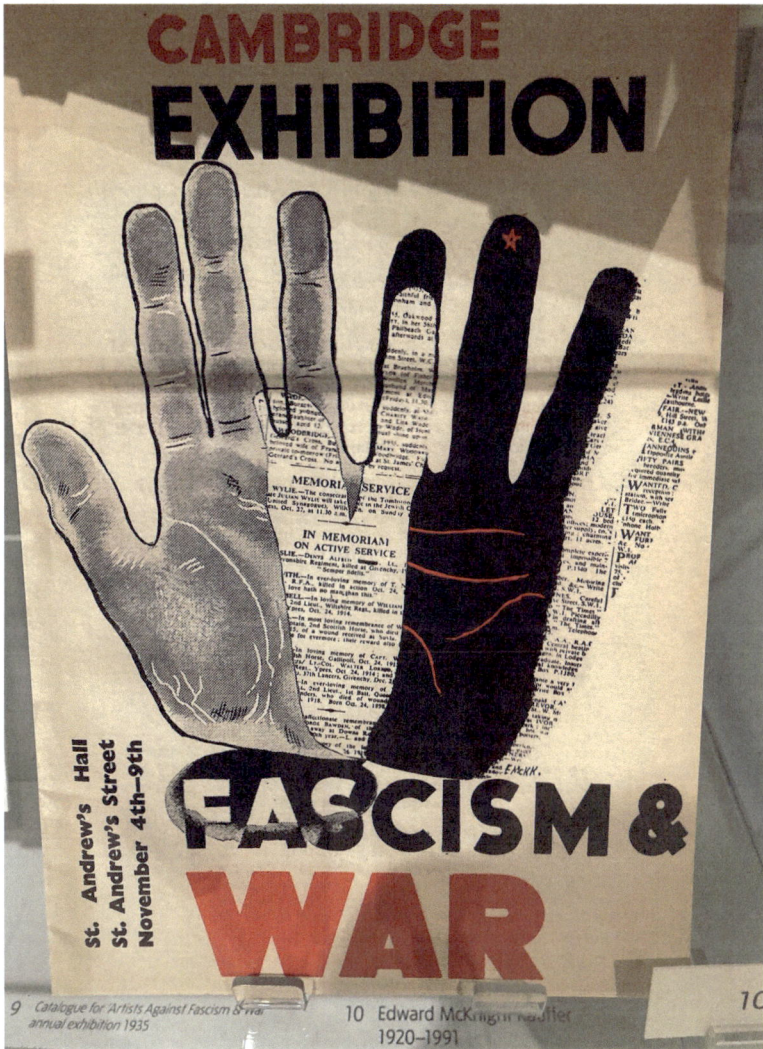

Edward McKnight Kauffer 1890-1954. AIA Exhibition poster, 1935, courtesy Tate Archive.

Norman King. Clement Attlee, Guernica Opening, Whitechapel Art Gallery
January 1939. Photograph, International Brigade Archive,
courtesy Marx Memorial Library.

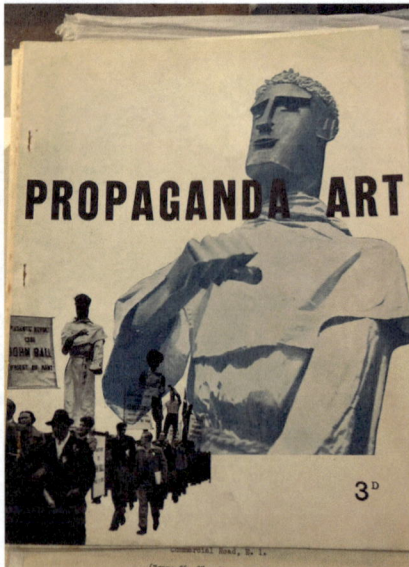

Norman King, Propaganda Art Course. Poster, courtesy
Whitechapel Art Gallery Archive

The Voice of East London 1939.
Press cutting, courtesy Marx Memorial Library.

The Voice of East London 1939.
Press cutting, courtesy Marx
Memorial Library.

Trades Union Poster 1939. Poster, courtesy Marx Memorial Library.

Ralph Laurier 1912 – unknown It's A Fascist Scheme! 1934. Cartoon, courtesy Tate Gallery Archive.

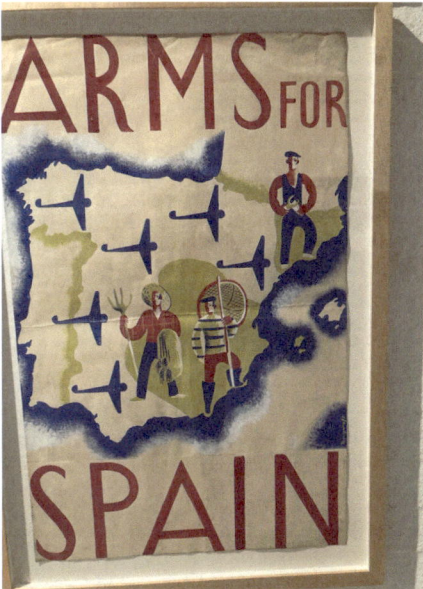

Priscilla Thornycroft 1917–2020. Arms for Spain 1938. Poster, courtesy Tate Archive.

Goshka Machuga The Nature of the Beast Exhibition installation, Whitechapel
Art Gallery 5 April 2009–4 April 2010. Photograph by Patrick Lear, courtesy the
artist and the Whitechapel Art Gallery Archive

The Keiskamma Guernica 2010. Courtesy Guernica Remakings.

Protest Banner September 2022. Courtesy Guernica Remakings.

Donald Rodney 1961–1998. Photograph of *Soweto/Guernica* 1988.
Lost work: oil on pastel on x rays and paper, Wolverhampton Art Gallery.

Tribune 28 October 1938. Press cutting, courtesy
Whitechapel Art Gallery Archive.

News Chronicle, May 1939.
Press cutting, courtesy Whitechapel Art Gallery Archive.

THE BEARD

Alinah Azadeh

It's insanely hot in here. The man shuts the door behind him, and shuffles in his cluster of thick, black, woollen robes towards the far end of the room, away from the window, out of sight of the eyes below, protected from the queues passing through the military gate into the building.

He sheds the robes first, to get some relief, then takes off his silver, square headdress, placing it on a huge, ornately carved walnut desk.

He's always been complimented on the volume and beauty of his beard, the thickest and longest in his close circle, with its enviable twists and curls, its signature indigo-black colour giving it motion, the light catching its shiny ridges. Many men coveted this beard, not just those within the justice department but among all the powerful government cliques. The beards of The Eminent Ones were the most substantial, commensurate with the power they wielded.

The man is panting, exhausted as he lowers himself onto the edge of a creaking sofa in the corner, sweating from the summer heat outside, and the stifling atmosphere of the courtroom. He has just finished pronouncing a series of sentences – thirty ritual cuts each to the forearms and calves, and varying periods of incarceration – on a long line of young women. *Down like dominoes.* He recalls the first defendant: on the video clip he was shown during the briefing last night, the girl's bright red hair rippled around her shoulders, her face increasingly ecstatic as she began to sing, at first quiet and moving to her own melody, then to a rhythm played by a young man with a small drum. Around them, a growing crowd, all smiling and waving at the camera.

Eventually, emboldened by those around her, she climbed onto the roof of an old, silver Mercedes, and sang the crudest of slogans across the crackling urban darkness. The girl stood tall, like a ship's mast against the sky, conducting a mass singalong to the music: *Freedom, freedom, freedom will be ours*. The man watched the screen as the girl lifted her arms, saw the delicate fabric of her neon orange shackles, stretched taut between her swollen wrists, glistening with the exquisitely embroidered gold initials of the man who owned her. Raising your arms above shoulder level – without explicit permission – was banned in public for women, was regarded as an act of heresy, yet this girl had offered them up into the night air triumphantly, as if she had just landed on the moon. It was the third night of full-blown demonstrations, triggered by the disappearance of yet another student caught disseminating anti-state propaganda, and this was not the girl's first transgression. Last year she'd had her feet bound together for a week, after being seen dancing in public.

Totally out of control, these little bitches, the man mutters to himself. They were supposed to be the children of the Great Coup, but they were nothing more than a public disgrace. *A serious threat to the moral fabric of this state and our reputation across the world!* he'd intoned before sentencing. *Just another whore to silence, who didn't learn from her mistakes.*

He enjoyed every single pronouncement of guilt he had made; thousands of them over the many decades since he first began working in this court, right at the beginning of the glory days of The Black Coup, as it had also come to be known. Named after the black robes The Eminent Ones wore, parading through the streets on the day the Palace was brought down. Named also after the viscous, black tar lines daubed across the eyes of the murdered Royal family, their decapitated heads hung by their hair from the ornately gilded balconies where they once made speeches, back in their days of pomp and spectacle.

He runs his palm over his sweating, shiny scalp. Too little left. He sighs.

The sudden hair loss had started yesterday at dinner over stew, then continued – in *public* – during a Judge's Council this morning. He had been listening desultorily when a series of beard hairs began littering the light cream table in front of him, like contorted fleas. He swiftly scanned the room to see if anyone had noticed, but everyone was distracted, so he sat back and stroked his beard casually, as the entire Council did when reflecting on dilemmas together, all very natural, moving his hands down to catch the renegade hairs loosening from his chin, slowly manoeuvring them to his edge of the table as discreetly as possible.

The pockets of his robes are full of hair, now.

He knows he needs a credible cover story for the inexplicable shedding. Perhaps he can say he has developed a rare skin condition, like alopecia, to explain the patchy beard? No, that would be seen as inherent weakness.

The powerful man unbuttons his white under-robe and the stiff corset beneath that. He wore extra layers today, to cover the changing shape of his body. Once a lithe revolutionary, a radical student used to hunger strikes and heroic abstinence, he's had many years as an Eminent One with an obedient wife, an affluent household, a useful and regular concubine, and many rich and tasty meals washed down with good wine. Slowly, he has expanded in all directions, can no longer see his genitals when he stands up, his hairy belly rising like some ancient, grassy, burial mound to meet him when he urinates. But he has grown proud of this belly, a symbol of his moral and actual wealth and status.

No, other things are changing.

He puts on his glasses to check if it's still happening. He scrutinises his nipples, those two previously rubbery, dark brown discs punctuated with thick, black curly hairs, crowning his flabby chest. The skin around these nipples is lightening, becoming completely smooth and hairless. And he swears they are starting to swell, as if injected with water. His belly, once seething with dark hair like spider's nests, is now bald in the middle. *Like a doughnut, a human doughnut!* A tiny, lonely crater of smooth skin which both shocks and fascinates him. How is this happening?

The man moves even closer to a long mirror in the corner to inspect his face. His beard is not thinning out naturally as might be expected with age, but conspicuously dotted with balding areas in the most irregular of places. He has occasionally fantasised, with a flicker of shame, about shaving this beard off completely, wondering what it would be like to run his fingers over smooth skin daily. Like a young girl's skin. An innocent skin. The skin of the women who once ruled this land centuries ago, with their false beards and baby-smooth flesh underneath. Of course, it would be utterly against protocol for someone of his status and role to do this, an outrageous insult to The Teachings.

His beard is interlaced with seven threads of high-grade gold, delicately spaced out and woven into his skin at the chin-line, identifying him as an Eminent One and ensuring fraud is impossible.

He will not be afraid. Abruptly, he looks down.

His penis, his most prized feature after his beard, is shrinking back slowly but steadily into his groin. *This can't be. Not that!* What will people say if it gets out, that one of the most notorious judges in the entire state is losing his masculinity before their eyes? *Someone is responsible for this*, he thinks, furiously. Toying with his diminutive penis, he wonders if it's his wife, conscious of his many infidelities, spiking the stew. No, she's too dependent on him to risk that. And so broken, she wouldn't dare. A political enemy, an inside mole perhaps, doctoring the air-con system. *Security's too tight for that, after the attempted poisonings last year.*

For a moment it occurs to him that this is divine judgement for what he keeps in the bottom drawer of his office desk, reappropriated from the previous regime's Unholy Archive of Imperialist Disrepute. He'd removed the single, battered pornographic magazine discreetly, before it was logged and 'filed' away for safekeeping. The artefact has been so well used – inspected and *analysed*, he reassures himself – that its pages are worn thin. And the images of flesh, hair and open red slits amorphously merging into one another through the wafer-thin paper, like a psychedelic landscape, are now too familiar to be quite as thrilling as when he first opened it. It was his job to assess the content. Designed to corrupt, hard to resist, even for a man of his moral standing and resolve!

When he pronounced sentence on women, on girls, they often collapsed, begging him for mercy, already worn and hollow after time in subterranean prison cells, all bail refused. It thrilled him, their tortured faces and pain. But sometimes, intertwined with this frisson of power, and remembering his own estranged daughter, he feels a flash of guilt. A specific thought arises, panicked, from deep in his stomach: he thinks of smoothness advancing, imagines his whole body changed – soft olive skin, curves, moist orifices. Imagines constant access to this new body's comforts and pleasures. He'd never be inconvenienced by a woman again, with their constant demands, failings and substantial overheads.

This man, who is one of the most notorious and revered of all The Eminent Ones, ponders, with a combination of dread and self-admiration, whether he has become so powerful now, that even his darkest, secret desires can materialise and take physical shape?

Over the next few days, the powerful man begins to realise he is not alone. He notices a number of his colleagues shuffling around the courthouse uncomfortably, changing in ways that seem familiar and connected to his own gradual metamorphosis. Their beards are in different stages of thinning: one has a mere crust of a goatee left, gold threads sprouting almost completely alone in several places. He is tempted to reach out to this man, someone he knows well, during a court break, but quickly stops himself, realising his own beard is disappearing so rapidly that there isn't much between them.

Better not to focus minds on his failings. Not yet.

More than a few of The Eminent Ones have double bulges on their chests that were not there before. They are not all heavy men with big bellies like himself, in fact one of them is remarkably slim for a man of his status, yet today he wears a massively oversized, tent-like robe, attempting to balance himself when he walks, in an increasingly clumsy and comical manner, unused to the extra weight in this most unexpected of places.

An atmosphere of insecurity thickens the air around these men as the week goes on. It is disconcerting for them all. Yet the powerful man starts to feel relief. *So, I am not alone. This is not my fault after all.* By midweek, there is an unspoken acknowledgement between them. Sideways glances bounce around the corridors of the courthouse. *If word gets out, this could be dangerous.* They agree to increase the number of bodyguards outdoors, to create a protective layer of defence. Inside the courthouse they worry less: the long-established fog of fear that hangs heavy in the air amongst the defendants and their families awaiting trial on corridor benches, the stress amongst the staff, preoccupied with stemming the chaos of this overflowing building, all this distracts from the judges' transmutation. Those awaiting trial are choked with anxiety, seeing nothing but an uncertain future, the terror of potential punishment, endless jail terms and the threat of separation from their loved ones. The thickness of a judge's beard or the shape of his chest is the last thing they care about in here.

Once it becomes clear that this metamorphosis is only happening amongst his peers, the man calls a Secret Emergency Council, the first in many months. Sitting together around a huge, boardroom table on the top floor of the building, their eyes flitting over each other's bodies with a mixture of shame, relief and growing solidarity, they discuss a proposed update to The Teachings. One of them suggests dropping the requirement to wear a beard at all. *Let's just keep the gold thread?* Another suggests false beards, like in days of old by the Fallen Matriarchs – but the reference back to the women who once wielded power is too risky and might remind the people of an alternative in these tumultuous times. And in any case, this alone wouldn't be enough, indeed any kind of change to The Teachings, which they had ruled unquestionable, unalterable, never to be challenged, would be too suspicious. *We cannot let the people know this is happening to us at all*, they conclude.

Despairing, they share conspiracy theories as to why and who is trying to strip them of their gender sovereignty, of all that shores up their power. One man whispers that The Pre-Eminent One seems unchanged. *Perhaps he has had enough of us, and this is a sign of his displeasure? He is the only human alive who could make this happen.* Another points out The Pre-Eminent One hasn't been seen in public for several weeks now, *haven't you noticed? We have no idea where he is. It is said he has gone east on sabbatical, but he left no instructions at all.* They stare at each other, and all take note. *Then we must follow his lead.*

Over the next few weeks, these black-robed men, with their distinctive silver headdresses and mini charcoal-grey-clad armies of mute bodyguards begin to slowly disappear from public view. They refuse all private audiences and media appearances and take refuge in their second apartments inside a high security compound, up on the far edge of the city, at the foot of a blue mountain range. They agree to tell their wives that urgent and serious state business will take them away for the foreseeable future, behind closed doors, working to counteract real and imminent threats to the state. They send out proxies to oversee court proceedings, deliver verdicts and suspend weekly addresses to their subjects, forced to trust those around them in lesser positions of power, communicating only via their most faithful aides.

But a smattering of subversive voices has begun to infiltrate the lower echelons of the justice department, spreading rumours that The Eminent Ones are in jeopardy, though no-one understands why. *They are cooking up something. We do not know what, but we will find out.* The diminishing presence of The Eminent Ones is quietly discussed on street corners, at family gatherings, in the markets. The citizens – or subjects as they are labelled, despite the allusion to the long-buried and hated monarchy – begin to wonder if these bearded ones still actually exist. Connections are made between their absence and the longstanding lack of action on rising costs of living, and life-threatening increases in food poverty and homelessness, a ripple effect of sanctions through conflicts with surrounding states. *And all this, whilst we know the wealth from their precious crystal mines continues to flow into the state reserves. Maybe they've pocketed the money and left the country!* Speculation is growing, though still no more than whispers and confidences.

Just one woman thinks she understands: his ex-lover. On the night before he severed their relationship – after seven years of weekly appointments at the apartment he moved her into – she wakes up to urinate and, seeing the bed empty next to her, follows the sound of his muffled voice. Perplexed, she hears lover's talk, coming from the second bathroom, further down the corridor, reserved for him only: *You pretty, pretty thing, look at this body of yours, isn't this beautiful? Ah yes, just there, just like that.* Catching a glimpse of him through the crack in the door, even in the half-darkness, she is relieved to see he is alone, but realises his body is not quite the body she knows and has loved. Utterly confused, a strong sense of self-preservation pulls her away and she tiptoes back to bed, shaking slightly as she slips beneath the cold sheets. She understands why he wouldn't let her touch him now or at any time over the last fortnight, but what the hell is going on?

She knew the end was coming, had felt a sense of dread as their appointments became less and less frequent, when during the last few encounters he'd refused to let her undress him or touch him anywhere except for his shoulders, through material, a short massage. *I must be coming down with a flu of some kind, no doubt, freezing inside the bones, I am sure you understand, my love.* Again, she noted something odd about his profile as he stood in the doorway before leaving. Yes, the landscape of his body had definitely changed, she wasn't imagining it. She couldn't believe it was possible. She knew of one person in the city who had had a black-market operation in a neighbouring country and then never returned, but for an Eminent One, no, it was heretical, impossible, utterly against The Teachings. He would risk losing everything. And so would she. *So, he got rid of me first, instead of confiding in me. He never trusted me, after all this time and so many moments of tenderness between us!*

Since he split from her and left his wife back in their city house, the man spends most of his time, alone, in this second apartment. At least he has neighbours and Council meetings can happen here quite easily, though none of them seems to know what to do about their bodies anymore. Doctors cannot be trusted, they agree, *they have betrayed us before.* It is as if they have surrendered to this inevitable change and lost all inclination to disrupt its course.

One cold, dry night the following month, the man, cursing the fact that he can now only move around outside in the dead of darkness, *like a fugitive, ridiculous!* is crossing the street from the private park near his apartment, where he often goes to take in the night air before sleeping. By now he has curvy hips, a hairless, stubble-free face, and a pair of bulging breasts that he cannot keep his hands off. Yet nothing about his new and nubile body can compensate for the absence of other humans and he misses those with whom he has known intimacy, however unequal the power balance. Thinking of his lover and her warm smile and touch, he trips over a pothole. The bulge of accumulated beard hair spills from inside his black robe pocket, his safe place, falling out in one mass onto the ground, and blowing unnoticed, against the kerb, as if settling there for the night.

In the light of the fullest moon anyone has seen all year, the cluster of hair forms a sizeable ball, and this ball gently blows downhill, collecting other hairballs which have also slipped from the pockets of Eminent Ones. They attract each other like pins to a magnet. Or a call from a long-lost lover. The discarded hairs, which they have all agreed are the equivalent of sacred relics and not to be disposed of until a conservation plan is hatched, manage to find pathways not only from robes but out from bedroom drawers, or slipping free from the folded pages of newspapers they have been wrapped in. Others escape from desks, bedside tables or from the shelves of slightly open bathroom cabinets. Buoyed by a gentle night wind, this spiky collective swarms, migrating to a particular spot in the centre of the city's main square.

It is the very spot where, half a century before, the henchmen of The Eminent Ones were commanded to make clear examples of those who refused to support the ideals of their new, shiny state, slicing open the throats of adults and children, allowing the square to fill with blood, flooding into the drainage system in the surrounding streets, a crimson invitation to join in their magnificent project, to create a common utopia, free of all abuses of power and redundant, imperialist ideology. This was also the place where anti-state protests would begin, approximately every decade, though never for more than a few hours or days, due to the brutal and well-organised security forces. Huge prison complexes were built on the edges of the city to contain the increasing numbers of dissenters, their population soon outnumbering that of the university campus downtown, where many of the troubles began.

Early the next morning, as he is setting up his cigarette and newspaper stall, a street vendor notices the enormous ball of debris, a metre in circumference by now – shed from the beards, heads and bodies of hundreds of Eminent Ones. He crouches in front of it, playfully poking it with his pen. People passing by stop and stare. Soon, fascinated disgust attracts a sizeable gathering.

From the top corner of the square, the powerful man's ex-lover approaches, weary from a noisy night at the hostel where she has been forced to relocate after his pitiful payoff ran out and her family refused to take her back. *Too much dishonour you bring on us. And you didn't even get a decent parting gift from such a wealthy man!* Full of grief and shame, she stops and stares hard at the mountain of hair, an impenetrable entanglement of blacks, greys, whites, and browns with the occasional streak of gold. It's a monumental version of the cluster of hair she had come across in her ex-lover's robe, rifling through his pockets before leaving their apartment for the last time, looking for a memento, or something she might use for a bribe if she got too desperate. She wondered why he kept the hair; some narcissistic attachment to anything that came from his own body? *He can let go of me, but he can't let go of his own body hair, what is this?* She had dismissed the hair as worthless and somewhat repulsive, but now she recognises it amongst this mass; its wiry, wavy texture and the shades of blue-grey and indigo-black are unforgettable. She has stroked and massaged it many times, at his request, as a form of foreplay.

During what turned out to be their final farewell, he had spoken as if they would meet again soon. *A few important affairs of state to attend to, we will be together again when it is sorted out, do not worry my love. Just a few weeks or so.* But he only communicated with her one more time, phoning to inform her in the language of a business professional that it was time to separate – *definitively* – that they had originally agreed this was a temporary arrangement. He told her where the severance money would be left. There was an odd fragility, a delicate tone in his voice towards the end of their conversation which she remained curious about for a long time. He had immediately blocked her number. Next came the raging silence, and with that, her regret at the losses incurred: two offers of marriage rejected, attachment to her family severed, a career as a nurse cut short because he had wanted her on call. The sense of abandonment was total.

As the woman stands in the main square amidst the crowd, facing this huge spectacle of a hairball, a wave of white anger takes hold of her, charging up through her body and finding voice. She whispers the truth out loud: the origin of this mass of shed masculinity; she exposes her lover's transformation, the cause of his detachment. Whispers her own despair and pain. She leaves enough words in the space to do their work, and then disappears; it might not be safe to stay.

The words quickly weave their way through the crowd, leaving everyone both stunned and compelled by the quiet foundation of the spectacle before them, in all its expended power.

Two students pick up the ball, raising it high above their heads for all to see, emboldened by no security forces in sight, despite the burgeoning crowd. *Is this all that is left of their so-called Utopian state, those cowards? A ball of grimy hair? Too ashamed to show their bald faces now the people are starving and there is no clean water, no affordable fuel, no nothing! People, is this not a*

*sign, a talisman? Surely it has been sent to us by the great forces they say protect
and guide them.*

An elderly woman, who many decades before had run into this square
declaring herself a revolutionary, ecstatic at the prospect of a new future,
a freer society, now steps forward with a lighter. *Let us burn it! Let us show
them what we think of what remains of their precious beards! Let me be the one to
start the fire, please! I've lost everything because of these bastards!*

And so, a clearing is purposefully and swiftly created and the hairy
mountainous ball, on being ceremoniously ignited, turns to a raging
fireball in seconds. The stench of burning hair is too much for many to
bear. The women use their delicate, deadly wrist shackles to cover their
noses against the smell, but then one of them, a young girl recently
released from prison, holds out hers just close enough to the fire to singe
and break through its centre, casting it with a shriek onto the sweltering
ball of fire. The scent of the perfumed fabric brings some relief, and her
bravery prompts others in the crowd to come forward, one by one, to do
the same. The core of the contracting, burning hairball is smothered and
sustained by layer upon layer of coloured strips of cloth. Neon orange,
yellow or green, denoting specific class or district, curling in the flames,
dancing with each other. Cheering and clapping ensues, singing and
drumming fill the square. By lunchtime, a mass celebration is in process.
And there is still no sign of the security forces anywhere.

After several hours, the henchmen finally arrive. They have been
focused on hundreds of sudden, suspicious deaths across the city and
beyond. They don't bother to coordinate a response to what they find
here; they are all too shell-shocked from the fresh sight of so many
unidentifiable and amorphously cross-gendered bodies, dressed in the
black robes of some of the most powerful officials in the land, collapsed
lifeless on apartment floors, in stairways, on the streets or inside their
smoked-glass, armoured cars. They have had enough trauma for one day
and the call to the main square, while Special Forces forensically
examine the bodies in the cramped morgues on the outskirts of the city,
is a welcome diversion.

Disarmed by the triumphant atmosphere, the men push their way
through the joyously raucous crowd, barely noticing the unshackled

women and girls waving their arms high, in time to the music, in the twilight. The crowd quietens as they move through and past, increasingly nervously, towards the epicentre of this illegal and momentous gathering.

They come to a still, smoking spot, and here they stop and stare at all that is left of their rulers; a charred pile of intertwined cloth strips and an array of singed, curled gold thread, glued fast like a series of distorted musical notes to the blackened ground.

'The Beard' was originally published in *Glimpse: An Anthology of Black British Speculative Fiction*, edited by Leone Ross (Peepal Tree Press, Leeds, 2022). *Glimpse* is the first anthology of speculative fiction by Black British writers, under the series editor Kadija George. 'The Beard' also appeared in *Best of British Short Stories*, edited by Nicholas Royle (Salt Publishing, Cromer, 2023).

THREE POEMS

Ibrayim Yusupov

My Mother Tongue

Bards have been borne by you, as on a winning horse,
Orators, arguing, have used you to arouse,
    Our Alpamises' battlecry, too, you have been,
Berdaq it was who honed you as an arm for us.

You are a tree, an old one, with an older root,
You are accomplished, you are accurate, astute.
    The Karakalpaks' heart, a bird that has to sing,
What wisdom we discover when your words ring out.

Our Gulparshins, within their breasts a burning brand,
Can sing their sorrows in sinsiw, the saddest sound,
    Wives of the khans, through you, made them much milder men,
Ajiniyaz could sing laments for his lost land.

Sayings of yours have stones inside a waxy rind,
You give a quick reply to an incisive mind.
    It was my father's courage that made you so strong,
It was my mother's milk that made you sound so kind.

You hit us with the truth, so straight, you never miss,
You have a voice as loud as any desert is.
    You are not one to flatter, one to flatly lie,
Goose after goose goes flying, frightened by your hiss.

I think of you as bread, that daily I digest,
A spirit in the syrup from my mother's breast.
    Since speaking, other tongues have not been strange to me,
You, though, my heart holds to it, the most closely pressed.

Set to a tune, you fly like starlings' airy throngs,
Sweetest of all to 'Ilme sultan' of all songs.
    How good that there are many that are kin to you,
That you are "close to me" is said by many tongues.

My mother tongue, distinction is what you endow,
The poet that I am is down to what you do.
    However harsh the exile, you have still survived
And I affirm, through you, that you are here today.

Cranes

With those wide wings of theirs, they beat the bright blue air,
In flight to some unknown and far-off land, the cranes.
Without them, there is loss and sorrow where we are,
    They take our happiness away with them, the cranes.

The sound of bugling is in my ears, their cries,
    From what are rolled-up paper trumpets in my eyes,
As if that is the way they broadcast their goodbyes.
    They go, they won't be back, so beautiful, the cranes.

With each turn of the earth, things turn for us on it,
A turn and we are lucky, a turn and we are not.
There is no seashore now, no waves that churn a net,
    Up, up, from flyblown ponds, away they go, the cranes.

Those islands where they bred dissolve and disappear,
Those moonlit wetlands, too, are arid and austere.
From high up in the sky, "quwaw-quwaw" we hear,
    What are those baleful bugles saying to us, cranes?

The cause of what we do is who we are. The curse
Of it is even rivers will reverse their course.
As if they say, "This land is now haram for us,"
     They leave us, flying high and crying out, the cranes.

The drum of waves no longer wakes me up at dawn.
What else will give me strength to get up, get things done?
Over they go now, over salt flat, dusty dune,
     Not stopping at the shoreline as they used to, cranes.

They are in high formation, each of them aligned,
I watch them and my heart is like a broken wind-
Ow. Why am I not free to flee my native land,
     Like you, up there, are doing, won't you tell me, cranes?

They Don't Understand

Its gaggle up and gone, there goes a lonely goose,
     Whose honking, lakes, so deep and still, don't understand.
A nightingale's scorched song of its love of a rose,
     Roses, that only blush at spring, don't understand.

For some, there is delight, for some, there is despair,
The world surprises us, what happens here and there.
A hurt gazelle seeks water, water anywhere,
     Through deserts that are dry and that don't understand.

This scourging of my soul, as if some spiteful sport,
This plucking of my heart strings, pitifully taut,
This suffering for you, for whom I am distraught,
     Thank God, a thousand times, more men don't understand.

Spring flowers, summer flowers, soon will pass their prime,
Let a hard frost not come when it is not its time.
To you, Ayaz, in love, I dedicate this rhyme,
     Satisfied souls and happy hearts don't understand.

Translators' Notes

IbrayimYusupov (1929–2008) is a Karakalpak poet. The Karakalpaks are a Turkic people whose homeland is Karakalpakstan, in the northwest of Uzbekistan. The translations here are taken from *Three Karakalpak Poets*, the first book of English translations of Karakalpak poetry, independently published in 2024 and translated by Andrew Staniland, Gulbahar Izentaeva, Shaxnoza Kengesbay qizi, Aynura Nazirbaeva, Nilufar Bayrambaevna Abdullaeva, Nargiza Urazimbetova and Gulnaz Jadigerova.

'My Mother Tongue' ('Ana tilime' in the original) was written in 1970. Yusupov's primary task was to maintain Karakalpak as a literary language. The poem also speaks on behalf of all those whose mother tongue is one of the world's minority and endangered languages. Berdaq and Ajiniyaz, his great predecessors, are the other two poets in *Three Karakalpak Poets*. Alpamis is the hero of a Karakalpak oral epic. Gulparshin is the heroine of the same epic. 'Sinsiw' is a sad song sung before getting married.

'Cranes' ('Tırnalar') was written in 1989. Yusupov was a witness, in his homeland, to the environmental catastrophe of the loss of the Aral Sea. Once the fourth largest inland body of water in the world, it lost 90% of its surface area from the 1960s until this poem was written, as water from its feeder rivers was diverted for cotton irrigation. His poems about the tragedy include this one, about the birds who used to migrate there, and 'Aral Elegies', a more wide-ranging and devastatingly powerful sequence of 25 poems (which is also included in *Three Karakalpak Poets*).

At heart, Yusupov was a lyric poet, and a lovely one too. 'They Don't Understand' ('Añlamas'), undated, shows him continuing the great Turkic-Persianate tradition of lyric poetry. Ayaziy was his nickname. He follows the classical tradition of including the poet's pen name in the final couplet of a ghazal and applies it to a poem of four-line stanzas, as Berdaq and Ajiniyaz had done before him.

THREE POEMS

Aicha bint Yusif

Distance

It is told that Israeli soldiers, upon raiding houses in the West Bank, hurry to put their hands on the hearts of young kids (mainly boys): if their heart is beating very fast, it means that they have been running and throwing stones, hence they're arrested. If their heart is calm and is beating slowly, it means they're not afraid of soldiers yanking them from the neck with a rifle dangling around their waist, so they terrorize them.

Either way – what good is a heart if it cannot beat at just the right pace?

Bread and salt

Sar fe ben-na khobez w meleh

One year and two months –
Spacious fields of wheat and endless skies of white salt

falling like snow,
making our wounds cleaner and sharper,
albeit more painful.
Sar fe ben-na khobez w meleh
He says with his northern accent, longer at the end,
sweet around the edges,
almost edible like fresh bread my sitti used to make on Fridays.
Before she died last May, she told me:

Be good. *Kone mleha.*
Did *mleha* come from *meleh?*
Sar fe ben-na khobez w meleh
What good is bread and salt, if there's no olive oil?
Olive trees, shade, roots, black tarp, omelette sandwiches for breaks

And olive pearls falling like sweet rain that waters our love?
Sar fe ben-na khobez w meleh
That's how things are, with time. Everything is inevitable.
Maktob in two nights and one day.
I write so I won't have it written, I tell him, We're different.
But we're also similar by the time the sun sets,
Huddling together, finding home in each other, across the Mediterranean.
Whispering:

A home is built with bread and salt.

Lines that will heal
after Julio Cortazar

Out of the open brachial vein, a line of blood extracts itself
                                        to solidify and extend along
the broken cemented slabs to reach the pit of the crater created
                                        by thousands of tons of
explosives shipped all the way across the Atlantic. It keeps climbing
                                        the other side of the pit,
passing by tufts of hair bulging out of the debris and takes a break
                                        over the hunched back of a
father who leans forward to collect the remains of his kids, hiding
                                        his tears from the intruding
cameras and phones. After a moment, it resumes its strenuous path
                                        to the top of an ambulance
that rushes through the grey city to the Awda hospital, where it is halted
                                        by khaki pants and a

foreign tongue. It climbs their rigid left free hand (the right one holding
                                                          a rifle), passing by
their rigid heart, morphing into sound bytes and waves to pass through
                                                    the phone all the way
to the pilot above the skies that is about to press another button
                                              to drop another bomb.

REVIEWS

}

LIBERTARIAN BASTARDS

Kostas Maronitis

On 10 July 2025, European Commission President Ursula von der Leyen survived a confidence vote put forward by one of the far-right factions of the European parliament. The text of the motion read that von der Leyen's Commission could no longer be trusted to 'uphold the principles of transparency, accountability, and good governance essential to a new democratic union'. A sizeable portion of the European Conservatives and Reformists voted against the motion and demonstrated once more the good working relationship the alliance has developed with the traditionally ruling centre-right European People's Party (EEP). Over the last year, the EEP has increasingly collaborated with the far right to pass amendments and resolutions on issues like immigration, security, and energy, often irking the liberal and left parliamentary alliances. The confidence vote showed that the far right or at least a fraction of it, see themselves as defenders of European values and more importantly as indispensable operators of the EU.

Quinn Slobodian, *Hayek's Bastards*, Allen Lane, London, 2025

Thus far, the rise and gradual establishment of the far right in Europe has been discussed and analysed through a cultural lens. A strong sense of national identity, an emphasis on a traditional national way of life, the importance of the nuclear family for social cohesion, all constitute a bulwark against social and cultural changes brought forward by globalisation. The distinction between 'the people' and 'elites' animates a battle for cultural hegemony that takes place in social media, TV studios, sports arenas, national and intranational parliaments. What usually remains absent from such conversations and analyses is the economic model the far right wish to implement or are implementing when they find themselves in governing positions. Quinn Slobodian's latest book *Hayek's Bastards:The Neoliberal Roots of the Populist Right* brings to the foreground the role of capitalism in the formulation of contemporary far-right politics via the latter's reliance on biology. As a historian Slobodian has set out to trace the intellectual journey as well as impact of the concept of neoliberalism. In *The Globalists:The End of Empire and the Birth of Neoliberalism* (2018), Slobodian argues against the conventional wisdom that neoliberalism is about the dismantling of state structures and regulations in favour of unrestricted markets. *The Globalists* contextualises neoliberalism as an intellectual movement and response to the dissolution of empires and the emergence of national self-determination in the interwar and postwar periods.

According to Slobodian, neoliberal economists and intellectuals such as Ludvig von Mises and Friedrich Hayek viewed the markets as fragile institutions which needed protection from democratic interference. Their aim, as Slobodian points out, was to restructure states and global institutions so that markets could function without disruption from democratic demands such as social welfare, redistribution of wealth, and nationalisation of industries and services. The contested topics of borders, fragmentation, and market fundamentalism inform the historical material and theoretical direction of Slobodian's 2023 book *Crack-Up Capitalism: Market Radicals and the Dream of aWorldWithout Democracy*. Slobodian shifts the focus from global governance to geopolitical disintegration, tracing how free-market ideologues have embraced political fragmentation, secession, and 'zone-ism' to realise their vision of a more anarchic than regulated capitalism. Instead of pursuing a borderless and frictionless market economy, libertarian thinkers like Peter Thiel, Murray Rothbard, and Hans-Hermann Hoppe are advocating for the digital and geographical crack-up of states in the form of special economic zones, freeports, tax heavens, and charter cities.

The apparent political convergence between the far right and the guardians of Europe's market economy is the product of a long ideological and operational transformation that can be traced back to the late 1960s. Amidst the 1968 Paris upheavals orchestrated by students and workers, a counter-revolution began to materialise. Confronted by the rising popularity of Marxism and its academic and artistic evangelists, the political philosopher Alain de Benoist tasked himself with rejuvenating and re-orienting the far right in Europe. The aptly named Nouvelle Droit (New Right) implicitly dissociated itself from the horrors of the Second World War and modelled itself to Europe's progressive popular movements. Nouvelle Droit's ideological and organisational predecessor was the Groupement de recherche et d'etudes pour la civilisation Européene (GRECE, Research and Study Group for European Civilisation). De Benoist and fellow GRECE members had long been involved in far-right politics and insurgencies, and their new movement was inspired by the campaigns and ideological direction of the European New Left.

Despite its aversion to Communism and Marxism, the Nouvelle Droit found in Antonio Gramsci's concept of hegemony the political and communicative strategy for assembling a mass appeal movement that cuts across class and generational divisions, gender, and occasionally ethnicity. The aim was to slowly infuse society with the ideas and rhetoric of the far right in the hope of achieving cultural dominance by establishing coalitions in religious organisations, capitalist enterprises, and trade unions, which would then allow for the assumption of political power. The tactic of social, cultural, and ultimately ideological expansion and elasticity meant that the far right could not and should not maintain an alleged ideological purity if it wished to survive and thrive inside and outside the world of parliamentary politics. Indicative of the New Right's ideological elasticity and political adaptability is its stance on Israel and the wider politics in the Middle East. The rudimentary antisemitism of the far right has been replaced with an unequivocal support for Israel and its exceptional status as a state that exists outside the confines of international law since the latter is increasingly viewed as the Eastern frontier and defender of European civilisation.

Three of the founding member states of the European Union, Italy, France, and Germany, have been politically and culturally transformed by the ideas and grand narratives of the Nouvelle Droit. Yet, the rather vague proclamations for the preservation and defence of European civilisation, the rejection of globalisation, and the ambiguous relationship they have developed with the EU makes their political and ideological classification impossible. The labels of nationalist populist, nationalist, far right, radical right, neo-fascist, and hard-right are used interchangeably to describe a loose network of political actors, journalists, and public intellectuals who might have different views on public administration, immigrant integration approaches, and foreign policy yet they all feel under threat by the irregular flows of immigrants and refugees from societies and cultures incompatible with the values of what has been described by de Boist as 'the European civilisation'.

Central to contemporary French politics is the conspiracy of the 'great replacement theory' put forward by the novelist Renaud Camus and supported by journalist turned politician Éric Zemmour. According to Zemmour and the allies and voters of his pop-up party Reconquête, a conspiracy is underway to replace white Europeans with people from Africa and Asia. Zemmour is not necessarily against the presence of non-white people in France but more accurately he wishes they remain a numerical as well as an ethnic minority. The somewhat administrative tone adopted by Zemmour the politician is offset by Zemmour the far-right public intellectual who claims that France is in a 'civilisational war' with Islam and only a 'state of cultural emergency' that suspends human rights can stop the 'invasion and colonisation' of France. Marine Le Pen is the only viable far-right contender for France's presidency. Not only did she modernise the politics of the far right by renaming her father's party from Front National to Rassemblement National but more importantly she normalised anxieties and fears over the status of white French citizens. The defence of European civilisation is a recurring theme in Le Pen's discourse. She portrays herself as the champion of Europe's Greco-Roman, Christian, and Enlightenment heritage. The civilisational argument underpins her opposition to multiculturalism and Islam, which she argues are incompatible with the European values of liberty, gender equality, and secular governance.

In Germany, the far right's activism and parliamentary voice coheres around the presence of Alternative für Deutschland (AfD). AfD began as a Eurosceptic party opposing the eurozone bailouts. Over time, it has evolved into a far-right, nationalist force within German politics. The party's platform reflects a sharp opposition to immigration, multiculturalism, and the European Union, underpinned by a racialised vision of national identity and a selective embrace of capitalist principles. AfD rhetoric constructs a narrow definition of *Germanness* rooted in ethnic and cultural homogeneity. It promotes the idea of a German Volk threatened by 'foreign infiltration,' particularly targeting Muslim immigrants and asylum seekers. The party has been repeatedly accused of normalising xenophobia and fostering links to extreme-right and neo-Nazi groups. In this context, race operates both as a boundary of belonging and a mobilising force for nationalist politics.

Italy, on the other hand, has always been considered the testing ground for post war far-right and fascist political experimentation. Giorgia Meloni' Fratelli d'Italia (Brothers of Italy) is the latest reiteration of a far-right ruling party and government. Whereas the name of her party derives in a simplistic manner from the opening verse of the Italian national anthem ('Fratelli d'Italia, L'Italia s'è desta...'), its politics paint a more complicated picture. As direct heir of the fascist party Alleanza Nationale and proud carrier of the fascist emblem of the flame, Giorgia Meloni's Fratelli d'Italia oscillates between contemporary forms of national populism and liberal political respectability. A pivotal moment in Fratelli d'Italia's political trajectory was Meloni's decision not to participate in Mario Draghi's coalition of a seemingly technocratic government comprising of independent technocrats and supported by far right Lega, Berlusconi's Forza Italia, the centre-left Democratic Party, the centrist Italia Viva, and the leftist Article One. While Meloni distanced herself and her party from the wider European consensus on rights, identity and public health mandates during the Covid-19 pandemic, she always intended to be part of a European mainstream that is closely aligned with ultra conservative social values pertaining to family structure, gender roles and national identity and at the same protecting Italy's and Europe's position in the postwar order as defined and nourished by the establishment and operation of the EU, NATO and the wider Euro-Atlantic political and military environment.

Slobodian's insistence on the use and wider relevance of the concept of neoliberalism appears to be at odds with contemporary political trends. Isn't neoliberalism after all a concept associated with the free mobility of people, goods, and services? A concept that provided fertile ground for the proliferation of ethnic and sexual identities and for reconsidering the purpose of both family and religion? The political presence and electoral success of parties whose message coheres around family, religion, and national identity are doing their best to dissociate their policies and governing practices from anything remotely liberal. The prefix *neo* adds another layer of confusion over the use and relevance of a concept that has been declared dead or redundant several times over. For Eric Hobsbawm neoliberalism had always been a problematic and politically speaking an undesirable concept. Not only did neoliberalism, or to be more precise its evangelists, fail to dismantle the welfare state but more importantly the consequences of removing social protection from citizens and potential voters would have been socially and electorally catastrophic. More recently, Perry Anderson drew parallels between regime change and the decline of neoliberalism in the West. In the absence of any meaningful opposition in the form of either revolutionary or reformist socialism, Anderson points out that the political-economic 'regime' of neoliberalism generated its own 'antibody' – namely populism. Populism and populist parties might assume different ideological guises, but they are united, Anderson claims, in their rejection of the neoliberal consensus – the neoliberal 'regime' of free market economics supported and propagated by the so-called centre left and centre right parties.

Slobodian takes a more cautious view with respect to the deaths of neoliberalism. The central premise of *Hayek's Bastard's* is that TINA — the famous political slogan arguing there is no alternative to liberal capitalism and the market economy — did not disappear with the emergence and establishment of the far-right populist parties. On the contrary, a reciprocal relationship is at play where neoliberalism gains popular legitimacy by incorporating the rhetoric and policies of xenophobia, limited definitions of national identity, and by exalting family as a vital economic and productive unit. On the other hand, far-right parties and populists claim a sense of economic and political respectability by interlinking national sovereignty and superiority with an efficient economy. Such a relationship is sustained by what Slobodian calls 'the three hards': 'hardwired culture', 'hard money', and 'hard borders'.

'Hardwired culture' supposes that inequalities in intelligence, behaviour, and social disposition are biologically determined and not necessarily shaped by the social environment and systems. The 'hardwired culture' discussed by Slobodian is part of a wider pseudo-science based on IQ and racial profiling that legitimises the 'natural' superiority or inferiority of specific groups of people. This type of biological determinism undermines efforts and demands for social change such as integration of migrants, expansion of the welfare state, and inclusive education system by alluding to a 'new fusion' of neoliberal economics and biological hierarchies. For Charles Murray, author of the bestsellers *The Bell Curve*, and *Human Diversity*, and one of the 'bastards' under examination in Slobodian's book, 'the explosive growth of genetic knowledge means that within a few years science will definitely demonstrate precisely how it is that women are different from men, blacks from whites, poor from rich, or for that matter the ways in which the Dutch are different from Italians'. In such a biological and economic environment social hierarchies are natural, fixed, and therefore untouchable—thus justifying economic inequalities and the rejection of egalitarian reforms.

'Hard money' alludes to a monetary philosophy that emphasises the need for currency stability, low inflation and resistance to political control. Fascination with the acquisition of gold and the gold standard, cryptocurrencies, and aversion to controlling central banks constitute the main traits of 'hard money'. In Slobodian's account of the fusion of neoliberalism and the far right, there is a deep suspicion of the way democratically elected governments and central banks dictate monetary policy – especially when they have to meet popular demands. Although blood and soil nationalism is very much present in the fusion of libertarians and far-right populists, the concept of 'hard money' provides the political and monetary tools for either fleeing a crisis or fortifying wealth from it. For Slobodian investing in gold is similar to the return to family and Christianity – a return to safety free from the interference of state agents. As the pages of the *Libertarian Review* attest, survivalism in a crisis prone economy is both a strategy and an investment. Gold surpasses national structures and regulatory frameworks yet retains a universal exchange value.

The third hard concept in Slobodian's account is 'hard borders'. The objective of hard borders is not limited to geographical control but more importantly it expands to the protection of wealth and private property. 'Hard borders' serve to insulate markets and their respective leaders from democratic control and redistributive pressures coming from NGOs, national and international institutions. 'Hard borders' represent an overarching ideological project to preserve 'natural inequality', cultural homogeneity, and private wealth by fortifying the boundaries and setting the parameters of who can be part of the neoliberal social contract. While classical neoliberalism championed open global markets, Slobodian shows that many on the populist right fused this with a desire for ethnonational protection. In this revised geo-political configuration, Hayek's bastards acknowledge the limitations and cultural borders of capitalism as well as the importance of the nation-state for the latter's protection and flourishing. For Peter Brimelow 'it's a curious fact that capitalism has developed and really came to fruition in the English-speaking world… beyond a certain point [capitalism] may not be [exportable]'. Subsequently, the nation-state is not an ideal that must be protected but more accurately a means to an end. 'Ethnic homogeneity had a material payoff: the nation-state, where everyone understands one another, is an efficient way of organizing human beings'. Gregory Pavlik, another prominent 'Hayek bastard', is quick to note that Brimelow's thoughts should not be interpreted as a call to protectionism. Actually the restriction of mobility informed by racial and ethnic criteria is beneficial for capitalism and free trade: 'free trade can replace immigration in public policy, allowing us to enjoy the benefits of the international division of labour without the social dislocations and destructiveness of mass immigration'.

In this detailed historical account of the fusion of economic libertarians and far-right populists, Slobodian deploys the cultural type of the bastard for indicating and analysing the mutations of economic and political thought. Even though Slobodian does not delve into the meaning, etymology and uses of the term 'bastard' in literature and the arts, there is the implication of impurity concerning the views and actions of Hayek's bastards. Dictionaries define bastard as either an unpleasant person or as a person born to parents who are not married to each other. Etymologically, for the French, bastard (*fils de bast*), refers to a packsaddle son – a child conceived on an improvised bed. For the German, bastard (*bänkling*) refers to a child begotten on a bench and not on a marriage bed. Yet the impurity of neoliberal thought implied by Slobodian has always been present within libertarian environments. In his opening address at the inaugural Mont Pélerin Society conference in 1947, the Swiss economist and diplomat William Rappard portrayed his fellow delegates as the heirs of Adam Smith's political and economic legacy. Rappard pointed out Smith's Scottishness and in particular his work ethic and prudence informed his philosophy and at the same time set a clear dividing line between the Occidental and the Oriental mind. Rappard recalled his travels to Algiers and the idleness of the Algerian Arabs sitting on the pavement in order to make the case that liberal capitalism can only thrive in conditions formulated by a very specific subject – the Occidental economic man.

A close look at the Mont Pélerin Society conference proceedings in conjunction with the development of neoliberal and far right populist thought and their application to diverse political and economic environments indicates that the 'bastards' under Slobodian's examination are now the rightful heirs and are not diluting, distorting or even debasing the ideas of great neoliberal father Friedrich Hayek. They might be lacking Hayek's intellectual depth evident in his political, philosophical and psychological studies such as *The Constitution of Liberty* and *The Sensory Order* but they communicate his ideas in an effective and persuasive manner. Mont Pellerin Society might seem a world away from the mafia but the latter provides a useful analogy regarding legitimacy and illegitimacy and the role of the outsider in official corporate and political environments. Popular culture provides us with an apposite example of the bastard turned rightful heir in the character of Vincent Mancini (played by Andy Garcia), the illegitimate son of Sonny Corleone and his mistress Lucy Mancini in the last part of *The Godfather* trilogy by Francis Ford Coppola. Vincent's status as a bastard carries cultural and symbolic weight in the mafia world and within the Corleone family. Traditionally, illegitimacy disqualified someone from being considered for leadership in dynastic power structures. But in the modernising and disintegrating world of *The Godfather III* this notion is challenged. Vincent's status as a bastard places him partially outside the family's formal power structures. The outsider status gives him a chip on his shoulder but also affords him a sense of independence. His 'bastard' origin symbolises a hybrid identity born of tradition but not bound by it. By the end of *The Godfather III*, Michael Corleone (played by Al Pacino) legitimises Vincent by naming him the new Don – Don Vincent Corleone. This decision marks a turning point: a 'bastard' becomes the head of the family, signifying a break from the rigid traditions of the past.

Who has the power to legitimise Hayek's bastards and pronounce them the new Dons? Like Vincent, the far-right populists and new libertarians present themselves as unpleasant, crude and as outsiders, fighting a system shaped by the alleged rise of identity politics, cultural rights, environmental activism, and central bank domination. Contra Hayek, they do not want to educate the elites but as Rothbard argues they want to rally 'the masses of people against the elites that are looting them, and confusing them, and oppressing them'. However, the elites in question are more than willing to accommodate Hayek's bastards. This development is due to the convergence of positions between the EU and the far right on critical issues such as the militarisation of borders, the criminalisation of immigration and asylum, and the defence of European civilisation against Islam through the unconditional arming of Israel. Slobodian's extensive genealogy successfully diagnoses the ways in which contemporary capitalism has deployed scientific racist fantasies in order to save itself but fails to acknowledge how such fantasies have entered the mainstream and turned into reality and a governing strategy in Europe and elsewhere. Despite the book's focus, Slobodian limits his scope to intellectual elites and inevitably ignores how and why the masses have come to accept the 'bastards' as their own.

MUSLIM CHICK-LIT

Alev Adil

Literature, in both its historical and contemporary forms, serves as a record of the values and beliefs of the time in which it was created. This reflection is particularly evident in commercial genres which reflect what is marketed most aggressively by mainstream publishers and is most popular with readers. The genre of chick-lit, not only captured the gender dynamics of its era but was also credited with challenging and redefining them.

The term 'chick-lit' was first defined by the academic Cris Mazza in 1995 whilst compiling the anthology *Chick-lit: Postfeminist Fiction*. Mazza identified the genre as: 'frank and wry; honest, intelligent, sophisticated, libidinous, unapologetic, and overwhelmingly emancipated. Liberated from what? The grim anger that feminists had told us ought to be our pragmatic stance in life. The screaming about the vestiges of the patriarchal society that oppressed us. Liberated to do what? To admit we're part of the problem. How empowering could it be to be part of the problem instead of just a victim of it?' Whilst the definition originates from an academic context, the genre was a runaway commercial success. A close relation of the romance or romantic comedy genre the chick-lit plot is usually centred around a romantic quest balanced with career aspirations. The challenges and pleasures of maintaining a financially precarious but consumerist lifestyle are often explicitly part of the storyline. The genre is marked by a self-deprecatory tone and an intimate form of address. The style of writing classically creates an imagined community of female bonding. Although the heroine is usually in her early thirties there is an informal intimacy, something of the high school best friend in the tone in which it is written. Heart break looms large and imposter syndrome or some sort of comic humiliation is often part of the narrative arc. In contrast to the passionate highs and lows of the romance genre, in chick-lit emotions are often demoted, made light of and rendered in a comedic register. The urtexts of the chick-lit genre, Helen Fielding's *Bridget Jones'*

Diary and Candace Bushnell's *Sex and the City*, were published in the same year, 1996. Neither were inherently novelistic works. Both started life as newspaper columns and swiftly became global phenomena that generated millions of dollars with the sales of the books and the ensuing long-running film and television successes that still grace screens across the world thirty years later. There is a wealth of academic literature debating the ideological parameters of the genre and whether chick-lit was merely a derogatory, and therefore misogynist, marketing ploy for popular female fiction, or a new mode of address that empowered and embodied new feminist realities. Either way, the category had lost its commercial pulling power by the first decade of the twenty-first century.

NussaibahYounis, *Fundamentally*, Weidenfeld & Nicolson, London, 2025.

Whilst chick-lit was no longer a fashionable label in terms of marketing in the West, the global iterations of the genre continue to have selling power. A closer look at Muslim chick-lit, in particular, reveals how this sub-genre navigates cultural and religious expectations, offering a unique perspective within the broader landscape of contemporary fiction. Raja Alsanea's *Girls of Riyadh* published in Lebanon in 2005 and then in the UK by Penguin in 2007 is the ground breaking, best-selling example of the global variant of the genre. The novel self-consciously adopts and adapts American televisual tropes. As in *Sex and the City*, we have a friendship group of four well-heeled Saudi women navigating the competing challenges of careers, sex and romance, although these twenty-something protagonists are set on marriage above all else. As in the Cecily von Ziegesar's series of young adult *Gossip Girl* novels published between 2002 and 2011, an omniscient anonymous narrator emails salacious observations about the privileged young protagonists to an online chat group. Despite their education and potential careers, these girls seek fulfilment chiefly through shopping and romantic love. They enthusiastically embrace consumerism. Like their New York sisters, the girls of Riyadh live lives of branded plenitude. They watch Hollywood blockbusters, carry miniature pedigree dogs in designer handbags, go to the gym, console themselves with rhinoplasty and chemical peels, drink daddy's secret stash of Dom Perignon and dance the night away in Badgley Mishka or Roberto Cavalli. However, sequestered under Sharia law with little in the way of basic human rights, they must display a great deal more ingenuity than their Western counterparts in order to meet men. Yet the impossibility of independent lives does not politicise or alienate them from Islamic fundamentalism. Indeed, they congratulate one woman for the 'bold spiritual step' of deciding to wear the full hijab.

The hijab and the burqa make women the most visible symbol of Islam, and also Occidental prejudices and anxieties around it. In June 2025, the newly elected Reform MP Sarah Pochin raised the issue at Parliamentary Question Time, when she invited British Prime Minister, Keir Starmer, to ban the burqa 'in the interest of public safety'. The symbolic fault line between the covered and the uncovered is one that reoccurs in Muslim chick-lit, just as much as it does in Western representations of Muslim women. The difference is that in some Muslim chick-lit the decision to wear the hijab is an act of self-expression and liberation rather than oppression and invisibility. It is central to both Ayisha Malik's 2015 novel *Sofia Khan is Not Obliged* and Uzma Jalaluddin's *Ayesha At Last* published three years later. Both feature diasporic Muslim heroines navigating a path towards professional fulfilment and love who seek empowerment through consumerism and individualism whilst also embracing traditional religious values and aspiring to find a way to build an identity and life where both can co-exist. In his essay *Algeria Unveiled,* published in 1965, the clinical psychiatrist and theorist Franz Fanon conjectured that the covered Algerian woman is perceived as a threat because she 'sees without being seen' and thus frustrates the colonial gaze. Her presence is unnerving because 'there is no reciprocity. She does not yield herself, does not give herself, does not offer herself'. To observe without the possibility of being seen defies the colonial order.

So, veiled or not, what exactly does the woman from a Muslim background observe when she sees? And how does she represent herself? How does she speak back in mainstream Occidental culture? Does the popularity and accessibility of contemporary genre fiction, namely chick-lit, written by Muslim women, liberate them by giving them a voice, and a chance to articulate hitherto unspoken identities that disrupt the Islamophobic presumptions about them? Or are these genre fiction narratives primarily addressed to a mainstream Western readership, designed to reassure and placate, to domesticate and neutralise the frightening spectre of the Muslim other? Within this political, social and cultural context, *Fundamentally* by Nussaibah Younis raises thought provoking questions about who the audience for these works are and what the authors are trying to tell them.

Shortlisted for the Women's Prize, Younis's debut novel has the key characteristics of Muslim chick-lit: we have a ditsy, libidinal heroine, a cosy demotic form of address, the hijab marks a fault line of identity and the plot tackles some weighty issues with humour. What is it that inspires the radicalisation of diasporic young Muslim women? Why do they become ISIS brides? Are the United Nations and NGOs effective in helping rebuild war torn regions? Younis's heroine Nadia is, like the author herself, an academic in her thirties with a Muslim heritage who takes a job leading a humanitarian aid project in Iraq. Younis has had an impressive career as an expert on peace building in Iraq. She has worked for the Atlantic Council as director of the Future of Iraq Task Force, where she led research on 'how the United States could best protect its national security interests and promote Iraqi interests' and has held Fellowships at European Institute of Peace, Chatham House and European Council on Foreign Relations. She has written articles on Iraq for *The New York Times* and *The Guardian* and weighty reports for the Atlantic Council. From 2019 to 2020 Younis worked, via an NGO, as an adviser to the Iraqi government, designing deradicalization programmes for women allegedly involved with the Islamic State. It was this latter role that inspired her debut fiction. *Fundamentally* is a world away from the serious articles and reports Younis penned, but just as prestigious, Weidenfeld & Nicolson won the rights to publish it after a fierce bidding war and the screen rights have already been snapped up.

Younis honed her authorial tone for the novel by doing stand-up comedy and the novel is littered with saucy one liners: 'I don't look a well-hung gift horse in the mouth', and bawdy jokes: ' how was your date with the student? He was so young my breasts tried to lactate when he sucked on them', that doubtless raised laughs in comedy clubs. Chick-lit is conventionally a gently comic genre. In *Fundamentally*, like Phoebe Waller-Bridge's *Fleabag* and Richard Gadd's *Baby Reindeer*, which are both successful television series developed via stand-up comedy, the plot is constructed around more robust humour and darker subject matter. Nadia is a feisty, foul-mouthed heroine who prefers comic monologues to contemplative ambivalence or soul searching. On arriving at the UN camp with her broken heart, new designer 'statement' handbag and a suitcase packed full of Primark suits, Matalan shirts, a copy of *Cosmo* with handy tips on rimming, her vibrator and plenty of spare packs of batteries she asks herself, 'what cunty-bollocking madness had possessed me to come here?'

In Muslim chick-lit, swearing is a signifier of empowerment. Swearing is one of the ways the Muslim female subject speaks back to power. Ayisha Malik's heroine Sofia, calls out the racist who identified her as a terrorist because of her hijab by calling him a cunt. Younis takes swearing to another level. Despite her PhD in criminology, Nadia's vocabulary is limited and unremittingly vulgar. 'I didn't move to Iraq for shits and giggles' she declares. She finds any words beyond the most basic vocabulary pretentious and states that 'when people start using the word "purview" that's when you know you're working with cunts'. Her swearing is unremittingly built around a disgust for female genitals. Sometimes her descriptions are graphic and surreal - 'he looked wounded, as though I'd bitch-slapped him with my oversized labia'. At other times her swearing is merely tautologous. 'Pierre wasn't a twat' she observes, 'he was a grade-A cunt'.

Any illusions that the world of humanitarian aid might be altruistic or ethical are swiftly disabused. Nadia observes that 'instead of becoming a beacon of democracy, Iraq had lunged from one civil war to another, and the UN had twisted around the carcass like knotweed'. The United Nations is as nepotistic, cut throat and corrupt as the world of finance or politics. Nadia's boss Lina is intimidatingly sophisticated with her expensive international education and extensive couture wardrobe. Her office is a stylish haven of Nordic designer furniture, where she doesn't seem to do any actual work, instead conversing with her beloved pet budgerigar in Lebanese Arabic. Nadia's colleagues are a hard partying crew, who spend most of their time getting drunk and getting off with each other in the UN tiki bar. They are an entitled and largely nepotistic crew. Pierre the son of the French ambassador to the United States, is constantly playing practical jokes when he isn't on Grindr. Apparently, Grindr has a very active user base in Iraq. His friend and fellow jester Charles is a scientist whose father worked with Mandela. Posh Priya sports 24 carat gold jewellery, a caramel balayage hairdo and a cultivated Delhi accent. Sherri, the Australian psychosocial support specialist is a woke yoga enthusiast with a red face and even redder hair. While Tom the Geordie, a muscular and well-meaning working class hunk loves his nana, resembles a Disney prince and is a fan of Lawrence of Arabia and Jordan Peterson. His sexism makes Nadia want to sit on his face, although he is so sexy it's not just to stop him from talking.

Nadia finds that putting her deradicalisation programme into practice requires much political manoeuvring and bribery, including expensive holidays to the Mövenpick in Beirut for the Minister of Humane Affairs and her lover. However, despite initial misgivings and lack of cooperation from her team Nadia settles into UN compound life where they 'fight like siblings, drink like college girls and work like deckhands'. Food fights in the breakfast hall and cocktails in the tiki bar are interspersed with trips to the camp where ISIS brides are detained indefinitely without charge or access to any due legal process. Nadia's ill-fated and incompetent United Nations programme employs an eccentric American imam. Sheikh Jason, a Californian revert in a Nirvana T shirt and shorts, espouses meditation, yogic breath work and the healing energetic of crystals as methods of deradicalisation. He comes across as more Buddhist than Muslim but he is chosen in preference to a Shia cleric who would alienate the ISIS women or the Sunni candidate who is anti-American and anti-Semitic.

In the internment camp Nadia meets Sara, a 'sweary' young East Londoner who joined ISIS at fifteen. She is a sharp, cheeky teenage Londoner who enjoys rollerblading, reading X-Men and eating gummies. Every sentence she utters is peppered with a hyperbolic contemporary masala of East London patois: 'swear down bruv … gwan … you been down my ends is it? You're kinda jokes'. Nadia becomes obsessed with saving Sara whilst bonding over a taste for Dairy Milk, McDonald's Filet-O-Fish, 'the staple Muslim order', and 'waxing nostalgic about discount handbags at TK Maxx'. Nadia soon forges a strong sense of identification with the young ISIS bride and risks everything in order to help her escape. Whilst Nadia represents the model of a Western assimilated Muslim woman: professional success, financial independence and sexual liberation, Sara is her antithesis: an uneducated working-class teenager who followed her best friend Jamila, her 'ride or die', to join ISIS. Sara's story echoes the Shamima Begum case. She has been widowed three times, stripped of her British citizenship, and is mother to a young daughter from whom she has been separated.

Fundamentalist Sara is both the polar opposite to secular Nadia and also represents a path she might herself have taken. Like the author herself, as a teenager Nadia attended a summer camp taught by Sheikh Anwar al-Awlaki, a charismatic Muslim cleric, whose compelling narratives about the suffering of Muslims at the hands of imperial powers lead her to flirt with fundamentalism. Anwar al-Awlaki is not a fictional character. Born in the United States in 1971 to Yemeni parents, al-Awlaki became an imam and taught in the US and the UK before returning to the Yemen where he worked as a university lecturer. He was incarcerated by the Yemeni authorities for eighteen months in 2006, after which he began to openly advocate violent resistance and jihad against the United States. Placed on the CIA kill list by Barack Obama in 2010, he was the first US citizen to be targeted and assassinated by a US drone strike, in Yemen in 2011. For Nadia, Sara's plight could so easily have been her own had al-Awlaki tried to radicalise her during that summer school. Nadia observes that Sara and ISIS brides like her 'were flogged a wet dream (only to be flogged for real when they turned up)'. Nadia is now in her thirties though and knows better, there is nothing tempting about Islam for her now that she has 'had enough sex to know that devout Muslims have tedious chat and give crap head'.

Younis's novel shows us that there is no single way to be a Muslim woman. We meet a range of women from different parts of the world and different classes. They range from the ultra-conservative to the ultra-liberal, rich and poor, from European teens groomed and kidnapped by fundamentalists to the bleached and Botoxed Iraqi Minister of Humane Affairs in her Chanel two-piece bought on a recent UNICEF trip to Paris. Their experiences and characters are shaped and vary according to their geography, sect, race and class. Some are cynical careerists like Lina and the Minister, some are brainwashed ideologues like the ISIS brides whilst Nadia, although highly educated is very naive. She confesses that 'live poultry probably grasped the political dynamics better than I did'. This plurality of representations challenges the singular stereotype of the uneducated, downtrodden Muslim woman as victim. Nadia is determined to deradicalise and save Sara but ultimately Nadia's values and motives are called into question. The book refuses easy certainties about heroism, trauma, or feminism. Sara sees Nadia as 'a coconut sell-out' and a 'slag with a saviour complex' and whilst Nadia is certain that in rejecting Islam, she has improved her life immeasurably, her career in the aid sector doesn't live up to her ideals, 'it felt shitty being on this side of the bulletproof glass: institutionalised, feckless and corrupt'.

Younis operates as a cultural intermediary introducing us to a world she is familiar with. The novel brings issues like citizenship stripping and refugee policy into genre fiction. The plot emphasises humane approaches to teenage recruits and argues, with humour, for justice not abandonment. Iraqi politicians are corrupt and self-serving whilst the foreign diplomats and NGOs are merely opportunistic hedonists lolling by the pool when they aren't partying in the tiki bar. Younis's depiction of the political establishment in Iraq, the British the diplomatic corps and the United Nations is dark and damning but it is also served up as entertainment, played for laughs. The joke is not only or always at the expense of the powerful however. Younis is able to make jokes no non-Muslim would venture without risking the accusation of prejudice. Younis is obsessed with Muslim hirsutism. Nadia in her hijabed youth was 'an unloved hairy little vole', a devout Muslim with 'a monobrow and a moustache topped off with a headscarf'. All Muslim men are terrible in bed, except for an American convert into choking. 'What makes sex halal?' Nadia quips, 'saying a prayer draining all the blood out and failing multiple heath inspections'.

At times Younis writes as though she is English. Nadia finds Middle Eastern food too heavy and oily. She tries 'not to grimace at the taste of aubergine' and tells us that 'my palate had not kept pace with my social climbing'. This might make sense if Nadia were a white working-class girl raised on baked beans, chips, and pizza, but she is a Pakistani girl from Leicester for whom aubergines would be a very familiar and homely vegetable and carry no particular social cachet. Jokes about a 'burning arsehole' caused by spicy kebabs and the warning that the body can adapt to local food 'but you may get tapeworm' are familiar squaddie or tourist humour. This is Muslim chick-lit for a white audience. Younis operates as both cultural intermediary and as native informant. For the literary theorist Gayatri Spivak, who developed the concept, a native informant is a go-between whose role is to offer up 'inside' information that authenticates and legitimises the colonialist's world view. Younis will reach a wider popular audience with her fiction and its screen spin offs than from her think tank reports but her prescription in both her fiction and her factual reports serve the same Occidental market driven ideology: a university education, 'moderate' family values, and a job in the private sector are what will save Muslim girls from being attracted to Islamic fundamentalism. Putting an end to American atrocities in the Middle East isn't in the equation.

EXPRESSIONS

Steve Noyes

Only Words is a late-career poetry collection by the transplanted Canadian Paul Sutherland, who converted to Islam in 2006, and is also named Abdul Wudud. *Only Words*, which follows his *New and Selected Poems* Valley Press, 2016, weighs in at more than 300 pages. A good eighty of those pages are available elsewhere, in the *New and Selected* or in *Poems on the Life of the Prophet Muhammad* Muslim Academic Trust, 2014.

Only Words is organised into four sections: Holy Week Sequence; Poems on the Prophet Muhammad; Seven Earth Odes; and New Mystical Writing.

Sutherland brings a long-honed craft and a determined humanism to religious or spiritual subjects which lifts the poems somewhat above the level of most devotional poetry, which has all too often relied on rhetorical formulas and ready-made phrases. The typical language of devotional poetry, borrowed from prayer, ritual and sacred text, is well-worn and replete with meretricious but unremarkable passages. Sutherland transcends this, though not without faults of his own. I have wondered why devotional poetry is particularly subject to this fault, and I believe that it has to do with the restrictive powers of reverence. Poetry charms by means of metaphor, its essential shiftiness; meaning has to move, to transport. By contract, the human language of devotion is relatively static, we have learned it by rote, and we count on it to conjure by its repetitive, sacred nature.

Paul Sutherland, *Only Words*, Vellum Press, 2023.

'Poems on the Life of the Prophet Muhammad' is a solid and closely-observed sequence that shows us the wisdom, courage, fine character, and compassion of the Prophet. Some of the poems are based on hadiths

collected in Sahih Bukhari but there are no accompanying notes that tell us
which hadiths, which is perhaps an oversight. By looking into the corners
of the many stories about our Prophet, and the people who surrounded
him, Sutherland surprises us with new insights about him, as in 'An
Unknown', when 'the trusted merchant' steps into the grave of his friend
(like Hamlet, like a medieval Christian monk), and lies there and begins
to recite the Qur'an, which cause the narrator to say:

> I thought I knew you
> but your unknown
> was more sweet
> than your knowing.

Sutherland uses a wide variety of poetic forms and storytelling devices
in this sequence, which is made vivid and believable by his deployment of
Arab physical culture in the Prophet's time: ceramic and clay bowls,
camels and their saddlery and tack, tents, palm-fibres, water-carriers, the
clay missile-pellets of Surah al-Fil (the Elephant). It is only occasionally
fanciful. 'The Bedouin' transports us to a magical time-stretching story/
place (the unknown, *al-ghayb*) where there is an allegorical rider and
where deer talk, which generates alternative meanings for the poem. The
best poems in the sequence run contrary to expectations, as in 'Entering
Makka' the Prophet is guided to the place of prayer by the animals of the
town, a lovely touch, or the poem 'A'isha', which is an impassioned
eulogy upon the Prophet's death that enumerates the many dimensions of
his many achievements and justifies, to my mind, in its eloquence and
discernment about what is important, in the entire sequence:

> he'd left us precious gifts
> that we stumble on with surprise
> everyday,
> shown how being trustworthy,
> honest, defeats any trickery,
> he'd disclosed that there are rewards
> that can't be seen

There are two issues that come up in these predominantly narrative poems. The first is the aforementioned relative dullness of devotional language set up to fail because it could not possibly do its subject justice. A poem called 'The Qur'an' is not going to match its subject in beauty, eloquence, or elegance. Could any prosody or imagery do the Qur'an justice? One can only marvel in Allah's direction: 'Infinite Nur, the Vast Shaper…', resorts to the devotional level of language. 'It came divinely forward…', et cetera. When Sutherland tries to imagine how the people in the market respond, we get some tautology (the Qur'an is elegant because it's elegant,) and the repetitive piling of measure upon measure:

> They understood each Surah's rhythm
> its colloquial elegance, in calls of a traveler,
> in shouts of the weigher of measures
> the words measured to their own meaning
> that frightened and soothed, that had to disturb.

Interestingly, this idea that the Qur'an's beauty is so because it resembles the language of the marketplace does not square with the responses of the early converts, who had never heard anything so obviously superior and removed from everyday discourse.

Closely related to this issue is the authenticity of the narrative voices in the poems when their sources constrain them, or, because the tone of hadiths is always reverent and centred on Muhammad, the characters who speak in these narrative poems can sound unconvincing, or not fully emotional in a realistic way. In the 'A Widow Remembers', (based on Umm Salama's story, I believe) the attempt of the poet to turn it into a narrative scene but not to invent (refusal of *bid'a*) can yield puzzling results. In this poem, Muhammad drops in on a wife, doesn't say anything to her initially, goes over and plays with the kids a while, and then tells the wife that her husband was killed in battle, and leaves. The matter of this incomplete sounding scene is an aspect of the devotional poet's default manner of discourse: reverence, with the newly designated widow closing with a comment about Muhammad's exceptional character, 'serene / greater humanity.' What, no grief? No, 'You could have told me that when you came in!' Instead:

He didn't need to come
but he came, bringing his blessing,
not that he would alter fate,
but he could and would
out of respect, share distress.
I knew he could perform
miracles but I didn't ask
or expect, it was
that kindly
man's serene
greater humanity
what he gave me
that I preserved
as that day
trailed
away.

Although the delay of Muhammad's delivering of the news was well done, and the poem visually tries to 'tail off' at the end, an attempt to signify her despondency, the new widow in her pious praise of the Prophet sails past her grief and has been unintentionally turned into a religious figurine. In a similar vein, Ayesha, reflecting on the incident where she becomes lost, and is found and accompanied back to the group by a man, the incident that in the Qur'an (Surah a-Nur, 24:10-20) becomes a condemnation of those who repeat the slander about A'isha's chastity, does not seem overly perturbed; she does not rage against the liars or even feel a sharp indignation or a sense of shame or even anger. Instead, she withdraws and patiently waits for Muhammad's decision about her. 'Your kindness, dear husband, / a little shaken. / I asked if I could return to my family / till you've made your decision about me. / You consented with ease.'

Though the impulse in these poems is to humanise these Ansari and other contemporaries of the Prophet, to draw us empathetically close to their humanity, sometimes this doesn't come off. A member of the Bani Qurayza argues back and forth to retrace the mental steps or possible calculations that the Prophet may have gone through as he deliberated whether to execute this 'eyewitness's' tribe (the final decision was actually delegated to another Jewish tribal leader) but doesn't seem to feel a natural human sorrow – fury, anger – that he no longer has any relatives left. His apologetic conclusion about the Prophet is unconvincing though politic and I thought his concluding self-abnegation rather bloodless.

> He called us to live in respect
> and value our differences
> … put away old hates
> through a common cause
> …
> After our betrayal he viewed
> almost everyone who wasn't a Muslim
> as an enemy. He didn't intend to create an Islamic
> State. We gave him no choice…

Sutherland converted to Islam with a Sufi bent and is also the author of *Servants of the Loving One*, Beacon Books his festschrift, if you like, for his Sufi Master. His Sufi sensibility provides him with the grand theme of 'Seven Earth Odes': the surprising, felicitous immanence of the Beloved in every part of Creation. This great truth notwithstanding, it must beam down into the realm of poetry, where literary values such as concinnity, proportion, shape and what Kundera called 'architectonic clarity' matter: If the poet squanders our attention in documenting every *apercu* in an experience, so much so that we can't remember the beginning of the poem, the poem suffers. If the so-so perceptions or metaphors vastly outnumber the striking ones, the reader suffers by extension.

The ode, mind you, is a loose and originally Greek form. It became popular in Neo-classical English poetics after the publication of the *Pindaric Odes* in the eighteength century. In Greek, this kind of long-form dedication were originally associated with sporting events, conformed to a metre, and were reinforced by brief refrains. These Pindaric Odes were the influence that blossomed into Wordsworth's 'Ode: Intimation of Mortality' and Keats's 'Ode to a Grecian Urn'. 'Seven Earth Odes' are suffused with Sutherland's gently questing seeking of the Beloved, and your response is a matter of taste: if you like your poems wandering, more like processes rather than artifacts, and you like your subjects radically

de-centred, you will like these Odes. There is real gold here, but you will
have to pan for it. You will have to be patient, and treasure the spots
where Sutherland rises above the generally prosey narration.

Oddly, where Sutherland impresses is when he comes upon a source of
imagery not usually associated with this sort of thinking-person's poetic
spirituality. We've visited enough churches, graveyards, and walked
through enough forests, the usual loci of the spiritualised insight. But to be
presented with the Beloved in unusual objects or circumstances, to draw
the holy out of the banal every-day – that takes a real poet, as here where
an Indian princess's grave starts his perorating imagination, which sends
him back to childhood, and a child's toy, a spinning top:

> making the scintillating top
> twirl faster,
> to release animals from their inscribed forms
> once they all run
> vanished in whirling bands of colour…
> as though a Saturn…
> with rings of bright reds, yellows and golds
> spinning on the air
> and faster, a sweet zinging against the ears.
> It has to crash, or wobbling on axis
> over-tilt, out of control, till collapsed
> with little to tell its old planetary self.

Or here, where Sutherland catches himself in a mall's mirrors and finds
himself in the company of future generations, himself the accident of time:

> Ah, the luck of first impressions!
> that column of mirrors in a department store
> that never failed to return a good expression.
> But I urge on forgetfulness, revoking that smiling face.
> Now my privileged places
> Faustian wrecking crews have demolished,
> a new generation capers through the glass colonnade,
> j-walks across a mirror-branched Arcadia — unaware.

In this and many other passages, as the Beloved is made plain or furtively elusive to us, Sutherland happily marries the concrete to the religiously abstract, the decoration with belief, and this grounds his odes, to some extent:

> Archaic craftsmen, stretching and intricately winding gold
> into winged filigrees,
> what does your handiwork betray:
> reconnaissance of afterworld reunion,
> lovers' afterlife entanglement?

However, there are a lot of signposting stanzas, summaries, rhetorical questions, and long-winded speculations featured in these odes, almost as though Sutherland is reminding himself *in compos* what the poem is about. When considering the adjectives to use in describing these odes – ruminative, wandering, expansive – I start heading in the direction of blowsy, unfocused, baggy. The discovery of transcendent beauty in the hitherto unremarkable is their strong point, but this happens intermittently. The poems' peripatetic habits start to seem more and more like the inability to find the centre of the poems.

In the last section 'New Mystical Poems', even though it tries too hard to be all-inclusive, to preserve all the recent Sutherland poems, there are many lyric gems here where the stanza-forms restrain Sutherland's tendency to drift, and the poems are better for being shorter, as in 'In Old Pentland Cemetery', which bristles in the stark stone keep of the dead,

> Near to the yard's pillared iron-gate lurks
> an estrange stone house. Through its transom
> families kept vigil to see that no man snatched
> their love ones' remains, left mounds unmarred
> to let at peace the deceased stroll to their Maker.

'Sawing' impressed with its gorgeous and miniature imagery – 'back and forth my limbs

ache / and sawdust disperses / a golden-like rain', 'on the antique spire /
an assortment of pigeons / re-shape to gargoyles'. In 'Meditations', which
uses the common Islamic imagery of roses to invoke the Beloved, many of
the themes of the 'Seven Earth Odes' are treated with greater economy
and with surprising referents: 'the prickles of bubbles / on each
submerged stem', 'An old empty Shipham's fish paste jar' and, bang on:

> You spread lit pigments and scatter
> neat spots on feeble petals then hide
> behind them like a shy girl at a party
> when the party's yours...'

In Paul Sutherland's best work, what he stumbles upon while looking
and sensing, *fi sabiil Allah,* is worth the journey.

LIFE OF FANON

Shamim Miah

Name one Black twentieth century political figure that has made significant contributions to radical politics? My guess is that you're thinking of Malcolm X or even Frantz Fanon! Both of these luminous figures were born in 1925 and died before their fortieth birthday – Fanon died at the age of thirty-six, whilst Malcolm X's life came to a violent end at the age of thirty-nine. Whilst their careers and radical politics overlapped there is no evidence to suggest that Fanon and Malcolm X ever met. Despite this, Eldrige Cleaver and Stokely Carmichael and other key figures within the Black Power movement considered Fanon as a French-speaking Malcolm X.

Malcom X's contribution to radical politics is well known and admired throughout the world. However, less is known about Frantz Fanon. This is starting to change. In recent years, there has been a growing interest in Frantz Fanon. Whilst Fanon's works have been widely available to the seasoned reader of postcolonial studies, throughout the last thirty years Fanon's complex political, intellectual and political ideas have attracted a wider audience, thanks to Isaac Julien's 1995 film, *Frantz Fanon: Black Skin White Mask* and David Macey's 2000 monumental biography, *Frantz Fanon: A Biography*. In 2014, the award-winning Swedish documentary filmmaker Göran Hugo Olsson, released the wildly acclaimed documentary on Fanon, titled *Concerning Violence*. Olsson's unique approach to documentary filmmaking through the usage of archival footages to convey important messages gained popular attention through his *Black Power Mixtape*, which was available through the popular streaming site – Netflix. Fanon's work was marred by controversy under Donald Trump's first term as President of United States, following the Michigan State Prison's decision to ban Fanon's book from its library in 2019. This was intensified by President Trump's much recent assault on US higher education in general and postcolonial studies in particular. Adam Shatz's most recent biography of Fanon is a much-needed counterbalance to the recent hysteria around post-colonial theory. Shatz is the US editor of the *London Review of Books* (LRB) and his work draws upon essays he was published through LRB.

Adam Shatz, *The Rebel's Clinic: The Revolutionary Lives of Frantz Fanon*, FSG Books, London, 2024

Who was Fanon? The answer to this question is complicated. He has often been described as West Indian, African, Algerian, and in some places as a Muslim. Paradoxically, he is very rarely described as French. Whilst Fanon has long been associated with the Algerian struggle against French colonial rule, he was in fact born in the picturesque city of Fort-de-France, capital of Martinique. Martinique, considered as France's *vieilles colonies* or 'the old colonies' was ceded to the French by Spain in 1635. The French colonial system which evolved from the seventeenth century was defined by a sense of continuity, that the sole purpose of West Indian colonies of France was to provide the metropolis with tropical produce. In short, Martinique's sole existence was to serve France. In fact, French law prohibited Martinique to develop its own economy or to accumulate wealth in its own right. Shatz's biography doesn't provide the reader with the broad historical context of Martinique, especially its legacy with slavery. To develop a much-detailed account of the different ways the French colonial enterprise permeated the Martinique's socio-political and legal system, one has to resort to David Macey's detailed biography of Fanon. This is because the colonial system Fanon was born into shaped his future.

During Fanon's childhood the first words he was taught to spell was *Je suis Francais* or 'I am French', despite his colonial education he maintained a degree of frustration against its leader's inability to exercise their power of agency over French colonial rule. Instead, they were 'prisoners of the white gaze' through internalising intricate racial hierarchies or in the words of the Saint Lucian poet and playwright Derek Walcott, they 'looked at life with black skins and blue eyes'. In many respects, Fanon's upbringing was relatively privileged and rooted in aspirational credentials with books, piano lessons, and a second home for the weekend and other vocational holidays. His father, Felix Casimir Fanon, was a customs inspector and his mother, Eleonore Felicia Medelice, a respected shop keeper. Fanon's paternal ancestors were free people. His great-grandfather, the son of slave, started off as a Blacksmith, a relatively respected position. His mother on the other hand, had a higher level of currency thanks to the French colonial system. She had white ancestry originating from Strasbourg, Alsace. During the Second World War, Fanon, then in his twenties, joined the French forces, and underwent essential military training. His time in the army brought him in close contact with other French colonies in North Africa, in particular Morocco and Algeria. Shatz, notes how serving in the Free French Forces, he witnessed the realities of Islamophobia and racism. Whilst Fanon was eager to join the Allied Forces, the realities of racism completely transformed his understanding of European society.

Fanon returned back to Martinque to start his studies at the prestigious Lycee Schoelcher in Fort-de-France, the same institution where the famous scholar, poet, and father of the Negritude movement, Aimé Césaire, taught. Contrary to speculations, Fanon was never taught by Césaire; nevertheless, it is clear that Fanon took inspiration from Césaire's work whilst advancing his own view of the world. After completing his Baccalaureate Lycee Schoelcher, Fanon embarked upon studying medicine with psychiatry at the University of Lyon. Although he did complete his studies in Lyon, his experiences of direct racism had a propound impact on his life. This is clear from the key chapter titled 'The Lived Experiences of the Black Man' in *Black Skin White Mask*. By echoing Ralph Ellison's classic *The Invisible Man*, published as a book in 1952, he notes: 'the Black physician will never know how close he is to being discredited. I repeat, I was walled in neither my refined manners nor my literary knowledge nor my understanding of quantum theory could find favour…I was up against the irrational'. It was during his studies in Lyon together with his travels through France that he came to the realisation that class privilege combined with cultural capital he inherited from his family in Martinique did not provide the protective layer against racism. Nor did his privileged education allow him to transcend the construction of Blackness within the White imagination.

After qualifying as a psychiatrist, Fanon completed his residency in psychiatry in 1951, and wrote his classic *Black Skin, White Mask*. Written in an autoethnographic style, *Black Skin White Mask* had significant impact when it was first published in 1952 and would continue to have a profound influence on activists, writers and academics throughout the decades.

Through combining poetic prose with clinical psychology, Fanon revealed the deep psychological impacts of racism on black bodies. His book aimed to 'liberate man of colour from himself'. Whilst the political impacts of colonialism and racism was well established, Fanon was one of the first writers to focus on the psychological impacts of racism. The collective impacts of racism on the sub-conscious were critical to the self. He noted how black people were enslaved by their inferiority and insignificance, they saw themselves through the lens of the 'other,' constantly seeking validation from their colonial masters. As Fanon notes at the end of *Black Skin White Mask,* 'the black man wants to be like the white man. For the black man there is only one destiny the unarguable superiority of the white man, and all his efforts are aimed at achieving a white existence'. The 'White Mask' aims to capture the intensity and significance of the deep-rooted psychological impacts of racism. As Shatz observes, the Black mask has been figured and assumed in the depths of the collective black psyche, forming the prism-or prison- through' which Black people see and 'misrecognise themselves'. The ideas explored within this seminal text would have a profound impact on Muslim academics. For example, Hamid Dabashi would extend Fanon's thesis in *Brown Skin, White Mask*, by examining the ways Muslim intellectuals act as facilitators of western imperialism.

Whilst working as a psychotherapist in Saint Alban, Fanon come into contact with Francois Tosquelles. Inspired by Marx, Tosquelles would aim to radically transform the normative approaches to psychotherapy from a racialised hierarchical system, in which doctors and other professionals aimed at curing patients to a more patient participatory approach. Fanon would also publish several articles challenging the racial model of psychiatry, as championed by Antione Porot, through his Algiers School of Psychiatry. By using pseudo-science of phrenology and biological determinism, Porot aimed to treat patients through a combination of racial ideology and psychiatry.

Fanon's approach to psychiatry would mark a paradigm shift from the structural racism of Porot. He used collective therapy, a system which puts a greater recognition on the role institutions play on the mental health of patients. Through greater institutional collaboration, between social workers, doctors, nurses, and patients, treatment is offered based upon the wholistic recognition of the person, community, and institutions. Fanon's relationship with Tosquelles would be marked by heated intellectual exchanges, akin to a scholarly bullfight. Nevertheless, both men had deep-seated respect and admiration for each other. At Saint Alban, Fanon would play a central role in advancing institutional psychotherapy through organising musical events, film screening with a view of nurturing 'therapeutic engagement' and 'inventing a new model of living'. Fanon's approaches to psychotherapy in general and his particular approach at decolonising psychotherapy would be one of the legacies which would outlive his relatively short life. Decolonising psychotherapy is an area that is increasingly attracting scholarly attention through the numerous articles and scholarly journals he had written.

In 1953, Fanon took the role of the director of the Blida-Joinville, Algeria, a country that is synonymous with Fanon the political activist. As Shatz, notes, Fanon arrived in Algeria as a French man and died as an Algerian citizen for a state that had yet to exist. He was already familiar with Algeria, especially given that it was the homeland of many of the patients he had treated in Lyon. He devoted the last decade of his life to Algerian independence from France; the struggle gave him a purpose, mission and a cause that occupied his final years. When Fanon landed in Algeria, the battle for Algerian independence against French colonial rule was already in full motion. France occupied Algeria since 1830, when it controlled the city of Algiers. In less than seventeen years, France took over all the territory and brought an end to 400 hundred years of Ottoman rule.

Other than the contacts he had with Algerian patients in France, Fanon had very little knowledge of the Algerian independence movement. In fact, there were no hints that Fanon advocated for Algerian independence, nor did he have a vision for Algeria's future when he first arrived in 1953, he had no revolutionary doctrine, apart from the politics of 'humanist solidarity'. In fact, there is little indication in his early work in Algeria of revolutionary violence with which his name is closely associated. But this all changed in the Algerian war of 1954, which marked France's most vicious and violent combat against Algerian independence. Fanon's name would later be inextricably linked with the Algerian independence through his active involvement with the *Front de Liberation Nationale* or National Liberation Front (FLN). The FLN was developed as a national liberation movement against the French occupation of Algeria often through the use of violence which it orchestrated via its armed wing, the National Liberation Army. Shatz sees Fanon's role with the FLN as providing ideological, moral and theoretical direction. On behalf of FLN, Fanon attended many diplomatic visits, including the All-African People's Congress in Ghana organised by Kwame Nkrumah and attended by many dignitaries associated with Pan African movement, including Patrice Lumumba.

Fanon's time with the FLN would preoccupy his intellectual energy in answering the central question, can the use of violence be justified against colonial oppression and for the pursuit of national liberation. The answer to that question came in *The Wretched of the Earth*. Considered as one of the central texts within post-colonial studies, it is studied and debated by academics and revolutionary activists. The loaded title of the book is taken from the poem *'Dirty Negroes'* by the celebrated Haitian Marxist poet, Jacques Roumain:

And here we are standing up
All the wretched of the earth
                          all the up holders of justice
                                    marching to attack your barracks
                                              your banks
like a forest of funeral torches

to be done once and for all with this
world of Negroes of niggers
          of filthy Negroes

The contents of the *Wretched of the Earth* is as relevant now as it was when it was first published in 1961, just few weeks before Fanon's death. Fanon was diagnosed with acute myeloblastic leukaemia in 1960. Whilst receiving treatment, initially in Moscow and later in the US, Fanon had rushed through the text, and the publication date would be slightly pushed back due to the outstanding forward of the book, written by Jean Paul Sartre. Sartre's preface would prove to be highly controversial, especially following his public defence of Israel's Six Day War, June 1967. This followed a call by many leading writers and political activists to the publishers of *The Wretched of the Earth* to omit Sartre's preface from any future publications. In many respects, *The Wretched of the Earth* was Fanon's last testimony which expanded his vision and reflections on the revolutionary potentials of armed struggle, especially within the journey from colonial exploitation through national liberation and finally to the period of genuine freedom. The written prose of the book, intended as a political manifesto, Shatz observes, 'brought together piercing analytical insights and militant theatrics, apocalyptic warnings and widely utopian projections'.

The overtly violent nature of colonisation, Fanon writes, is 'marked by violence,' indeed, their 'existence together – was created by dint of a great array of bayonets and canon'. The statues built by colonial rulers, celebrate, glorify, and legitimises the use of violence. As colonialism is 'violent in its natural state', Fanon argued, it will 'yield when confronted with greater violence. The process of decolonisation for Fanon is aimed at changing the order of the world – a new ordered world free from colonial legacies, requires cultural, political, and psychological change.

Fanon's book shared the same legacy of other seminal political texts, including Marx and Engels' *Communist Manifesto*, Thomas Paine's *Common Sense* or *The Social Contract* by Rousseau. The lasting legacy of *Wretched of the Earth* weaved a political message which would inevitably lead political and psychological awakening of cross section of leaders throughout the world through the use of violence in their own self defence. The centrality of violence as a process of psychological liberation and its re-humanising potential should be understood through social political context of Algeria's violent history with French occupation. Fanon's own work as a psychiatrist taught him about the deep-seated psychological trauma inflicted, especially to a society 'where the aggressive instincts of the settler were given free reign, whilst those of the native were thwarted altogether'.

Fanon died in Maryland, US, he was buried in the *Shuhada* or Martyrs cemetery, *Ain Kerma*, in Algeria. Shatz's biography makes a worthy contribution to his complex life, demonstrating the enduring legacy of Fanon on the questions surrounding race and empire. Shatz documents the moment 'when colonised people make their present felt by men and women, rather than as "natives," "subjects" or "minorities," seizing the world for themselves, asserting their desire for recognition, and their claim to power, authority and independence.'

ET CETERA

}

ON TARNISHING
THE GOLDEN ROAD

Hilman Fikri Azman

'Stop the Islamic takeover of the West' Although the sticker was faded, fastened over a palimpsest of even more faded stickers coating a wall on a street in London, these words read disturbingly clear. I nearly dropped the book I was holding in my hand, the Scottish historian William Dalrymple's *The Golden Road: How Ancient India Transformed the World*. It struck me odd that the former Orient, the exotic and intriguing place of desire that the West formerly colonised, is now colonising the West. How the tables have turned! But if colonialism is to be understood as the systematic control of another subject's ontology in political, economic, legal, and cultural terms, then it is far from reality that 'the West' now is in the position of being subjugated. While this sticker exemplifies the heightened ethnocentrism and xenophobia witnessed across the Western hemisphere, segments of society subscribing to such notions appear to forget how the Orientalist project – the categorisation of nature and humankind into typology and reduced nomenclatures still being perpetuated today – was built on the foundational structure of Western domination over 'the Other'. This kind of amnesia is quite concerning and speaks to devastating impacts that have gone global.

According to British Pakistani writer and critic Ziauddin Sardar, Orientalism is not an outward gaze of 'the West' towards the East, rather a form of inward reflection, preoccupied with intellectual concerns, problems, fears, and desires of 'the West' that are visited on a fabulated, constructed object by convention called the Orient. Orientalist scholarship was the scholarship of the politics of desire. It codifies western desires into academic disciplines and then projects these desires onto its study of the Orient. What is then regarded as universally scientific, legal, and rational is defined by 'the West', in total neglect and dismissal of the contributions of other major civilisations preceding it. 'The West' then becomes the apex of all civilisations, responsible for ushering modernity into the contemporary world. As such, they become the ultimate standard and reference for the rest of the world. But, 'the West' itself has never been the stable and coherent category it would claim. Such notion dates back only to the sixteenth century following the Protestant reformation and the rise of the Ottomans. Before that, it was Christendom. And this was why the historical encounter with the Orient has much more to do with the clashes and aggressions, like the Crusades against the Islamic empires, rather than the Orient in its broader sense which includes major civilisations such as China, India, Southeast Asia, and Japan. Nonetheless, to be Orientalised, as the Palestinian American academic and critic Edward Said would call it, is to be created and subjected to the positionality of being inferior to 'the West' in a cultural hegemonic relation, regardless of geographical positions. Such obsession then matures through history by way of notions, evolving yet set to the West' definitions of the nation-state and sovereignty.

Cultural hegemony perpetuates Orientalism through such fundamental features of a thriving civilisation as language. The British direct rule for almost a century in the Subcontinent has left everlasting impacts on the psyche, culture, and attitude of the natives, all of which were formed by the languages they used. English was taught and even used as the primary language in some schools, particularly the convent schools, and the English that was taught was of a particularly posh British accent. When an Indian student from the mainland gets enrolled in the school, his accent will be noticeably different from the rest of the North Eastern students, enmeshed in somewhat thick Hindi pronunciation. European schoolteachers will then have to habitually correct them, advising a minimised usage of 'only', a word frequently used by mainland Indians in daily conversations but considered improper in formal Queen's English. North Eastern students had to submit to the idea that *their* English was incorrect, and that, to quote the American author and social critic bell hooks, 'one is worthy of being heard only if one speaks in standard English'. As English gained dominance in daily conversation, North Eastern mother tongues and cultural identities began to erode. Gradually, fluency was lost in languages like Angami, Nagamese, or Assamese – a tragedy described by the Kenyan writer Ngũgĩ wa Thiong'o as psychological violence of the classroom – whereby one is alienated from her 'natural and social environment… reinforced in the teaching of history, geography, music, where bourgeois Europe was always the centre of the universe'. Students even developed an internalised racism, coming to see native languages as substandard or lacking usefulness, and thus preferred to speak only in English. In addition to that, they were also taught to eat using cutleries at the dining table. Using hands to eat, just like the rest of the mainland Indians, is subconsciously accepted as a sign of barbarism. British colonialism displaced native languages and cultures, and postcolonial India continued the work.

The British rightly criminalised *sati* in 1829, a Hindu practice in which a widow self-immolates during her late husband's funeral, but it was probably the only legal reform effected to permanence throughout a century of colonial rule. However, it was not initiated by the first British Governor-General, Lord William Bentinck. Rather, the regulation came much earlier, first brought up by the Mughal empire in the sixteenth century by the likes of Emperor Akbar I and Emperor Aurangzeb who were averse to such practices! These are historical facts that neither the British nor the Indian leaders can suppress. Nevertheless, later history textbooks and a plethora of publications on this matter would only acknowledge the role of the British – framing them as the promulgator of human rights in India by banning *sati*. It must be mentioned here that Lord Macaulay, as a member of the Supreme Council of British India, later did compromised on the law, allowing several *sati* incidences to take place, supposedly out of empathy. Aside from this half-hearted attempt, enshrined in a romanticised alternative history, the British can be said to have undertaken next to no social reform while ruling over India. They failed to stop child marriages, a religious and cultural practice that is still prevalent in many parts of India today. As of 2023, 23 percent of young Indian women under the age of eighteen were already married or in union. Statistically, one in three of the world's child brides live in India. UNICEF declared the country home to the largest number of child brides worldwide. The British also failed to bring religious tolerance and unity to its colony and may not even have had the intention to embark on such an ambitious mission. According to the

Indian intellectual and politician Shashi Tharoor, in 1857 there is evidence
of Hindu and Muslim soldiers pledging a joint allegiance to the enfeebled
Mughal monarch. It was the British who eventually pitted them against one
another, resolute that *divide et impera* was vital to ensure the unchallenged
continuance of empire. Lest we forget that the British, too, facilitated the
separation of India and Pakistan in 1947, which led to massive population
displacement and widespread violence, resulting in the displacement of an
estimated 15 million and approximately one million deaths.

The British colonial administration was often content to work with
oppressive structures rather than against them so long as they preserved
order and tax revenue. Education was limited, gender equality was never
championed, while democracy remained limited to members of nobility
and higher class. The civilising mission, it turns out, was a well-crafted
fiction. Apologist looks to the trains and other public infrastructures
undertaken by the British Raj, but it is important to note they did not hold
a monopoly on such endeavours. The Mauryan, Gupta, and Mughal
empires have respectively brought advancements to the region and built
landmark monuments that exists until today. Over two hundred years
before the common era, the Mauryan, under Ashoka the Great, built cities
and roads which were often inscribed with edicts on morality and
governance. The Guptas patronised the renowned library-monastery of
Nalanda, which became a global centre of learning without parallel,
attracting devoted students from all over the world. The Mughals built
roads, irrigation, bridges, and dams while pushing further urbanisation of
several major cities. These 'pre-modern' Indian empires laid enduring
infrastructural foundations well before colonial times. One must not deny
the Orient its history and civilisation, its power and wealth. The British Raj
plundered more than what they worked on in India.

With the independence of India in 1947, the country embarked on a
new era of self-government while experimenting with democracy that had
few precedents: to fuse the chaotic diversity of caste, faiths, language, and
culture into a modern democratic republic. The architects of postcolonial
India did not envision democracy merely as a procedural form of
governance. They saw it as a fundamental ethical paradigm, a secular
covenant between the state and its diverse citizens. For decades, leadership
changed hands, but this moral vision for the republic endured. But the

gambit was always dubious. Recently, a darker wind has begun to blow across the Ganges plain. India now finds itself at a menacing precipice as the Bharatiya Janata Party (BJP), under the influence of Hindutva ideology, steered the country's 1.4 billion population into a dangerous territory of extremism. Its main leader, Narendra Modi – a man moulded in the crucible of the Rashtriya Swayamsevak Sangh (RSS) – has ushered in an era of ethnoreligious nationalism where religion and power intertwine. The RSS finds its roots in Vinayak Damodar Savarkar, the main ideologue and progenitor of Hindutva, who seeks not the secular state tolerant of all faiths, envisioned in independence, for India, but a *Hindu Rashtra*, that is a Hindu nation. Savarkar's Hindutva is not inspired by the faith of the Vedas and the Upanishads, nor the mysticism of the Bhakti poets. It is a narrow nationalist ideology crafted when he was incarcerated. Identity was conflated with ethnicity, and citizenship measured in cultural conformity.

The question of identity has always been at the crux of debates of any emerging nation. When the Irish political scientist Benedict Anderson theorised about what binds communities together despite differences and with few commonalities, the framework that he had in mind was the dialectics of power between nations. However, when an essentialist framework is employed to analyse what makes a nation from an inward perspective, no theory is one-size-fits-all. As each community is unique, we may need a set of different tools and perspective to understand what identity is to them. In the case of India, we saw a reversal of the idea of imagined communities that laid emphasis on the transition from the decline of religion and faith to the rise of nation-states based on territorial sovereignty. The secular territory downplayed religion and ethnicity, creating an identity vacuum that Hindutva rose to fill. Hindutva has seen a surge in the influence of Hindu teachings in the public sphere, and it has consequently redefined what it means to be a true and authentic Indian. Being an Indian means being a Hindu, able to speak in Hindi, and adorn oneself with *Patola sarees*, and *kediyu* with *dhoti* – a redefinition accepted by many based on *Hindu Rashtra*.

Nothing feels more like neocolonialism than when a language is imposed at the expense of one's native language. Factually speaking, Hindi is only an official language alongside English, and there are twenty-two other languages that are acknowledged and enshrined in the Indian Constitution under the Eighth Schedule. Regardless, the mainlanders have the impression that Hindi is the only language that all Indians should speak, and for that reason they felt entitled to impose Hindi upon everyone. It is not much of a stretch to think why some of them, particularly in the North East, felt like they are being colonised by India. And if there is anything that will bring the different tribes together, it is resistance against any kinds of imposition by those in power. And the North Easterners are not alone in the feeling of being colonised. Muslims in India face similar experiences of systematic control and epistemic arrests.

With over 220 million people living in the country, the Urdu speaking Indian Muslims, who are native to the country, find themselves cast not as citizens of equal dignity, but as second-class citizens. They suffered decades of physical and systematic discrimination, like the North Easterners. Under the BJP government, their fate has only gotten worse. In December of 2019, the Parliament of India passed the Citizenship Amendment Act (CAA), offering a pathway to citizenship for religious minorities like Hindus, Sikhs, Buddhists, Jains, Parsis, and Christians – but not Muslims! – from neighbouring countries, allegedly to protect these individuals who are fleeing religious persecution. The CAA works in tandem with the National Register of Citizens (NRC), under which 1.9 million people were left off. The new amendment could protect the Hindus excluded from the NRC by offering them a citizenship route but will render many Muslims stateless as they might be unable to provide the necessary documentation to prove their citizenship. This legal segregation and privilege policy is a clear echo of apartheid South Africa. It is also the first time in India's history that religion has been introduced as a criterion for citizenship. And what is to become of protections for minorities? As the Rohingya Muslims, Ahmadis, and Shias are excluded, it suggests that the motivation is political rather than humanitarian. The BJP government also rescinded nearly all provisions of Article 370 of the Indian Constitution, which conferred special privileges upon the people of the state of Jammu and Kashmir to have their own constitution and the freedom to make laws related to permanent residency, property ownership, and fundamental rights. Indians from outside the state used to be barred from purchasing property or settling there. But with the abrogation of Article 370, non-Kashmiris are now permitted to acquire as much land as is desired in the region, thereby altering the demographic composition of this predominantly Muslim state. Sovereignty of the region was taken away unilaterally without consultation and without consent from the 12 million souls living there. Thousands were then detained, and communications were disrupted as the government acted to suppress dissent. In India, the cow is protected, but the dissenter is not. Streets once humming with prayer now echoed only with military boots and drone flights. And the question hangs heavy in the air like incense in a desecrated shrine: is this democracy or apartheid? The absence of Muslim voices in politics is due to the small ratio of Muslim parliamentary members, who represent less than 5 percent of the house. Hence why the gavel of justice rarely falls in favour of the marginalised.

Meanwhile, in classrooms and textbooks, the Mughals' ruling in India for over 600 years is simply mentioned in passing or, in some cases, even left unheard. Their roles and contributions are effectively erased from history lessons. The BJP understands very well the power to name and the power to define. Beyond the covert defining done in the classroom, the BJP resorts to overt changes. The 435-year-old name of the city Allahabad has been changed to Prayagraj, simply because the name refers to God in Islam, and was given previously by a Muslim ruler of the Mughal empire. The same went for Aurangzeb Road – named after the magnificent Mughal emperor – which was renamed to A.P.J. Abdul Kalam, in honour of India's former president. With the renaming trend kickstarted, every other place bearing a Muslim name stands under threat of erasure, including the cities of Ahmedabad, Hyderabad, and Aurangabad. To have a perspective on this matter, India had experienced a similar trend of renaming in 1995. As a result, it restored the names of the cities of Bombay, Bangalore, Calcutta, Cawnpore and Jubblepore to their indigenous names – Mumbai, Bengaluru, Kolkata, Kanpur and Jabalpur respectively – to emphasise its independence from Britain and reject the legacy of colonial linguistic symbols. But now, the act of renaming is being strategically weaponised to systematically erase the long and indisputable heritage of Muslims in India, to rewrite a new history in such a way that aligns with the aspiration of the ethnoreligious nationalism of Hindutva influence. As if those were not enough, the BJP also abused the law by instructing state councils under their influence to demolish the homes and businesses of Muslims at the whisper of unrest. They masqueraded behind the law using the pretext of these spaces being 'illegal structures'. Without warning and without warrant, homes are reduced to rubble. Cow vigilantes roam with sacred rage, lynching men on suspicion of transporting beef. Their impunity is protected by silence – or worse, smirks – from power. The police and security personnel, in many cases, become not protectors, but perpetrators. The violence against Muslims is the new normal. Hatred against Muslims went even further than mixed marriages to encroach on love itself, criminalised when it crosses the sanctioned borders of religion. Indian Muslims are portrayed as seducers in the grand scheme of 'Love Jihad', as conspirators in some mythical plot to influence or convert Hindu women across India. India is not only turning into a pariah state due to its problematic ties with neighbouring countries like China and Pakistan, but inherently a fascist one as well from the way it treats its North Easterner and Muslim citizens.

Under Modi and the BJP, India is now trembling with fascist proclivities. The secularism enshrined in India's constitution is no longer a shared value, but a contested terrain. What is hidden within India is Hindustan. 'It is that which tacitly shapes the state and determines the frontiers between freedom and repression, what is allowed and what is forbidden,' to quote the British philosopher and historian Perry Anderson. In fact, one could not help but find a plethora of shared commonalities in terms of systematic discrimination and elimination of the subalterns between India and Israel. Hindutva and Zionism, two peas in a pod, proport that they represent countries that are faithful to respective religions – Hinduism and Judaism – but the endgame of their endeavours have more to do with politics and power consolidation than pleasing God. While Israel builds illegal settlement in the West Bank, India has its own 'West Bank' to annex too: Kashmir. In fact, Indian politicians openly call for 'Israel-style' settlements for Hindus and demographic reengineering in Kashmir, replicating the settler-colonial infrastructure including militarised walls, checkpoints, and discriminatory planning. The revoking of Article 370 further paving the way to settle non-Kashmiris in the region in order to reduce Muslim populations' influence, the same way Israel similarly significantly reduced Palestinian populations through settlements, land expropriations, and ethnic cleansing. In addition to that, both countries pursue cultural erasure: Israel Judaizes Palestinian land through renaming and colonisation, while India Hinduizes name of places and curriculum, while marginalising Muslim histories. Mythology and religious texts are recast as historical fact to dominate the national narrative. Both states also weaponize 'anti-terror' laws to imprison dissenters, academics, activists, and human rights defenders. Critics are labelled as anti-nationalists or terrorists, with state agencies engaging in surveillance, harassment, and even digital evidence fabrication. The way Indian supremacists use lynching and vigilante violence against Muslims and Dalits over matter like beef consumption or interfaith marriages also parallel the settler's violence in Israel toward Palestinians. The unholy alliance of these states in sown in deeply Islamophobia that informs their policy and public discourse. The Hindutva extremists admire Israel's hardline tactics against Palestinians and adopt similar narratives against Indian Muslims. And just as those who supported the creation of the State of Israel in 1948 could hardly imagine where we'd find ourselves less than a century later, it is hard to imagine the founding fathers' fight for independent is honoured in the present actions of the Indian government. All the measures taken ostensibly point to an indubitable phenomenon rupturing Indian society: neocolonialism.

The celebrated polymath and Nobel laureate Rabindranath Tagore had foreseen the pervasive peril of such narrow ideology over the universality of humanity. In 1908, he wrote, 'patriotism can't be our final spiritual shelter. I will not buy glass for the price of diamonds and I will never allow patriotism to triumph over humanity as long as I live'. Tagore could easily be deemed anti-nationalist read through the lens of hardline BJP members today. But the harmonious presence of different religions and ethnicities was not entirely alien to India. In fact, during the precolonial period, India boasts the record of being the home to emerging different societies. The Silk Road that connected India with the wider world was an important route for economic trade. In addition to that, it also empowered people with exchanges of religious, artistic, and intellectual ideas. For that reason, it was also called the Golden Road. Dalrymple argues that India's soft power strength lies in its religious pluralism. It used to absorb and reinterpret ideas across time and geography, within its own civilizational matrix, thus demonstrating an inclusive and adaptive culture rather than an isolated one. Such a thriving heterogenous tradition that it became 'a confident exporter of its own diverse civilization, creating around it an empire of ideas which developed into a tangible 'Indosphere' where its cultural influence was predominant'.

India was not meant to be an ethnostate. It and many other multicultural states always had the potential to be a pluralistic sanctuary, a peaceful realm where Hindus, Muslims, Christians, and Buddhists could all call the same land their own. India and other nations like it still do. The point of the nation-state model was to give voices and power to communities, not pit them against one another. The infusion of fundamentalist Hindutva ideology into the veins of governance threatens to unravel this vision. Fascism is bleeding Mother India, just as it has bled Palestine, and threatens to bleed other areas of multicultural beauty around the world.

Will India, the world's largest democracy, return to embrace its pluralist promise or will it wander further into the darkness of hatred and fanaticism, where difference is intolerable, and silence is survival? The world watches. But more importantly, history watches. And history has no erasers—only pens.

TEN FARCICAL FASCISTS

C Scott Jordan

Fascism has delivered some of the greatest evil humanity has ever had to experience and endure. The horror's wrought are nigh incomprehensible. The twentieth century is a century we may not ever be able to truly understand. If one good thing came out of the devastation of that century, it is that we learned to revere the 'fascist'. Today the debate continues, attempting to make sense of what has come to pass as well as what is happening in the present. Yet, fascism, contrary to popular opinion, did not go anywhere. It remains. The stigma is so strong, that card carrying fascism, when called out, must seek immediate rebuttal. Godwin's Law – a rule stating that the longer an internet conversation goes on, the more likely someone is to be compared to Hitler and the Nazis – stands as a testament to fascism being the extreme of inhumanity and wrong. Ideally, fascist might replace the Big Bad Wolf, or the evil witches of the tales parents tell children. However, the shamelessness of our contemporary world allows fascist to again parade and march unphased by how much they mimic the images history asks us to beware. It is one thing to be aware of the repetition of history, or even to heed French critic Jean-Baptiste Alphonse Karr's words, 'the more things change the more they stay the same', but it is something far graver to not see that as a problem.

Time and again we need a reminder. Some of us need to be violently shaken from our slumber on a bed of apathy. And our good friends who take up the Antifa flag set that watchman and certainly declare what they see, loud and clear. However, there is something that reaches more to the masses. Popular culture. And while many songs and art instillations do their work to put fascism in its place, I feel film is the realm where certain concepts can be taken on more completely. Film gives us the ability to play with what otherwise might be illogical, inconceivable, and confounded by multiple interpretations and perspectives. Most importantly film can give and take away power where otherwise, in the real world, this can often seem an impossibility.

There is no shortage of antifascist films. Indeed, one of the greatest films of all time is 1985's *Come and See* from the Russian filmmaker Elem Klimov. Described as a film belonging to both the horror and tragedy genre, this film stands against war, fascism, and human violence. Its visuals combine with the arch of its teenage protagonist, Flyora, to take us along for a ride through the history of human suffering during the Nazi occupation of Belarus in the 1940s. Nothing quite captures the lengths of humanity's ability to make itself suffer than the lens of the loss of childhood followed by the violent thrust into adulthood. Though, it must be noted that this is no film for the masses, especially those with weak constitutions. Even the most well-adjusted viewer will get up from the credits shook, and quite possibly changed. This may not be the best way to take on fascism. We often need a keen look in the mirror, though a mirror distorted just enough can help us see what is otherwise not necessarily clear.

While distortion should be undertaken with extreme caution, funhouse mirrors in particular help broaden our perspective on things. While realism in film certainly brings things home, it is comedy that can really capture the absurdity of something so terrible as fascism. So, to begin our antifascist journey through cinema here is my list of ten films that highlight the silliness of fascism. In laughing at the clowns, perhaps we can remove their power in the real world. So, sit back and let's enjoy some lovely films and take the piss out of those fascist bastards!

1. My imaginary friend, Adolf Hitler

If one film could be seen as the comedic spiritual opposite to *Come and See*, it would have to be Taika Waititi's 2019 satire *Jojo Rabit*. Our protagonist is a ten-year-old member of Hitler's Youth, Johannes 'Jojo' Betzler, who is accompanied by his dreamt-up approximation of Adolf Hitler, portrayed by Waititi himself. This is one of a very short list of films that begins with a young impressionable boy being given a pep talk by his imaginary Hitler and shouting 'Hail Hitler' multiple times, growing exponentially in volume and intensity before the title card. Waititi's Hitler becomes both the angel and devil figures of conscious as Jojo asks him increasingly difficult questions until he runs out of the ability to rationalise the worldview he is imposing upon the boy. The situation is further complicated when he discovers that his mother, a voice of peace and stability in a Germany-gone-mad, is hiding a Jewish girl in their attic. A packed cast includes Rebel Wilson, who embodies the apathetic German who follows her orders, unaware of the full extent of the Nazi's doings, and Sam Rockwell, the leader of the local Hitler Youth organisation slowly realising his identity and the worldview he preaches are incompatible. The 'Hail Hitler' opening shouted at the audience is brilliantly juxtaposed with Jojo, becoming aware of the buffoon that is his imaginary friend and by extension Hitler, shouts 'fuck you Hitler' before kicking him through the window of his bedroom, effectively severing his devotion to Nazi propaganda. The film also cleverly shows us how fascism literally causes a city, a nation, and a people to spoil and decay while juggling tearjerking tragedy and chortles of gut-wrenching comedy.

2. Adenoid Hynkel

Adenoid Hynkel represents the classic, farcical analogue of Adolf Hitler. The 1940 film that brings Hynkel to life, Charlie Chaplin's *The Great Dictator* is the standard of antifascist satirical cinema. Chaplin portrays both Hynkel and a former Jewish soldier, suffering from amnesia, who becomes a barber in the fictionalised German nation of Tomania. Even Benito Mussolini was taken on through the dictator Benzo Napaloni of Bacteria, the fictionalised version of Italy. Coming out at the height of World War II, the targets of this satire was made obvious by the use of certain motifs and symbols. *The Great Dictator* also represents a rare case where the subject of the satire was still alive and at large. Following a botched assassination plot against Hynkel, that the barber was roped into, the barber is suddenly mistaken for Hynkel just as he undertakes the invasion of Osterlich, a fictionalised version of Austria. With all the troops gathered, the barber takes to the stage, all thinking he is Hynkel, and gives one of the greatest antifascist speeches put to film, announcing that he has had a change of heart and will abandon his dictatorial ways, ushering in a new era of democracy for Tomania. The film was largely popular in the United States and would become an essential piece for British propaganda during the war, although it was produced while Great Britain had a policy of appeasement with Germany.

3. 'Springtime for Hitler: A Gay Romp with Adolf and Eva at Berchtesgaden'

As a young American Jewish man, having served as a combat engineer in the US Army during World War II, Mel Brooks had always seen Adolf Hitler and Nazi fascism as his greatest adversary. Hitler and the Nazis in fact feature, even in small ways, in almost all of his films. But it was his 1967 film *The Producers*, where he crafted them into the ultimate clowns. When wanning theatre producer Max Bialystock is faced with indiscrepancies with his taxes, his accountant Leo Bloom discovers that he could make more money if he was certain that his next show would be a flop. To ensure this plot could come to fruition, they search for the worst play imaginable. They come across 'Spring Time for Hitler: A Gay Romp with Adolf and Eva at Berchtesgaden', written by a Hitler-loving Nazi in New York, pairing this with the worst director and cast they could find. They were certain the show will close before the end of Act I. After a bombastic and overly offensive opening number Bialystock and Bloom are sure that all will go to plan, but the direction and cast are so bad that, in actuality, the production comes off as a clever parody of the script as originally written. The actor who was cast to play Hitler is such a bad actor he plays him as himself, a smooth-talking beatnik which transforms Hitler into a fool which enraptured the audience in laughter. Instead of being the quickest cancelled shows in history, it becomes one of the most popular shows. Landing themselves in prison they start over with a new production: 'Prisoners in Love'. With Hitler personally pacified in this film, it stands as one chapter in Mel Brooks's long career of removing the fangs from such evils as fascism, xenophobia, and hate.

4. Standartenführer Hans Landa

Quentin Tarantino's brand of filmmaking blends violence, witty dialogue, and absurdity to place this entry more firmly in the category of black comedy. While his 2009 film *Inglorious Basterds* goes to great lengths to paint Adolf Hitler and Joseph Goebbels in a less than favourable light – especially in the third act – the crosshairs of his satire are focussed on Christoph Waltz's portrayal of SS officer Hans Landa. In Landa, Waltz perfectly incarnates evil in a blend of cold-hearted anger, eloquent speech, eccentricity, and hypocrisy. Landa is the ultimate hunter of Jewish people in one of the greatest cold openings seen on the silver screen. The story positions Hans Landa as coincidentally placed in the path of the Basterds – a black ops commando unit of Americans led by Brad Pitt's Aldo Raine, who collect the scalps of the Nazis they kill and carve swastikas into the foreheads of those they allow to live only so that they may spread tales of terror to other Nazis. When the Basterds are called in to assist British forces in a plot to assassinate Adolf Hitler at a film premiere in France, Landa is presented with an opportunity. As a 'fan' of the Basterds he has longed to make contact with them, to see if the stories told of them are true. So enamoured by them, when he catches a couple of them at the film premiere, he agrees to allow their plot to carry on if they can promise him safe passage if he turns cloak. In Tarantino's alternate history World War II film, things rarely go as planned and violent delights always get their violent ends.

5. Dr Strangelove

The 1964 film *Dr Strangelove or How I Learned to Stop Worrying and Love the Bomb* is lauded as Stanley Kubrick's magnum opus and one of the most influential films ever made. Ostensibly, *Dr Strangelove* stands primarily against nuclear proliferation and the absurdities of the Cold War. However, underneath this classic Cold War farce is a looming shadow of fascism in the shape of the titular Dr Strangelove, a wheelchair-bound former Nazi, nuclear war expert played by Peter Sellers. Dr Strangelove is introduced within the war room where the American president and Soviet premiere meet to try to prevent nuclear war between their two countries. Aside from a case of alien limb syndrome, where Dr Strangelove involuntarily extends his right arm in a Nazi salute, the quirky character appears the ultimate embodiment of fascism propaganda, welcoming the end of the world as others race to prevent the strike. A world where fascism is denied the reigns of global dominance is best a world destroyed in cumulatively expressed in Dr Strangelove rising from his wheel chair at the moment when all hope is lost proclaiming to his 'Führer' that he could walk again. Fascism is portrayed here not only as a worldview of the insane, but one that even dements and twists the body as it did with Dr Strangelove.

6. High Chancellor Adam Sutler and the Norsefire Party

Acclaimed novelist and wizard Alan Moore's graphic novels all contain major antifascist themes, but none go so directly as *V for Vendetta*, adapted to 2005 film of the same name by James McTeigue and the Wachowskis. Set in a dystopian future Britain ruled over by a fascist authoritarian regime helmed by the ubernationalist Norsefire Party and High Chancellor Adam Sutler, an ironic portrayal where John Hurt, having formerly played Winston Smith in 1984's *1984*, now plays a Big Brother equivalent in Sutler. Propaganda drives a society that imprisons and executes all undesirables including immigrants, those of different sexual preferences, those who worship alternate religions, or who embrace other ideas or lifestyles. In a tightly controlled society, one vigilante stands up against the totalitarian system, an individual known as V, who sports a mask in the likeness of Guy Fawkes, a controversial figure of resistance and antifascism infamously one of the conspirators behind the gunpowder plot of 1605. Where Sutler is certainly the face of fascism in this film, the complacency of a people and the well-oiled propaganda machine of complete media control go so far that even as the party leaders being purged, the show goes on. The film proports, along with our vigilante, V, that ideas are stronger than anything and outlast regimes and oppressive policies.

7. The United Citizens Federation

Paul Verhoeven's 1997 film *Starship Troopers* is one of the most misunderstood films, as it parodies fascist society to the point of almost appearing to be arguing for it. The film is roughly based on the 1959 book of the same name from the controversial sci-fi novelist Robert A. Heinlein. However, Verhoeven's vision comes from a much more absurdist and violent lens than Heinlein's book. Known for his over-the-top displays of death and destruction – as seen in 1987's *Robocop* and 1990's *Total Recall* – he blends blood and gore with intercut advertisements, that are beyond-the-pale absurd in their displays of commercialism and propaganda, to reveal the true satire at play here. Constant and repeated messaging from the universe of this film ask us to be more violent humans and join the United Citizens Federation's fight against the enemy. *Starship Troopers* is essentially a coming-of-age story on a future Earth which found itself at the brink of total destruction, only to be united in a struggle against the threat of an insect-like alien that surfaced following a colonialist exercise by the United Citizens Federation on a distant planet. We follow a group of friends as they finish school and join the Mobile Infantry charged with fighting and killing the alien threat. We see first-hand how generational violence, all of the mentors in Mobile Infantry are horribly maimed and have seen all their friends killed, propels a fascist society with the help of propaganda and a heavily controlled education system. In case the fascist point was not made clear enough, the highest ranking in the Mobile Infantry wear uniforms and long coats that are oddly similar to the uniforms seen in Nazi Germany. Any character who might be able to make a difference is killed as the complacent and conformist characters survive and work their way up the ladder. Empathy for the alien 'Other' is completely denied. This entry is a rather nihilistic one, but fascism, especially in the future is not likely to be rainbows and sunshine.

8. Illinois Nazis

American Nazis have always been a strange phenomenon that many in the US wish to remain ignorant of their existence. However, since 1998 gave us Tony Kaye's brutal film *American History X*, white supremacy in the US has been given increasing attention from film and popular media. But before this the American Nazi Party was lampooned in John Landis's 1980 film *The Blues Brothers*. Some Americans' first exposure to American Nazis was through this *Saturday Night Live* sketch turned film following two musically talented brothers, putting together their old band for a 'mission from God' to prevent the shutdown of the orphanage that raised them. Along this sojourn around the Chicagoland area, they run into a demonstration put on by the Nazi party that they decide to crash after John Belushi's character utters the famous line 'I hate Illinois Nazis'. By driving their car through the demonstration they add the Illinois Nazis, their leader portrayed by the affable Henry Gibson, to a coalition of enemies that include the National Guard, firefighters, law enforcement officers, a country music band they upstaged, and a mysterious shotgun-wielding woman out to kill the brothers, all on their tails as they try to pull off one big gig. Although the film is certainly in the genre of goofball comedy, the scene featuring the Illinois Nazis is a sobering display of white supremacist and antisemitic rhetoric set to the backdrop of foaming-at-the-mouth Americans disgusted by their presence and the police in between upholding their constitutional rights to free speech and demonstration. An image that looks quite different nowadays!

9. Team America:World Police

Trey Parker and Matt Stone, of *South Park* fame, bring us an interesting addition to this list with 2004's *Team America:World Police*. At hindsight you would think the films 'protagonists' are fighting the fascists. However, in their bombastic demonstration of militarism, racism, and destructive foreign policy, this film highlights the fascist nature of American society that was kicked into overdrive following 9/11 and into the 'War on Terror'. Team America is an international counterterrorism force that ends up seeing out their ends regardless of the collateral damage, which in the opening scene is most of Paris, including the Eiffel Tower, the Arc de Triomphe, and the Louvre. In taking on a coalition of 'Islamic terrorists' and liberal actors led by Kim Jong-Il, the former dictator of North Korea, the fascist face behind the US's foreign actions is brought front and centre. It is interesting how the use of puppets in this film plays at the uncanny valley, giving an eerie distorted mirror on American exceptionalism and quest for supremacy. Although largely focussed on critiquing the ongoing wars in Afghanistan and Iraq of the time, the film could be easily remade today with a few names and locations switched out. Although a clear satire of American exceptionalism turned fascism, the film is readily quoted by Americans on both sides of the political divide. Should 'America, Fuck Yeah,' one of the films memorable themes, be played, numerous Americas are ready to sing along at full volume. Some ironically, and some not.

10. Donald Trump Analogues

Donald Trump is an interesting character. Numerous films made throughout his life have antagonist characters that have been modelled after him and what he represents, even before he was elected President of the United States in 2016. There are even some characters that predate Trump's birth that make you do a double take when looking at Trump's actions today. Montgomery Burns from *The Simpsons*, Biff Tannen from *Back to the Future*, and Gordon Gekko from *Wall Street* have all been tied to the inspiration of Donald Trump. But, since his leaving office in 2020, a proliferation of characters have featured on the silver screen with funny hair, odd accents, or lots of money and a rude, bullying demeanour. One example is Pedro Pascal's character Maxwell Lord in 2020's *Wonder Woman 1984*, a failed businessman who works to save his company and gain power and influence by stealing a stone that grants people their dreams. Another is 2025's *Mickey 17*, featuring Mark Ruffalo's Kenneth Marshall, a failed politician turned leader of a deep space colony to the planet of Niflheim. His arrogance, funny speech patterns, and even Ivanka Trump-like wife Yfla, played by the talented Toni Collette, ooze with a Trumpian sentiment – even though filmmaker Bong Joo Hon denies anything like Trump to be his intension when writing the character. We are even seeing portraits of Trump himself, such as Sebastian Shaw's embodiment of the Donald in 2024's *The Apprentice*. Though perhaps it is too early to rule on the fascistic tendencies of Donald Trump, but a quick glance at his supporters, his policies, and the 6 January 2021 incident, one cannot help but think. If the shoes fits...

CITATIONS

Introduction: Springtime for Fascism
by Hassan Mahamdallie

Hannah Arendt's *The Origins of Totalitarianism* is available as Penguin Classic, 2017. Richard Seymour's *Disaster Nationalism: The Downfall of Liberal Civilisation*, Verso, 2024, is a provoking and rewarding read with a plethora of useful citations. For a good concise account of the rise of the Nazis I recommend Benjamin Carter Hett's *The Death of Democracy. Hitler's Rise to Power*, Windmill Books 2019. Cas Mudde and Cristóbal Rovira Kaltwasser's *Populism: A Very Short Introduction*, Oxford University Press, 2017, is a good starting point on what is right wing popularism. The NAACP's website https://naacp.org/ contains many educational resources on the fight against racism and for civil rights. Naomi Klein and Astra Taylor's long form essay *The rise of end times fascism*, Guardian newspaper 13 April 2025, is an excellent survey of the outer shores of supremacist survivalism, and contains many links to useful further reading. It can be found at https://www.theguardian.com/us-news/ng-interactive/2025/apr/13/end-times-fascism-far-right-trump-musk

What is Fascism? by Donny Gluckstein

European Social Surveys can be accessed at: https://www.europeansocialsurvey.org. The quote is from 2017 survey, p16.

On Jews in Italian fascist party, see: https://www.dubnow.de/en/research-project/schmeing-jews-in-the-italian-fascist-party and https://www.quest-cdecjournal.it/italys-fascist-jews-insights-on-an-unusual-scenario/

The quotes are from: Anca Ulea, 2023, 'Europeans are becoming more socially liberal, according to a new study', *EuroNews*, https://www.euronews.com/culture/2023/03/12/europeans-are-becoming-more-socially-liberal-according-to-a-new-study and Adrain Lyttelton, *The Seizure of Power. Fascism in Italy 1919-1929,* Weidenfeld and Nicolson, London 1973, pp. 85-6

See also: Donny Gluckstein, *Nazis, Capitalism and the Working Class*, Haymarket Books, 2012, and *A People's History of the Second World War: Resistance versus Empire*, Pluto, 2012 and Donny Gluckstein and Janey Stone, *The Radical Jewish Tradition: Revolutionaries, Resistance Fighters and Firebrands,* Bookmarks, 2024.

The Far Right in Europe by Louis Ordish

I have mentioned the following works: Aijaz Ahmad. *On Communalism and Globalization: Offensives of the Far Right*, 2nd ed. (New Delhi: Three Essays Collective, 2016); Vijay Prashad, 'Ten Theses on the Far Right of a Special Type," *Tricontinental: Institute for Social Research*, 15 August 2024. https://thetricontinental.org/newsletterissue/ten-theses-on-the-far-right-of-a-special-type/ (Accessed: 11 May 2025); Enzo Traverso. *The New Faces of Fascism: Populism and the Far Right* (London: Verso, 2019), p22.; Richard Seymour. *Disaster Nationalism: The Downfall of Liberal Civilization* (London: Verso, 2024), p192.; and Tariq Ali. *The Extreme Centre: A Warning* (London: Verso, 2015).

Women and Fascism by Judith Orr

For detailed accounts of women's involvement in past fascist movements historian Martin Durham's book, *Women and Fascism* (Routledge 1998) broke new ground. He covered the role of women in both the Italian and German fascist movements as well as looking at the women in the British Union of Fascists (BUF). Julie V Gottlieb's *Feminine Fascism* (IB Tauris, 2003) is another thorough study of women in the BUF. To learn about the experience of the US the work of US academic Kathleen M Blee is a good place to start. Blee has spent years researching women in the Ku Klux Klan and racist movements in the early 20th century, her publications include *Inside Organised Racism: women in the hate movement* (University of California Press, 2002). Cécile Simmons looks at the part played by social media in the promotion of misogyny online in *CTRL HATE DELETE* (Policy Press 2025); Eviane Leidig's *The Women of the Far Right* (Columbia University Press, 2023) also looks at how far-right women influencers are using social media to win new recruits to the movement. Sophie Lewis looks at the ideas of right-wing women in her *Enemy Feminisms*, (Haymarket Books 2025). Lois Shearing investigates the experiences and ideas of women within far-right movements such as the trad wives and online influencers in her excellent *Pink Pilled* (Manchester University Press, 2024). Hilal Elver's *The Headscarf Controversy* (Oxford University Press, 2012) looks at the rise of Islamophobia and the specific targeting of Muslim women in both Europe and the US.

The Chetnik Genocide by Marko Attila Hoare

The sources used in this article are, for the most part, original documents written during World War II by participants in events; above all, by members of the Chetnik movement. They include three collections of published documents. Fabijan Trgo, ed. *Zbornik dokumenata i podataka o narodnooslobodilačkom ratu jugoslovenskih naroda* is a monumental collection of documents of all participants in World War II in Yugoslavia assembled and published over the course of several decades by the Military Archive in Belgrade. Vladimir Dedijer and Antun Miletić, eds, *Genocid nad Muslimanima, 1941-1945*, is a collection of documents and eyewitness accounts relating to the Chetnik genocide. Dragoljub M. Mihailović, *Rat i mir đenerala*, is a comprehensive published edition of the wartime papers of the overall Chetnik leader, Draža Mihailović. All three of these collections are primarily drawn from documents found in the Military Archive in Belgrade. Its Chetnik Collection contains the world's most important collection of documents of the Chetnik movement, two of which I have cited in this article. The Historical Museum of Bosnia-Hercegovina hosts the most important archive of documents in Bosnia-Hercegovina relating to World War II; in particular, its UNS Collection contains valuable documents of the Ustasha Surveillance Service (UNS), a wartime intelligence service that produced reports on Chetnik activities. Finally, Rodoljub Čolaković, *Zapisi iz oslobodilačkog rata* is the published memoir of one of the leading Bosnian wartime Communists and resistance leaders.

The quotes, in order of appearance, are from: Valdimir Dedijer and Antun Miletić, eds, *Genocid nad Muslimanima, 1941-1945: Zbornik dokumenata i svjedočenja* (Svjetlost, Sarajevo, 1990), p8-16, p33-44; Dragoljub M Mihailović,.*Rat i mir đenerala: Izabrani ratni spisi*, vols 1-2, (Srpska Reč, Belgrade, 1998), p2 and p10; Rodoljub Čolaković, *Zapisi iz oslobodilačkog rata*, vol. 3 (Svjetlost, Sarajevo, 1966), p3 and p756-77; Dedijer and Miletić, p8-16 and p33-34; Mihailović, p2 and p10; Čolaković p76-77; Dedijer and Miletić, 1990, 99-100; Military Archive, box 170, folder 3, document 51; Mihailović, p1 and p212); Military Archive, box 222, folder 5, documents 23+24; and Historical Museum of Bosnia-Hercegovina, UNS collection, box 3, document 927; and Fabijan Trgo, editor., *Zbornik dokumenata i podataka o narodnooslobodilačkom ratu jugoslovenskih naroda*, pt 14, vol. 2 (Vojnoistorijski institut, Belgrade, 1983), p182-185.

See also: Marko Attila Hoare is the author of *Genocide and Resistance in Hitler's Bosnia: The Partisans and the Chetniks, 1941-1943* (Oxford University Press, Oxford, 2006); Max Bergholz, *Violence as a Generative Force: Identity, Nationalism, and Memory in a Balkan Community* (Cornell University Press, Ithaca, 2016); and Jozo Tomasevich, *War and Revolution in Yugoslavia, 1941-1945: The Chetniks* (Stanford University Press, Stanford, 1975).

Hindutva by Sufyan Hatia

The following works are mentioned in this article: *Modi's India: Hindu Nationalism and the Rise of Ethnic Democracy* by Christophe Jaffrelot (Princeton University Press, 2021); C. Christine Fair, review of Jaffrelot's *Modi's India* in *The Journal of Asian Studies* 81, no. 3 (2022): 612–14, https://doi.org/10.1017/S0021911822000894; Walter K. Andersen and Shridhar D. Damle, *The Brotherhood in Saffron: The Rashtriya Swayamsevak Sangh and Hindu Revivalism* (Vistaar Publications, 1987); Thomas Blom Hansen, *The Saffron Wave: Democracy and Hindu Nationalism in Modern India* (Princeton University Press, 1999); Priya Chacko, 'Marketizing Hindutva: The State, Society, and Markets in Hindu Nationalism,' *Modern Asian Studies* 53, no. 2 (2019): 377–410, https://doi.org/10.1017/S0026749X17000051; Ahmed Osama Tahir and Memona Mujahid, 'A Critical Constructivist Analysis of Global Media Framing of Hindutva Narratives and Their Impact on Indian Muslims,' *Global Social Sciences Review* 10, no. 1 (2025): 243–53, https://doi.org/10.31703/gssr.2025(X-I).21; and Prateek Ghasiya, Georg Ahnert, and Keita Sasahara, 'Identifying Themes of Right-Wing Extremism in Hindutva Discourse on Twitter,' *Social Media + Society* 9, no. 3 (2023), https://doi.org/10.1177/20563051231199457.

Luton's Fear of Freedom by Ghazal Tipu

The books mentioned are: Erich Fromm, *The Fear of Freedom*, Farrar and Rinehart, 1941; Nafees Ahmed, *Alt-Right,* Byline Books, 2025; and Hsiao-Hung Pai, *Angry White People: Coming Face-to-Face with the British Far Right*, Zed Books, 2016.

On the report by UN's Special Rapporteur see, 'UN rights expert hails UK for anti-racism action but raises serious concerns over Immigration Policy, Prevent programme and Brexit':https://www.ohchr.org/en/press-releases/2018/05/un-rights-expert-hails-uk-anti-racism-action-raises-serious-concerns-over. The 'Fear and Hope 2024' report can be downloaded from: https://hopenothate.org.uk/fear-and-hope-2024/

Friendly Far Right? by Sean Goodman

"Christian Zionism 101," https://politicalresearch.org/2024/04/24/101-christian-zionism; Hal Lindsey, *Late Great Planet Earth*, Zondervan, 1970; Talia Lavin, *Wild Faith: How the Christian Right is Taking Over America*, Legacy Lit, 2024 "A Collective Call to the Global Church from Middle East Evangelical Leaders" 5 August 2024 https://togetherme.org/; "Statement on the Holy Land War," 16 October 2023, https://levantministries.org/holy-land-war/; David Austin Walsh, *Taking America Back: The Conservative Movement and the Far Right,* Yale University Press, 2024; Candace Owens Tweets on Brenton Tarrant can be found here https://x.com/RealCandaceO/status/1106391443457888257, her tweets about Afghan refugees can be found here https://x.com/RealCandaceO/status/1426986532284637188; Stuart Wexler, *America's Secret Jihad: The Hidden History of Religious Terrorism in the United States,* Counterpoint Press, 2015; Christogeana.org, "What is Christian Identity?" 12 December 2010.

https://christogenea.org/articles/what-christian-identity; Christogeana.
org, "Christianity is not evil, Islam is Evil! Where is the outrage?" 27
December 2010 https://christogenea.org/articles/christianity-not-evil-
islam-evil-where-outrage; Christogeana.org, "The Arab Question, Part 1"
22 February 2019 https://christogenea.org/podcasts/historical/arab-
question-part-1; Talia Lavin, "Forward" in *No Parasan! Antifascist Dispatches
from a World in Crisis,* Ed. Shane Burley and David Renton, AK Press, 2022;
Spencer Sunshine, *Neo Nazi Terrorism and Countercultural Fascism: The Origins
and Afterlife of James Mason's Siege,* Routledge Studies in Fascism and the Far
Right, 2024; Leila Al-Shami and Shon Meckfessel, "Why Does US Far
Right Love Bashar Al-Assad?" Chapter in *No Parasan! Antifascist Dispatches
from a World in Crisis,* Ed. Shane Burley and David Renton, AK Press, 2022;
Bruce Hoffman and Jacob Ware, *Gods, Guns, and Sedition: Far-Right Terrorism
in America,* Columbia University Press, 2024; Katherine Keneally and Zoe
Manzi, "Hate United: Neo-Nazi accelerationist support for Hamas,"
Institute for Strategic Dialogue, 13 November 2023

https://www.isdglobal.org/digital_dispatches/hate-united-neo-nazi-
accelerationist-support-for-hamas/; Shane Burley and Ben Lorber, *Safety
Through Solidarity: A Radical Guide to Fighting Antisemitism,* Melville House,
2024.

Gods, Monsters and Ernst Jünger by Boyd Tonkin

Ernst Jünger's voluminous writings, the subject of massive scholarly
editions in Germany, can only be patchily sampled in English. Luckily,
three titles at the core of his achievement exist in first-rate recent
translations: *Storm of Steel* (translated by Michael Hofmann; Penguin
Classics, 2004); *On the Marble Cliffs* (translated by Tess Lewis; New York
Review Books, 2022); and *A German Officer in Occupied Paris: the War Journals
1941-1945* (translated by Thomas S Hansen and Abby J Hansen; Columbia
University Press, 2019). *The Glass Bees* (translated by Louise Bogan and
Elizabeth Mayer; New York Review Books, 2000) is a strong example of
his postwar turn to speculative fiction. *The Worker: Domination and Form*
(translated by Bogdan Costea and Laurence Paul Hemming; Northwestern

University Press, 2017) shows Jünger the scattergun theorist at his most eloquent – and most sinister.

Unfortunately, the most accessible biography available in English (translated from French) comes from one of the 'New Right' intellectuals who adopted Jünger as a mascot and mentor, and is predictably partisan: *Ernst Jünger: a Different European Destiny*, by Dominique Venner (Arktos Media, 2024). However, solid, searching and balanced accounts of his career, output, and reputational afterlife come from two American scholars: Thomas Nevin, *Ernst Jünger: Into the Abyss 1914-1945* (Constable, 1997), and Elliot Y Neaman, *A Dubious Past: Ernst Jünger and the Politics of Literature after Nazism* (University of California Press, 1999).

On the aesthetics of Fascism, see Susan Sontag, 'Fascinating Fascism', in *Under the Sign of Saturn* (Penguin Modern Classics, 2009), and Walter Benjamin, 'The Work of Art in the Age of Mechanical Reproduction', in *Illuminations* (translated by Harry Zohn; Bodley Head, 2015). Curzio Malaparte's *The Skin* (translated by David Moore) and *Kaputt* (translated by Cesar Foligno) are published by New York Review Books (2013; 2007), and Louis-Ferdinand Céline's *Journey to the End of the Night* (translated by Ralph Manheim) by Alma Classics (2012).

For the culture and politics of the Weimar Republic, see Eric D Weitz, *Weimar Germany: Promise and Tragedy* (Princeton University Press, 2018); and for France under occupation, Julian Jackson, *France: the Dark Years 1940-1944* (Oxford University Press, 2003). Susan Ottaway's *Hitler's Traitors* (Leo Cooper, 2003) covers the range of civilian and military opposition to the Third Reich, while Ian Kershaw's *Luck of the Devil: the Story of Operation Valkyrie* (Penguin, 2009) explains the origins, course and consequences of the Stauffenberg plot.

Excavating the Warsaw Ghetto by Martin Smith

The following works were referenced in this article: Primo Levi, *The Drowned and the Saved* (widely available); Vassily Grossman, *The Treblinka Hell* can be accessed at https://msuweb.montclair.edu/~furrg/essays/

grossmantreblinka46.pdf; Samuel Willenberg, *Surviving Treblinka* (Wiley–Blackwell 1989); Emanuel Ringelblum, *Notes from the Warsaw Ghetto: The Journal of Emmanuel Ringelblum* (McGraw-Hill 1958); Abraham Krzepicki, *Człowiek uciekł z Treblinek*, found in the Ringelblum Archive and published in 2017 by the Jewish Historical Institute; Martin Gilbert, *The Holocaust: The Jewish Tragedy* (HarperCollins 1989); Chil Rajchman, *Treblinka: A Survivor's Memory* (MacLehose Press 1989); Richard Lukas, *Forgotten Holocaust: The Poles Under German Occupation 1939 – 1944* (Hippocrene Books Inc. U.S. 2001), Marek Edelma, *The Ghetto Fights* (Bookmarks Publications 1995); Jurgen Stroop Report, 'The Jewish Quarter of Warsaw is no more' - *A facsimile and translation of the official Nazi report on the destruction of the Warsaw Ghetto* (Secker & Warburg 1980; Yitzak Zuckerman (Antek), *A Surplus of Memory: Chronicles of the Warsaw Ghetto Uprising* (California University Press 1993).

Interviews with author: Samiel Willenberg (Interview with author 5 August 2013); Ada Willenburg (Interview with author 5/6th August 2013); Estelle Glaser Laughlin (1st September 2021).

For further Reading: Yitzhak Arad, *Belzec, Sobibor, Treblinka. The Operation Reinhard Death Camps* (Indiana University Press 1999); Yisrael Gutman, *The Jews of Warsaw 1939 - 1043 (Ghetto, Underground, Revolt)* (Indiana University Press 1989); Bella Gutterman - *Fighting for her People (Zivia Lubetkin 1914 – 1978* (Yad Vashem Publications 2015); Raul Hilberg, *The Destruction of the European Jews* (Yale University Press 2003); Gitta Sereny, *Into that Darkness. From Mercy Killings to Mass Slaughter* (Andre Deutsch Ltd 1991).

Guernica: Things to Come
by Marjorie Allthorpe-Guyton

Guernica has generated an academic industry and an extensive literature. The painting returned to Spain in 1981 and is exhibited in the Reina Sofia Museum of Contemporary Art whose website Rethinking Guernica chronologically presents research data on the work comprising c 2000 documents. For this essay, I have consulted the archives at Whitechapel Art

Gallery Archive WAG/EAR/4,62,62A,63,64 and Marx Memorial Library, London SC/EPH/21/2/6 1936-39.

On Guernica see: John Richardson, *A Life of Picasso*, vol.4, *The Minotaur Years 1933-43*, Jonathan Cape, London 2022; the scholarly and highly readable biography by Gijs van Hensbergen, *Guernica: The Biography of a Twentieth Century Icon*, Bloomsbury, London 2004, from which citations p.3, 4,7,11 are from pp.35, 83,77,122; Simon Martin, *Conscience and Conflict; British Artists and the Spanish Civil War*, Pallant House Gallery, Chichester in association with Lund Humphries, UK 2014, citations pp.4,5 are from p.121; *The Whitechapel Art Gallery Centenary Review*, Whitechapel Art Gallery, London 2001, citations p.8, from pp.13,19; John Berger, *Success and Failure of Picasso*, Penguin Books 1965, Writers and Readers, London 1980, citation p.11 from p.179.

For Picasso and Communism see: Sarah Wilson, 'The Picasso Files', *Tate Magazine*, issue 2 Spring 1994, pp.28-32; Sarah Wilson, '*Guernica*, Agit-Prop and the Grand Style,' *Picasso, Marx and Socialist Realism in France*, Liverpool University Press, 2013, pp.66-90 ; Lara Pucci, 'Guttuso, *Guernica*, Gramsci: Art, History and the Symbolic Strategy of the Italian Communist Party', *Tate Papers* , no.33, 2020 , https://www.tate.org.uk/research/tate-papers/33/guttuso-guernica-gramsci-art-history-symbolic-strategy-italian-communist-party, accessed 9 July 2025.
For Guernica Remakings: an ongoing project by Nicola Ashmore mapping contemporary interpretations: Http:guernicamakings.com; Nicola Ashmore, *Guernica Remakings*, University of Brighton 2017. And on the Artists International Association: Lynda Morris and Robert Radford, *The Story of the AIA 1933-1953*, Museum of Modern Art Oxford 1983, citation p.10 from p.55; Robert Radford, *Art for a Purpose: The Artists International Association 1933-1953*, Winchester School of Art Press 1987; Andy Friend, *Comrades in Art, Artists Against Fascism 1933-1943*, Thames and Hudson, September 2025.

The excellent archive exhibition 'Artists Against Fascism and War', curated by Andy Friend, Tate Britain 2025-May 2026. The AIA destroyed many records, concerned for their safety under possible Nazi occupation, but the

Tate Archive recently acquired the Central Committee minute book 1938-1940 from the estate of artist Morris Kestelman; for recent research on propaganda in British art of the period, see Helen Atkinson, *Showing Resistance, Propaganda and Modernist Exhibitions in Britain 1933-53*, Manchester University Press 2024. For the many thousand of posters produced during the Spanish Civil War, see Alexander Vergara , *The Visual Front, Posters of the Spanish CivilWar from the University of California Southworth Collection*, 1998.

Last Word: On the Tarnished Golden Road
by Hilman Fikri Azman

The following works were referenced in this article: William Dalrymple, *The Golden Road: How Ancient India Transformed the World,* Bloomsbury, 2024; Ziauddin Sardar, *Orientalism*, Open University Press, 1999; Edward Said, *Orientalism*. Penguin, 2019; Bhimrao Ambedkar, *Writings and Speeches*, Dr. Ambedkar Foundation Ministry of Social Justice & Empowerment, 1979; Benedict Anderson, *Imagined Communities: Reflections on the Origin and Spread of Nationalism*, Verso, 1983; Perry Anderson, *The Indian Ideology*, Three Essays Collective, 2012; bell hooks, 'This is the Oppressor's Language/Yet I Need to Talk to You: Language, a Place of Struggle' in *Between Languages and Cultures*, edited by Anuradha Dingwaney & Carol Maier, University of Pittsburgh Press, 1995; Ngugi wa Thiong'o, *Decolonising the Mind*, Boydell & Brewer, 1986; V D Savarkar, *Hindutva:Who is a Hindu*, Hindi Sahitya Sadan, 1928; Rabindranath Tagore, *Selected Letters of Rabindranath Tagore*, Cambridge University Press, 1997; Shashi Tharoor, 'But what about the railways ...?' The myth of Britain's gifts to India. *The Guardian*. 2017: https://www.theguardian.com/world/2017/mar/08/india-britain-empire-railways-myths-gifts

CONTRIBUTORS

● **Tahir Abbas** is Professor of Criminology and Global Justice at Aston University ● **Alev Adil** is Reviews Editor of *Critical Muslim* ● **Marjorie Allthorpe-Guyton** is former President of the International Association of Art Critics (AICA), British Section ● **Alinah Azedeh** is a British-Iranian writer, artist and cultural activist based in the UK ● **Hilman Fikri Azman** is pursuing his postgraduate dreams ● **Sean Goodman** is a scholar of far-right movements ● **Donny Gulkstein** is a lecturer in history at Stevenson College, Edinburgh ● **Sufyan Hatia** is an MSc candidate in Conflict, Security and Development at the University of Edinburgh ● **Marko Attila Hoare** is an Associate Professor, Department of Political Science and International Relations at the Sarajevo School of Science and Technology ● **C Scott Jordan** has recently been appointed Deputy Director of the International Institute of Futures Studies (IIFS) in Malaysia ● **Hassan Mahamdallie** is busy writing yet another oeuvre in his recent theatrical renaissance ● **Kostas Maronitis** is the author of *Robots and Immigrants* and other books ● **Shamim Miah** is Course Lead for MA Education, University of Huddersfield ● **Steve Noyes** won the 2024 BP Nichol prize for his chapbook *The Conveyor* from Alfred Gustav Press ● **Louis Ordish** is a contributor to the Institute of Race Relations, where he compiles the Anti-Fascism and Far Right section of the Institute's Calendar on Racism and Resistance ● **Judith Orr** is author of *Sexism and the System* and other books ● **Martin Smith** is writing a comprehensive account of life and resistance in the Warsaw Ghetto ● **Ghazal Tipu** is a writer and poet based in Cardiff ● **Boyd Tonkin** is a well-known literary critic ● **Robin Yassin-Kassab** has rediscovered his itch to travel ● **Aicha bint Yusif**, poet and medical student, was born in northern Palestine, surrounded by its hills and history ● **Ibrayim Yusupov** (1929–2008) is the most beloved modern Karakalpak poet, his work spanning the post-war Soviet period and the first decades of an independent Uzbekistan.